DETAINED IN the DESERT & OTHER PLAYS

By JOSEFINA LÓPEZ

WPR BOOKS: LATINO INSIGHTS

CARLSBAD, CA

WPR BOOKS: Latino Insights
3445 Catalina Dr., Carlsbad, CA 92010-2856
www.WPRbooks.com 760-434-1223 kirk@whisler.com

TABLE OF CONTENTS

INTRODUCTION

A WOMAN OF HER WORD(S): JOSEFINA LÓPEZ

Josefina López was born in Mexico in 1969. At the tender age of five she was brought to this country illegally settling with her family in Boyle Heights, East of Los Angeles. She started grammar school the following year and thus began the process of "Chicani-zation" in the school system and in this society. From her first day in school, López knew that although her parents had green cards, she was undocumented and therefore lived in constant fear of being deported. But she used her vivid imagination to get her through, living a kind of shadow existence for several years until she became a Temporary Resident through the Amnesty Program in 1987. The threat of deportation would inform several of her plays, becoming a kind of leitmotif in the lives of her characters. According to López, she "became a Chicana" at the age of twenty, ostensibly when she no longer feared deportation.

López first started writing plays in the fifth grade. However, her major influences were the televised version of the Teatro Campesino's *La gran carpa de los Rasquachis,* retitled *"El corrido,"* and the live production of Luis Valdez's *I Don't Have to Show You No Stinking Badges.* She had seen *"El corrido",* when she was in the 9th grade.[1] *"El corrido",* was taped in part as a stage performance and López could see the possibilities in the live, staged version. Watching the program, the impressionable and imaginative author felt liberated from the constrictions of realism:

I thought, wow, I didn't know that theatre could be this way . . . that's how I think. . . . that's what I loved about it, that one moment you're in Mexico and the next [you're in the US]. . . transitions

4

and transformation--that's how I think; that it could be an epic, adventuresome . . . it doesn't have to stay in one place. [2]

While attending the Los Angeles County High School for the Arts, López saw *I Don't Have to Show You No Stinking Badges,* written and directed by Luis Valdez at the Los Angeles Theater Center in 1986.[3] Yet, while Valdez's play was an inspiration to the young playwright, it also inspired her emerging feminism. As she searched Luis Valdez's works for a monologue to perform in her acting class, López discovered that Valdez's female characters "were very flat--all mothers and girlfriends."[4] It is important to remember that López was studying acting in high school with the intention of becoming an actress. Like many female actors who become playwrights, López decided to create her own vehicles to perform. If the male-dominated, sexist Chicano Theater Movement was not going to satisfy López's desire to act, she would take matters into her own hands. This volume is a testament to her commitment to create theatre that is relevant for all audiences, especially women.

In the years since she first gained the attention of producers, critics and directors, Ms. López has fulfilled all of her girlhood dreams. She earned a B.A. in Liberal Arts from Columbia College Chicago in 1993 and an MFA in Screenwriting/(Playwriting) from the School of Theater, Film & TV, UCLA in 2000. As this volume and the accompanying first volume demonstrate, our playwright has never stopped writing, acting, directing and producing. The list of awards she has garnered ranges from local to national recognition for her efforts to bring the Chicana and Latina voices to the attention of her community and beyond. A partial list of awards includes, Latina of the Year by *Latina Magazine,* 2002; Gabriel Garcia Marquez Writing Award from the Mayor of Los Angeles, 2003; Woman of the Year for the First District of L.A. from County Supervisor Gloria Molina, 2004; Mujeres Destacadas – LA OPINION, 2009; and Woman of Action – Assemblyman John Perez, 46 Assembly District, 2010.

In the year 2000 López fulfilled her dream of creating her own theatre space, CASA 0101. The following narrative is from the CASA 0101 website:

CASA means house or home in Spanish. 0's and 1's are the binary language computers use to operate. Casa 0101 was founded at the dawn of digital age. . . . Early on Josefina Lopez taught a few digital video classes and Casa 0101 was meant to become a home of the digital revolution. Though the organization subsequently focused its energies on theater and not digital filmmaking, the name stuck. 0 and 1 can also mean nothing & everything, yin and yang, male & female, and many more dual opposites. Through storytelling and theater and other art forms Casa 0101 is committed to exploring the

5

world and oneself, the good and the bad, the light and the darkness of our soul and our world to the point where there are no borders and "0" and "1" are one.

"Good versus Evil" is at the heart of most dramas, comic or serious and Lopez's oeuvre demonstrates her ongoing struggle to bring Justice to all oppressed individuals and communities. Usually she does this with her characteristic comic flair, her love for parody, farce and characters that remind us of ourselves as well as of our enemies, the good and the bad. These plays are published in chronological order and together confirm the playwright's place as a force in the American theatre. Like all plays, these should be read as if they were being performed, for the stage is where they live because the stage is where the playwright lives and thrives. In the year of this publication, 2011, CASA 0101 will add another venue to its roster, a 5,000 square foot performance, gallery and rehearsal space down the street from the original venue, lovingly referred to as "Little CASA 0101." As she predicted in her youth, Josefina López has put Boyle Heights on the cultural and political map of Los Angeles, having inspired an entire "Arts District" in this once-neglected part of the City of Angels. As her plays will show, devils and angels abound in our communities but one thing is certain: Josefina López will go down in history—or should I say, "Herstory" as one of the Good Angels.

WHO'S THE ALIEN: DETAINED IN THE DESERT

Detained in the Desert was first produced in 2010 at Casa 0101, directed by Hector Rodriguez.[5] While López has confirmed her place as a playwright who observes life around her through a comic lens, in *Detained in the Desert* she takes a serious look at one of the most urgent issues of our times. This is her assured response to Arizona's SB 1070, the controversial bill that would allow police officers to question the citizenship of anyone whom they think could be undocumented. The major reaction to this was the fear that racial profiling would occur unabated; dark-skinned people being the targets of this lawful practice. Informed by extensive personal and analytical research into the responses to "those illegals" in Arizona, Lopez has created a biting indictment, not only of the Arizona law, but by inference, of the country as a whole.

Like most of her plays, this one is cinematic in structure, moving back and forth from locale to locale. This calls for fast, efficient transitions, designed to keep the momentum going, to keep the tension building. In the world premiere production the transitions worked, carrying us from one setting to the other with minimal set pieces and props as well as music and sound effects. The play follows two stories, focusing on Sandi, a young woman who has lost her sense of her Mexican heritage and a radio talk-show host who foments anti-immigrant hysteria among his listeners along the Arizona/Mexico border. Sandi is traveling with her Canadian boyfriend when a police officer stops them because she "looks like an alien; the irony is that her Canadian boyfriend is undocumented. Sandi refuses to "show her papers" and ends up being arrested. The irony, that she is a citizen while Matt is not, is compelling and enhances the notion that this law will promote racial profiling.

The nemesis of the play is a small-town talk radio host, Lou Becker. This despicable man promotes hatred against immigrants through his radio show. When he is kidnapped and left to die in the desert, his discovery of Sandi, who has escaped the ICE bus and is wandering in the desert, he has revelations that occur somewhat naturally. Although this is a play about real people in real situations, López invokes the supernatural, bringing-on two ghosts crucial to the plot. Whether you call this "magical realism" (which Ms. Lopez decries) or not, it worked for me. As she said in the after-show talk-back, "Our people believe in ghosts." Most importantly, this play forces us to consider the consequences of laws like SB 1070 as well as the actions taken to kidnap the Lou Becker character.

A MEXICAN BROMANCE: TRIO LOS MACHOS

Trio los Machos received a workshop production in 2008 at the CASA 0101 theatre and will receive its world premiere in the new theater space directed by Eddie Padilla in 2012. This is a play with music that focuses on the trio of the title, Lalo, Paco and Nacho. We first meet the trio in the present, fifty years after they first began singing together. They are singing in a Mexican restaurant on Olvera Street and as they sing, their voices become distorted to the point that they are let go by the owner of the restaurant. These three are over-the-hill and capture our sympathies as they reluctantly leave, wondering how they will survive. Through flashbacks we discover that they first met as braceros during World War II, got deported, became fast friends, crossed back into the US and have remained friends ever since. The play is full of farcical humor and relies on three "clowns" to pull-off these lovable viejos. Two of the men are always arguing, usually over inanities that only old friends can put up with. Because they are musicians and singers, the play is rich with popular music of their era, adding a wonderful sense of "history" to the play.

As the play progresses we learn about the men's failed relationships with women, their reliance on one another to get by and their deep love for one another. When Lalo suffers a stroke the other two are helpless to take care of him. When he has a bowel movement the other two are appalled at the possibility of having to change his diaper. But Life must go on and they deal with the situation as best they can. If this were a film (which it could certainly be) it would be called a "bromance," if not simply a "buddy movie" but these are old timers in the autumn of their years and it's difficult not to fall in love with them. In true Hollywood fashion, there is a surprise ending and we are left to believe that these three will live forever, if not on this Earth, at least in our minds. Perhaps most importantly, López has created three good men, flawed like the rest of us, but worth our attention as we watch them struggle through life.

WOMAN POWER: WHEN NATURE CALLS

When Nature Calls premiered in 2009 at Breath of Fire Latina Theater Ensemble, in Santa Ana, California, directed by Elsa Martinez Phillips. In that production this series of monologues was played by seven actresses. The "Nature" referred to in the title is actually "Mother Nature" and each woman discusses her relationship with Mother Earth. The characters are distinct in many ways, beginning with a Chinese woman, named "The Battery Queen" because she sold so many batteries in her village. However, she discovered how dangerous cheap Chinese batteries were and has begun to collect all the batteries she can to keep them from being dumped in the ground, polluting the ground water. Her discourse teaches us about the importance of recycling from a very different perspective thousands of miles across the sea. We next meet Alma, who cannot sleep because the slain women of Juarez haunt her imagination. She sees these unsolved, brutal murders as if she were a victim herself, narrating different deaths from the perspective of the women. "You can't kill so many women without it affecting the land," she tells us, hoping to bring about justice for the hundreds of murdered women.

Although she claims not to be an activist, the "Tree Woman" fights for the environment in response to being a battered woman. When her vigil is interrupted by a miracle, she gets down from the tree made aware of the power of the Four Elements and the need to balance these forces of Nature. Sally is an American in Paris who decries the smoking and the dog litter on the streets of that city. Her response is both comical and sad, as the reader/audience will discover. Moe is a middle-aged Chicana who finds herself organizing refugees in the Cajun Dome in the midst of Hurricane Rita, which followed Katrina. She relates how she came to this place and how the tragedy gave her a new understanding of her role in the cosmos. Soledad comes to a hypnotist to discover that in all of her previous lives she had killed herself, leading to the pain she is suffering today. She relates how she lived in different time periods and how, as a woman, she was always oppressed by men, but that she too was a man and oppressed others and played every type of role. The final speaker is Thelma, who is conducting a workshop titled "Getting in Touch With Your Inner Goddess." Though sometimes comic, Thelma's purpose is to liberate the women in her workshop (and the actual audience) from old paradigms of what a woman should be and replacing these stereotypes with how a woman can be extraordinary. She is interrupted by a phone call from a surprise visitor, who ends the evening with a bang.

HOME IS WHERE THE HEART . . . : BOYLE HEIGHTS

The world premiere of *Boyle Heights* was directed by the team of Tony Pacheco, Josefina López and Buster Rojas in 2004. In *Boyle Heights* Lopez returns to the themes she explored in her first play, *Simply Maria, or The American Dream*; however, she now writes in the genre of realism.[6] This is another Mechicana/o family in crisis but with characters and situations that are not allegorical figures (such as the Three Marias) or other extensions of reality the young playwright observed in the Valdezian actos that first inspired her. The settings change and the plot travels back and forth in time but we are asked to consider these changes as if they were really happening. This is actually a cinematic text that will challenge an imaginative artistic staff but it can work as we follow the trials and tribulations of two generations of the Rosales family of Boyle Heights.

As the title suggests, this play is a love song to the playwright's hometown. As Dalia, the central character says towards the end of the play, "Everyone thinks you're East L.A. But I know who you really are," meaning her beloved Boyle Heights is more than an idea, it is a real place, the place where she grew up. Unlike Simply Maria, this play is not for children; perhaps not even for young adults, as the characters explore their sexuality and other adult themes conservative barrio parents might find excessive. When the Bohemian Dalia talks about all of her boyfriends, as well as her sexual adventures, or when we discover that her mother got pregnant out-of-wedlock, having an affair with a married man (Dalia's father), we've entered the realm of Adult Themes. There are comic references to *telenovelas* in this typically Mechicano family and this play has its own brand of melodrama as well.

Ultimately, *Boyle Heights* is another autobiographical play, written years after Lopez's first exploration into how a Chicana daughter of Mexican

immigrants can come to terms with herself as a liberated woman yet retain her love for her community and her people, however dysfunctional. Like the playwright, Dalia is college-educated, writes poetry and lives to experience all that she can of Life, with a capital "L." Sitting on the Rosales roof, looking down at all the neighbors and their *"chismes,"* Dalia isn't superior to them, she's just more adventurous. When her father declares he is taking her mother back to México we witness the fantasy of many Mexican immigrants, especially those (like my father) who fled the Revolution of 1910-17: to go home. As the corrido, *"Mexico Lindo y Querido,"* states, "If I die away from you [Mexico], tell them I'm asleep and take me home to you."

ABUELA'S SECRETS:
LOLA GOES TO ROMA

The playwright directed the world premiere of *Lola Goes to Roma* in July of 2004 at CASA 0101. In this cinematic play López explores the consequences of a marriage that should never have been as we learn about Lola, the just-widowed family matriarch. In a series of multiple settings we follow Lola and her youngest daughter, Roma, on their travels through Western Europe. Roma has just defended her dissertation in anthropology and to celebrate she is taking this trip. When none of her siblings want to have their mother live with them, Roma agrees to take her with her to Europe. While on their travels we discover that Lola is a very liberated woman, in sharp contrast to Roma, whose whole life has been academic and free of romance.

It should come as no surprise that our playwright has taken on such a controversial subject, focusing on a grandmother, an abuelita who is not your typical *madre sufrida,* or all-suffering Mexican mother in black but a sexually liberated woman. Lola has a great deal to teach her daughter about Life and Love as we watch the two women explore different European cities, the men they encounter and, ultimately, themselves. This play is not for children but rather, for an adult audience willing to "go along for the ride," literally and figuratively. The many scenes and characters will challenge the production team in the serious yet often comic travelogue. Chicanas in Paris? Who would have thought, if not for Josefina López.

Sincerely,

Jorge G. Huerta

Jorge A. Huerta, Ph.D.

Jorge A. Huerta, Ph.D. Chancellor's Associates Professor of Theatre, *Emeritus,* University of California, San Diego

BIBLIOGRAPHY FOR HUERTA'S INTRO

Broyles-Gonzales, Yolanda. *El Teatro Campesino: Theater in the Chicano Movement.* Austin: 1994.

Huerta, Jorge A. *Chicano Theater: Themes and Forms.* Bilingual Press, 1982.

_____. *Chicano Drama: Performance, Society and Myth. Cambridge,* 2000.

Huerta, Jorge A., Lopez, Tiffany Ann and Morton Carlos. Discussion/ Review of *Detained in the Desert. Gestos,* Spring 2011 (in press).

Green, Judith. "She's at that stage," *San Jose Mercury News,* 12 November 1989, Arts and Books, p. 5.

Hurtado, Aida. *The Color of Privilege: Three Blasphemies on Race and Feminism* (Michigan, 1996), p. 56-57.

Maria Teresa Marrero, "Real Women Have Curves: The Articulation of Fat as a Cultural/Feminist Issue," *Ollantay,* I (January 1993): 61-70.

McFerran, Virginia Derus. "Chicana voices in American drama: Silviana Wood, Estela Portillo-Trambley, Cherríe Moraga, Milcha Sanchez-Scott, Josefina López," PhD dissertation, University of Minnesota, 1991 (Ann Arbor, 1991).

Valdez, Luis. *I Don't Have to Show You No Stinking Badges* in *Zoot Suit and Other Plays* (Arte Público Press, 1992):23-94.

FOOTNOTES

[1] The televised version of *La gran carpa de los Rasquachi,* retitled *"El corrido,"* was first produced and broadcast by PBS in 1976. López saw a re-broadcast version.

[2] From an unpublished interview with Josefina López in Chicago, Illinois, 3 October 1992.

[3] *I Don't Have to Show You No Stinking Badges* is published in Luis Valdez, *Zoot Suit and Other Plays* (Arte Público Press, 1992):23-94.

[4] Judith Green, "She's at that stage," *San Jose Mercury News*, 12 November 1989, Arts and Books, p. 5.

[5] For a discussion/review of *Detained in the Desert* see Jorge Huerta, Tiffany Ann Lopez and Carlos Morton's discussion in *Gestos,* Spring 2011 issue.

[6] *Simply Maria, or the American Dream,* is in Volume One.

DEDICATIONS

This book is dedicated to my wonderful and loving husband Emmanuel who is the biggest supporter of my dreams.

I also dedicate this book to my manager Marilyn Atlas, my "Fairy Godmother" who has been fighting for my dreams to become real on the big and small screen – for being a visionary and getting the big picture.

This book is especially dedicated to all the wonderful people at CASA 0101 like Hector Rodriguez, Gaby Lopez de Denis, Eddie Padilla, Corky Dominguez, Miriam Peniche, Ramona Gonzales, Selene Santiago, Luke Lizalde, Luz Vasquez, Emma Nava, Mark Kraus, Elizabeth Otero, and all the rest of the CASA Familia who has helped make a dream come true by creating a cultural center in my barrio. Thank you for your energy and generosity to my community!

This book is also dedicated to all the women and men who have acted in my plays – thank you for breathing life into my characters.

Thank you Jorge Huerta for believing in me and not letting me give up on my writing.

Acknowledgements

DETAINED IN THE DESERT Special thanks to Hector Rodriguez and the wonderful cast who was adventurous and courageous enough to put their whole heart and selves into this story. Special thanks to Carey Fox for giving such humanity to Lou. Thank you to the Border Angels who came to support it and spread the word.

TRIO LOS MACHOS Special thanks to Eddie Padilla who brought this beautiful "bromance" to life, BRAVA Theater for their support in developing this play, Bill Virchis for his wonderful workshop production that showed me how much more this play could be... To the wonderful casts of both productions and the reading at Brava.

WHEN NATURE CALLS Special thanks to Corky Dominguez for his beautiful direction of the first workshop production, to Elsa Martinez Phillips who did the world premiere at BREATH A FIRE – an amazing production – to all the women of BREATH OF FIRE thank you for what you do! A very special thank you to the fantastic cast of the CASA 0101 workshop.

BOYLE HEIGHTS Special thanks to the wonderful cast of the first CASA 0101 production...and to Tony Pacheco and Hector Rodriguez for their wonderful direction.

LOLA GOES TO ROMA Special thanks to Katie Laris who did an amazing production at SBCC. To Ludo Vika for her kick ass performance and to Minerva Vier and Fabrizio Imas for being so wonderful, and the rest of the ensemble in the CASA 0101 production who created original characters with their wonderful improve.

SPECIAL DEDICATIONS

DETAINED IN THE DESERT This play is dedicated to Enrique Morones, founder of Border Angels, for his courage and generosity of spirit, and to all the activists and humanitarians who risk their lives and make sacrifices so that others may live, and to all the migrants who have died crossing – you are not forgotten.

TRIO LOS MACHOS This play is dedicated to all the men who served in the Bracero Program and to all the Latino men who make their living singing.

WHEN NATURE CALLS This play is dedicated to the real Battery Queen for inspiring me to write this play, to Lorena Mendez and Diana Valdez-Washington, who risked her life and sacrificed so much let people know about the horrors happening to innocent women in Ciudad Juarez, Moe Lopez who experienced first hand the Cajun Dome and was a light in the darkness for so many, to Butterfly Woman, to all the women healers and "Shamamas" who hear the call of Mother Nature.

BOYLE HEIGHTS This play is dedicated to all the wonderful people who live and have lived in Boyle Heights and have lived their lives with dignity.

LOLA GOES TO ROMA This play is dedicated to Keisuke Fukuda, a long lost love who taught me a lot about destiny and soul connection. This play is also dedicated to Lupe Ontiveros who inspired the character of Lola.

CASA 0101 Presents

DETAINED
IN THE
DeSert

A New Play by Josefina Lopez

WARNING: THIS PLAY IS FOR MATURE AUDIENCES ONLY

OCT. 1 - NOV. 21, 2010

Artwork by Luke Lizalde

INTRODUCTION
BY TIFFANY A. LÓPEZ, PH.D.

Detained in the Desert received its world premier in Los Angeles, California, at CASA 0101 (October 1 – November 21, 2010) located in the heart of Boyle Heights, where López herself grew up. The play's story pivots around two people detained in the desert, how they got there, and the impact the experience has on their thinking about immigration and the role they both occupy within the specific political landscape of Arizona. Significantly, López wrote this play during a time of national conflict so as to prevent herself from falling into a state of despair and to lend her voice to the struggle of those in Arizona working against the rhetoric of hate that has come to permeate the cultural landscape, from the legislature to the media. To write this play, López conducted research that included following the evolution of SB1070, listening to talk radio, and studying performed struggles at the U.S. Arizona-Mexico border between humanitarian activists and vigilante Minutemen types, the latter known to aggressively follow and sabotage the efforts of groups such as Border Angels by targeting for shooting practice the containers of water they leave throughout the desert for desperate crossers.

López's play is written in a genre she describes as "cineatro," a form that brings to the dramatic script key cinematic elements, such as a sense of highly directed framing and editing, including the appearance of jump cuts. The play signals the conventions of film and works from familiar modes of reading in order to expand the narrow frames of reference that shape and inform our thinking. *Detained in the Desert* positions its audience to bear witness to the impact of anti-immigration activities on public interactions as well as interpersonal relationships. López begins by featuring emblematic talk radio conversations that insistently focus on disenfranchisement. The climate is one in which people perceive the world through affect, asserting that they don't enjoy the privileges they used to enjoy and, more importantly, felt and still feel entitled to. The play's focus on a protagonist

who is a shock-jock radio host serves to illustrate how an infotainment narrative of disenfranchisement has come to replace political analysis of historical and material disenfranchisement. Significantly, the play's second featured protagonist is a college student, a Chicana who upon completing her Master's degree is in the process of returning home to her community. What she will do with her education remains a question that charges the play.

Detained in the Desert is also clearly interested in the shock wave that Arizona has sent across the country as other states model legislation on SB1070. Well over a month after López's play premiered, the media reported Jared Loughner's shooting of Arizona's Rep. Gabrielle Giffords. Significantly, in the information about Loughner that the media has unfurled, there appears a consistent thread of logic permeating Loughner's world-view: that there is no reliable or trustworthy structure on which to build his life. He ranted about being rejected by the military, employers, and college. Information has been unearthed that suggests he obsessed about Giffords' not adequately answering a question he posed to her in 2007 at one of her political events. Among his obsessive rants against government, he is reported as having said, "What is government if words have no meaning?" Notably, his comments emphasize that he felt completely disenfranchised. In a post-traumatic response to the shooting, James Fuller, a Democratic activist and former campaign volunteer for Rep. Giffords, threatened a Tea Party spokesmen, "You're dead! It looks like [Sarah] Palin, [Glenn] Beck, Sharon Angle and the rest got their first target." Notably, the majority of news stories insistently focused on the shooting as solely a freak event perpetrated by a mentally unstable young man on a downward spiral; very few reports discussed the larger historical and cultural contexts framing the event and linking it to other acts of violence born from a shared cultural climate. In Arivaca, Arizona, May 2009, nine-year old Brisenia Flores was shot in her home at point blank range; Shauna Forde, the alleged mastermind behind her murder, publicly represented anti-Latino hate groups, including the Minutemen and the Federation of Americans for Immigration Reform. In their recent publication, *Solderdera de Amor: Mujeres de Maiz Flor y Canto* (2011), the collective dedicate the zine to Brisenia and comment, "Her murder represents the violence that follows when hateful and dehumanizing rhetoric and the groups that promote it go unchecked." Read in tandem with current events, Josefina López' *Detained in the Desert* offers an incredibly timely and important call to analyze the many convergent factors, but most especially the rhetoric of violence, that shape thinking about citizenship.

PLAYWRIGHT'S NOTES

I was in Arizona on vacation when it was announced that SB 1070 had passed. Quickly I got texts from immigrant rights organizations telling me where the protest would be that night. I was seriously considering going, but my husband's family was having a family reunion, and he would not let me skip it. I wanted to do something more than just protest, so I decided to write this play to show the ridiculousness of this law but also to explore the motives of "hate talk" which in the past few years has led to a 40% increase in hate crimes toward Latinos. When I read about the many hate crimes that have happened and the similarities between them, it made me wonder if the men at the forefront of this "hate talk" and fear of immigrants are aware that they have blood on their hands. They have a right to freedom of speech, but they must realize that spreading hate causes more hate. All of us must realize the power of our words to separate humanity or bring humanity together. I hope with my words I have created some degree of understanding that goes beyond the immigration rhetoric and fear mongering that is happening right now in this country. Hopefully with this play I've shed some light on the darkness of ignorance.

Josefina López
October 2010

DETAINED IN THE DESERT

SCENE

TIME: Over a period of a few days in the summer of 2010.

SETTING: Multiple locations in the state of Arizona – KRZT 1070 radio station DJ booth; front seat of a car; a tent somewhere in the desert; a road somewhere in the desert; a Detention Center in the desert; a Water Station; and Ernesto's SUV.

CHARACTERS

SANDI BELEN, 20s, second-generation Latina who does not speak Spanish but is dark skinned and looks almost Native American.

LOU SANCHEZ, 50s, a portly, Anglo conservative talk show host who criticizes "illegal aliens" on his shows and encourages Americans to "Take Back America." This slogan is also the title of his radio show.

ERNESTO MARTINEZ, 50s, an activist who distributes gallons of water throughout the desert to provide aid for migrants crossing. He is founder of Angels of the Border.

MATT WILLIAMS, 20s, blond-haired and blue-eyed, Sandi's boyfriend of six months. He is an undocumented Canadian.

MILAGROS, 20s, a soon-to-be deported woman who befriends Sandi at the detention center.

TALL FIGURE/SAUL, 20s, Latino, an angry man who lost his brother to a hate crime.

SHORT FIGURE/J.C., 20, Latina, an angry woman who lost her brother to a hate crime.

MEDIUM FIGURE/CHUY, 20s, Latino, an angry man who lost a brother to a hate crime.

FEMALE GUARD at the Detention Center, 40s, African American, sympathizes with Sandi.

ARIZONA POLICE OFFICER, 40s, a racist cop who racially profiles Sandi.

CARL DUNLOP (VOICE), a Minuteman who eventually becomes the next host of Take Back America.

KEN BEAVERS, 40s, radio producer of the show Take Back America.

DOCUMENTARY FILMAKER & her CAMERAMAN, both from England.

ARTEMIO HERNANDEZ, 40s, a dark-skinned man who was murdered in the desert.

MRS. ARTEMIO HERNANDEZ (VOICE), 40s, a woman who writes to thank ERNESTO for returning her husband's bones.

SCENE ONE:

In the darkness we hear short bits of audio from various radio stations as the dial moves in search of a station. Spanish language radio plays for a second or two, and then the dial stays on a station that is broadcasting in English. A jingle identifies the radio station as KRZT 1070. LIGHTS FADE in on LOU BECKER sitting at a DJ booth welcoming his listeners.

LOU: Good morning Phoenix! This is KRZT 1070. Welcome to Take Back America. My fellow Arizonans I am so proud of us for finally taking the correct measures to keep all the illegals out. Our lousy Government and the Bozo in office has been too weak to get the job done, so it was up to us to do it…and for that, many hate us. It took courage to do what we did. We have to stand proud in the face of adversity. We shall overcome. While protests at the state capital continue, we must hold firm to the belief that we are doing the right thing, even if the snobs in California and New York think we are racists. This is not about racism or racial profiling. We are just sick of paying for all those illegals that come to our country and state to live and breed like cockroaches. What do you think? I want to hear your thoughts. What can we do to stay strong and continue the fight to take back America? We're going to the phones... Oh, look, it's lighting up like a Christmas tree. We have a lot of callers on the line. So let's get this tea party started. (*LOU presses a button.*) We have Thelma from Scottsdale. Thelma, what do you do to stay strong?

THELMA (*voice over, a white woman in her 70s*): I just think it's so unfair that everyone thinks we're racist when we're not. So, when someone calls me a racist, when I'm out there holding my protest signs defending Sheriff Arpaio and our fine Governor against all those Latino protestors, I just look up to God and ask for patience and peace.

LOU: That sounds like a great idea. Patience and peace.

THELMA: It's just awful what they are doing to Sheriff Arpaio... He is so brave for standing up to the criminals. So what if he makes his prisoners wear pink underwear. Don't come to this country illegally, if you don't like it.

LOU: Did you know that one third of the prison population is made up of illegal aliens?

THELMA: No, I did not know that, but I suspected it.

LOU: People call us racists, but we just really love this country. I'm a patriot, not a racist. I don't want this country to go to the pits, the dogs, hell-in-a-hand-bag, or whatever you want to call it. I don't want tuberculosis and whatever diseases those vermin bring across the border.

Photo by Josefina López

Lou hosts his talk show on KRZT 1070.

THELMA: That's right. My granddaughter got lice the other day from some dirty Mexican kid who gave it to her. Why should my granddaughter be exposed to that? I pay my taxes, and my husband and I have worked hard to give her a great life. Lou, you are a great man to stand up for us.

LOU: Thank you, Thelma. I'm just a humble servant to all my listeners... (*LOU presses some buttons.*) Now we have Adam from Flagstaff. Adam, welcome to Take Back America.

ADAM: Lou, I am fighting back by encouraging all my friends and family to participate in a "Buy-cott." I bet you that there are more people who are for us than against us.

LOU: Yes, more people are in support of our law than against it. Before you know it, ten more states will be passing this same law. Florida is getting ready to pass even tougher laws, so I know we are not alone in this.

ERNESTO MARTINEZ appears close to the DJ booth.

LOU: Thank you Adam.

LOU signals for ERNESTO to come in and sit down next to him. ERNESTO puts on the headset, knowing the routine.

LOU: Ladies and gentlemen, as all my listeners know, I am not afraid to

speak the truth and to speak it on this station in public and in private, and I have always invited all these idiotic liberals who believe that the border is an imaginary line to come debate me on my show. Do they ever take me up on my offer? No! At the heart of all those liberals, there's nothing but a coward. However, today is different. I got a call the other day from a man some of you know as the "Minutemen's Enemy Number One." Now, before anybody accuses me of sympathizing with this man, let me just say that as a law abiding American, I respect a U.S. citizen's right to exercise his First Amendment right, which is free speech. I do not agree with this man, but I wanted to give him the opportunity to tell his side of the story. So let's welcome Ernesto Martinez, founder of Angels of the Border, an organization that provides relief for illegal—

ERNESTO: Migrants. We help people in need of help in the desert regardless of legal status—

LOU: They are illegal! They break the law. They're illegal – what's so difficult about saying what it truly is?

ERNESTO: They are human beings. I help human beings.

LOU: Why are you breaking the law?

ERNESTO: All I do is put water out in the desert—

LOU: Aren't you encouraging people to cross the desert by putting water out there? Aren't you enticing them to cross the border by making it easier to cross the desert?

ERNESTO: It's seventy-six miles of desert! No human being would cross the border and risk their life just to get my water. Things have to be dire and desperate for someone to decide to cross the border. Everyday one person dies crossing that border.

LOU: If they cross the border illegally, then they deserve it!

ERNESTO: No human being deserves to die alone in a desert trying to feed their families. Everyone has a right to survive and strive for a better life—

LOU: Yada, yada, yada... You idiotic liberals always give me the same emotional bullshit! You have no respect for the laws that clearly state you can't come and live in this country without the proper documentation —

ERNESTO: Lou, you know that you can't legislate morality. You know there used to be laws that barred blacks and women from voting, Jews from—

LOU: They broke the law!!!

ERNESTO: Were you a good history student?

LOU: Yes, I do fancy myself a history buff.

ERNESTO (*affirmatively*): Then I'm sure you know about the treaty of Guadalupe Hidalgo and how Americans constantly broke the law and crossed the Mexican border illegally and eventually stole Arizona, Texas—

LOU: That's a lie! Don't come on my show and distort the truth! We did not steal it!

ERNESTO: And I don't need to remind you how this land originally belonged to the Apaches and all the Native Americans before it was stolen by the Mexicans and then your "forefathers"—

LOU (*sarcastic and disgusted*): So what's your solution? Giving it back?

ERNESTO: The solution is immigration reform. New humane laws need to be created that are compassionate towards families and that give opportunities to those who are here —

LOU: Why should we reward people who break the law? Criminals don't get rewarded in prison—

ERNESTO: They are not criminals. No human being is illegal or a criminal for—

LOU (*staring down ERNESTO*): Yes they are, and so are you! What you do is criminal! You should be arrested—

ERNESTO: I take orders from a higher source. Laws, like men, are flawed, so God has told me to do this, and until God tells me to stop, I will continue. Until then, I must do what is right.

LOU: So God told you to do this?

ERNESTO: Yes.

LOU: You know how crazy that sounds? So God told you to break the law?

ERNESTO: In Matthew—

LOU: Shame on you for bringing God into this. Don't bring God into this!

ERNESTO: I will bring God into this. What kind of God do you believe in that allows poor people to die in the desert and children to get separated from their families? Or do you believe in God? Or do you believe that only white people are God's children?

LOU breaks his stare down with ENRIQUE and changes the subject.

LOU: Now, let's take a break for station identification. (*LOU presses a button*

and the show's identification jingle plays, severing the tension.) Would you like some coffee or water?

ERNESTO (*civil*): Water would be great. Can never have enough water.

The jingle ends and Lou takes the mike again.

LOU: Welcome back to Take Back America... Today my guest is Ernesto Martinez, founder of Angels of the Border. (*To ERNESTO.*) I have a surprise for you. (*LOU pushes a button.*) Caller, you're on the air.

CARL (*voice over, a white male speaks with a Texas twang*): Hello Lou, thanks for having me on your show. Ernesto, my name is—

ERNESTO: Carl. I know who you are. You're a poor confused man who thinks poking holes into the gallons of water I leave out in the desert is a patriotic act. Or taking shotguns to the border and dressing up like G.I. Joe is an act of—

CARL (*V.O.*): I am a proud member of the Minutemen, and I am defending this country against the illegal invaders who want to—

ERNESTO: That makeshift green uniform that you proudly wear, trying to imitate a Border Patrol Officer, is made by undocumented labor. I know that because I've visited those factories where undocumented people get paid pennies to make your uniform. That rifle that you use for target practice in the dessert, those parts are assembled in Mexico by Maquiladora workers who are exploited by NAFTA. That cap that you wear—

CARL (*V.O.*): Now, that's made in China so don't even lie.

ERNESTO: Yes, it's made in China by forced prison labor.

LOU: Carl, you're out there defending the border.

CARL (*V.O.*): Yes, I'm right here now.

LOU: Do you think what Ernesto is doing should be considered a crime?

CARL (*V.O.*): Yes, it certainly is!

ERNESTO: Gentlemen, I can see we are not going to come to any understanding, and I have a lot of water to deliver. This is going to be a very hot week, so I better get back to work. I just hope that one day you see the light, but hopefully not before you...finally see the light... Goodbye. (*He gets up and exits, leaving LOU and CARL to insult him in the wake of his absence.*)

LOU: See. These liberals know they can't stand up to me....

LIGHTS FADE OUT.

SCENE TWO:

LIGHTS FADE IN on the front seat of a car. It is night. SANDI drives with MATT. She spots something outside as they drive by.

SANDI: Did you see that?

MATT: No, what?

SANDI: There was a strange man by the side of the road. I wonder if he was waiting to cross, or if he wanted a ride.

MATT: What man?

SANDI: He was on your side.

MATT: No, I didn't see anything. It's so dark outside, except for all the stars.

SANDI: Yeah, it's kind of scary. This reminds me of a horror film I saw once... I would hate to have a tire blow out and get stuck here. (*SANDI turns on the radio. She dials it. A Ranchera song comes on.*) God, I hate Rancheras. Not another Ranchera station. (*After a few seconds she moves the dial and settles on a station broadcasting Take Back America. We hear part of the show we just witnessed, the moment when Lou Becker tells Ernesto that what he does is criminal.*) This show is so stupid. (*SANDI turns off the radio.*) People in Arizona are so stupid.

MATT: Where are we?

SANDI studies the map and fully opens it to follow a route.

SANDI: I can't wait to get a job so I can buy a car with GPS. This old clunker is ready to die...I just hope it gets us to California.

MATT (*sarcastic, joking*): With your Master's degree in English, you should be able to get a high paying job.

SANDI laughs. She continues studying the map.

SANDI: We are...we are...in butt-fuck Arizona... Some stupid route close to the border... Why did you get off the Eight Freeway?

MATT: I didn't know I got off...it just sort of kicked us off and put us on this road.

SANDI: We gotta get back on the Freeway, or it's going to take us longer, and I told my mother we'd be there for lunch.

MATT: Well, let me know when you see an opportunity to get back on the freeway.

SANDI: I'm so glad we're going to California now. If I hadn't gotten a scholarship to the University of Texas, I would have never gone to Texas. Man, I should never have left California. I miss San Diego.

MATT: I'm glad you did, otherwise we would have never met.

SANDI: We would have met. I know we were destined to meet... I can't wait for my mother to meet you.

MATT: Are you sure your mother is not going to mind me staying with you over the summer?

SANDI: I spoke to her. She says it's fine.

MATT: I really appreciate it, but you don't think it's going to be awkward... with your mother in the other room?

SANDI: Whoa. Don't tell me you have sexual hang ups?

MATT: No...I just know that if you came to my parents' house in Vancouver, and we slept in the room next to theirs...well...I just wouldn't feel right... My parents are conservative, and I probably couldn't sleep with you in their house, unless we were married.

SANDI: Your parents are definitely more conservative than mine...than my mother. My mother is pretty hip. She's had several boyfriends since my father and doesn't believe in marriage anymore so don't worry about it.

MATT: That's interesting that my parents are more hung up on these things, when you're Mexican and Catholic.

SANDI: I'm not Catholic, and I'm not... Well, I'm different. I am not a typical Latina like the other girls you might have met in college.

MATT: That's true. None of the other Hispanic girls would go out with me.

SANDI: Yeah, the freshmen ones are all afraid their parents are gonna kill them if they lose their virginity while away in college...especially to a gringo.

MATT: I'm not a "Gringo" - I'm a Canadian—

SANDI (*joking*): Any man as pale as you automatically is a "Gringo."

MATT: Yeah, well, I'm the only "Greengo" who doesn't have a "Green-cardo."

SANDI laughs. MATT doesn't. There's a pause in their conversation as SANDI stares at MATT, quickly figuring out that what he is saying is not a joke.

SANDI: No way.

MATT: I can trust you with that information, right?

SANDI: Of course. Of course. I feel honored that you are confiding in me. Your secret is safe with me.

MATT: Good, because you're the only person I've ever told this to. Not even my mother knows.

SANDI: Wow...I never imagined...hmmm.... Well, I feel special knowing you trust me...

MATT: Of course I trust you... I love you.

SANDI: I love you, too. *(BEAT)* How did you get all those scholarships?

MATT: I lied about my status and nobody has asked.

SANDI: What about law school? You mean nobody has figured out you're using a fake social security number?

MATT: Oh, it's a legitimate one...I got it from a dead person.

There's a pause as SANDI slowly turns to MATT not knowing if he is just joking. The information takes a few seconds to sink in.

SANDI: Hey, you aren't some serial killer that is gonna take my car and leave my corpse in the desert?

MATT: Why would you ask that?

SANDI: Oh, using dead people's social security numbers isn't something I take lightly.

MATT: Oh, no, no...I paid some guy in Vancouver, and he got me one and... It's actually easier than it sounds... I didn't go to someone's grave and pick out a name or anything like that...

SANDI: So what's your dead man's name?

MATT: Matthew Williamson.

SANDI *(after a BEAT)*: So what's your real name?

MATT: I can't tell you.

SANDI: Why not?

MATT: Because then I would have to kill you. (*He tickles her and they laugh. The laughter settles down, and he caresses her cheek.*)

SANDI: So come on; tell me your real name.

MATT: Ah... It's Dylan Thompson...

SANDI: Wow, almost like the English Poet...

MATT: Ah, yeah... Just don't call me by that name, OK?

SANDI: OK.

MATT: So forget what I told you, OK?

SANDI: Sure... So what if somebody found out?

MATT: Ah... If I don't go to jail for using a fake social security number, then I guess they'll just deport me back to Canada.

SANDI: That will be the day!

MATT: It could happen. One Canadian friend did not renew his Visa, and he was sent back.

SANDI: I would hate for you to be forced to leave this country... *(BEAT)* I would marry you.

MATT: Huh? What did you say?

SANDI: I said...I would marry you if it meant keeping you in this country... I know we've only been dating six months so I don't want to creep you out by making you think I want to get married...like right now...but I truly care about you.

MATT: Wow. That's the most beautiful thing anyone has ever said to me...If I weren't driving, I would kiss you.

SANDI: You should pull over soon at the next gas station. We're almost out of gas.

MATT pulls over and stops the car.

SANDI: What are you doing?

MATT grabs SANDI'S face and plants a kiss on her lips. SANDI kisses his neck and makes her way down to his crotch. MATT sticks his hand behind her back and unhooks her bra. She is about to unzip his pants when they hear footsteps, and a light in the distance interrupts their foreplay. An ARIZONA POLICEMAN approaches their car and stands next to the driver's side window.

ARIZONA POLICEMAN: Good evening. Is everything all right?

SANDI and MATT just nod. SANDI looks away trying to adjust her bra.

ARIZONA POLICEMAN: What are you doing parked on the side of the road?

MATT (*cautiouslt*): Ah... We got lost. We were trying to figure out where we are on the map.

ARIZONA POLICEMAN: Aha... The border is just a few miles away from here.

MATT (*still cautious*): Yes, we know.

ARIZONA POLICEMAN: So what are you doing here so close to the border?

MATT (*remaining cautious*): Like I said. We got lost.

The ARIZONA POLICEMAN stares at SANDI who is acting suspicious with weird movements as she tries to discreetly place her breasts back into her brassiere. He walks over to the passenger side of the car. SANDI looks up and freezes.

ARIZONA POLICEMAN: Oh, I think I know what is happening here...

MATT: You do?

ARIZONA POLICEMAN: Who is this woman?

MATT and SANDI turn to look at one another. SANDI is about to open her mouth, but MATT answers.

MATT: She's my girlfriend.

ARIZONA POLICEMAN: How long have you known her? Or do you even know her?

MATT: Excuse me?

ARIZONA POLICEMAN: Where did you pick her up?

SANDI: Hey!

MATT shoots SANDI a look that communicates, "Let me handle this."

MATT: Officer, this is my girlfriend of six months. We met in college and—

ARIZONA POLICEMAN: Let me see her documents.

MATT: Documents?

ARIZONA POLICEMAN: Son, it is a crime to transport an illegal alien in exchange for sexual favors.

SANDI: What?! I'm not an illegal alien!

ARIZONA POLICEMAN: Then show me your residency card...please!

SANDI: I don't have one!

ARIZONA POLICEMAN: Well, then step out of the vehicle.

SANDI: No! I don't have a "Greencard" or any documents with me because I am a U.S. citizen, and I don't need to carry any!

ARIZONA POLICEMAN: Well, if you can't prove you have a legal right to be here—

SANDI: I'm a U.S. citizen! I don't have to prove it!

ARIZONA POLICEMAN: You are six miles away from the border and you look – I mean...you have given me reason to suspect that your status—

SANDI: He's in the same car with me. Why haven't you asked him to show you his papers?

MATT: Sandi! (*MATT shoots her another look that indicates for her to chill out and let him handle it.*)

Sandi refuses to show her ID to the Arizona policeman.

Photo by Josefina López

ARIZONA POLICEMAN: Please step out of the vehicle.

SANDI: No! I won't step out of the car. Why don't you ask him for his documents? How do you know he's not an "illegal Canadian alien?"

MATT (*annoyed*): Sandi!! God!!

ARIZONA POLICEMAN: Lady, you are interfering with my job. I have a right to ask you for your papers and to ask you to step out of the vehicle—

SANDI: Well, I'm not showing you any documents.

MATT: Sandi, just show him your California I.D. – I'm sure that's all he needs to see.

SANDI: No! I am not showing you no stinking badges, cabrón!

ARIZONA POLICEMAN: Did she just call me a "cabrón?"

MATT: No! She called me a "cabrón!"

SANDI: I'm speaking to you in English. Do you notice I don't have an accent, and I'm not afraid of you? Doesn't that tip you off that I am an over-entitled American who went to college and is exercising her right to civil disobedience?

ARIZONA POLICEMAN: Lady, I don't care what you think you are. You are now resisting arrest. I'm only going to ask you one more time. Step out of the car at the count of three, or I'll have to personally remove you from the vehicle. (*He begins to count slowly.*) One….

MATT turns to SANDI with pleading eyes and begs her to stop her "civil disobedience."

MATT: Sandi, please, just show him your driver's license and your college I.D. Come on, baby, this could end badly, for both of us.

SANDI: No. He's called me an "illegal alien" and practically called me a "whore." How can you just sit there and let him do this to me?

MATT: What can I do?

SANDI: You went to law school. Think of something.

MATT: Officer, you have no right—

ARIZONA POLICEMAN: Yes, I do... Two!...

MATT: Come on! Show him your I.D.

SANDI: No!

MATT grabs her purse and searches for her I.D. She snatches her purse back from him.

SANDI: How dare you! You have no right to do that for me!

MATT (*whispers*): I don't want to get deported.

SANDI: Dylan, this is wrong!

MATT: Sandi, stop this, now!

SANDI defiantly throws her purse out the car window.

ARIZONA POLICEMAN: Three.

SANDI crosses her arms and sits silently in protest.

LIGHTS FADE OUT.

SCENE THREE:

LIGHTS FADE IN. In the darkness we hear a phone ringing. The call goes to voicemail.

VOICEMAIL MESSAGE (*voice over*): Hey, this is Saul. Please leave a message. Hola, soy Saul. Dejame un mensaje.

YOUNG MEXICAN MAN (*voice over*): Saul, es Raul. Te estoy llamando para decirte que por favor le mandes dinero a mi Ama porque ésta semana necesito comprarle ropa a mi niña y con la renta – pues... [Paco, I'm calling you to ask you to please send money to my mother this week because I have to buy clothes for my daughter and with the rent-- well...] (*Footsteps are heard in the background of the message.*) Qué quieren? [What do you want?]

YOUNG WHITE MAN #1 (*voice over*): You fucking wetback, go back to your own country!

We hear the sound of a bat making contact with flesh and then a bloodcurdling scream.

YOUNG MAN #2 (*voice over*): Take that you scum of the earth! You fucking criminal!

YOUNG MEXICAN MAN (*voice over*): ¡Auxilio! ¡Ayúdenme! [Help! Help me!]

YOUNG MAN #3 (*voice over*): You piece of shit alien! Bringing leprosy and tuberculosis – you deserve to die!

YOUNG MAN #1 (*voice over*): Let's kill the cockroach!

YOUNG MAN #2 (*voice over*): Die cockroach! Die!

There are sounds of spitting, feet stomping hard against the ground, and bats pounding on flesh, followed by screams of agony. There are also other undecipherable sounds.

YOUNG MEXICAN MAN (*voice over*): ¡Por favor! ¡Ayúdenme! [Please! Help me!]

The sounds of the attack subside. A final blow is heard as it smashes the cell phone, and after that, nothing else is heard. The voice over abruptly ends. LIGHTS FADE IN on a tent. (The tent is located in the desert, but this is not yet made clear to the audience.) LOU is tied to a chair, gagged and blindfolded. Dried blood is caked on his head and nostrils. He is full of sweat and surrounded by THREE FIGURES who all wear ski masks and appear male. They take off his blindfold and remove the duct tape covering his mouth. LOU is jolted by their appearances. He looks around, horrified.

LOU: Who are you? What do you want? Where am I?

The THREE FIGURES stand in menacing silence.

LOU: Why did you kidnap me?

They remain silent.

LOU: How did you...? How did you...bring me here? What do you want from me? Who are you?

The THREE FIGURES turn to each other and nod. The tallest one presses a button on a digital device and plays for LOU the horrible murder sequence documented on the YOUNG MEXICAN MAN's voicemail message.

LOU: Who are you? Are you terrorists? Do you speak English?

TALL FIGURE: The only thing you should be asking is how are you getting out of here.

LOU: How can I get out of here? Are you holding me for ransom? Who have you called? What did my wife say? How much money are you asking for?

TALL FIGURE: This isn't about money.

LOU: No? Then what else do you want?

The THREE FIGURES turn to each other and nod. The TALL FIGURE presses a button and replays the audio of the murder. LIGHTS SLOWLY FADE OUT. (BEAT) LIGHTS FADE IN on LOU still tied to a chair and surrounded by the

THREE FIGURES with the recording of the murder in progress again.

LOU: Stop! Stop playing it! Stop!!! Why are you doing this to me?

TALL FIGURE: Why do you do it?

MEDIUM FIGURE: Why do you spread so much hate?

LOU: Who are you? What group are you with? Are you illegal aliens?

They remain silent. They turn to one another and nod. The TALL FIGURE pulls out a gun and points it at LOU who immediately gasps in horror. The other two FIGURES grab a brush and a bucket full of a dark liquid. The SHORT FIGURE brings a bag with clothes, and the MEDIUM and SHORT FIGURES put the items close to LOU. The MEDIUM FIGURE releases LOU from the chair and places him directly in front of the SHORT FIGURE

SHORT FIGURE: Take off your clothes!

LOU: What!

SHORT FIGURE: You heard me, fuck face!

LOU removes his clothes and turns away from them, keeping on only his boxers.

SHORT FIGURE: All of it!

LOU takes off his boxers and stands completely naked. The short figure gives him a pair of pink boxers.

SHORT FIGURE: Put this on!

LOU: What kind of a sick joke is this?

MEDIUM FIGURE: You are the sick joke. Now put them on before I shoot your balls off!

LOU puts on the pink boxers.

LOU: This is so childish.

TALL FIGURE: Shut up asshole!

The SHORT FIGURE proceeds to take photos of him.

SHORT FIGURE: These are going to be so funny. People are gonna love these on the internet.

LOU: Come on, how much money do you want? I'm not a rich man, but I can get you at least twenty-five thousand—

TALL FIGURE: I told you this is not about money!

LOU: Oh, so then what? You just want to humiliate me? Is that it? Teach me a lesson?

TALL FIGURE: Shut up!

LOU: You're not going to get away with this.

MEDIUM FIGURE: This fuckin' pink pig needs to be taught a lesson!

SHORT FIGURE: Let's get started.

The TALL FIGURE gets close to LOU and points the gun at LOU'S head. LOU winces, thinking he is going to get shot.

LOU: Don't kill me! Please don't kill me!

TALL FIGURE: Take that brush and dip it into the bucket.

LOU does as he is told.

TALL FIGURE: Now, paint yourself with it.

LOU brushes the brown liquid on himself and stops to smell it.

LOU: What is this?

MEDIUM FIGURE: Just keep brushing!

LOU: This is bar-be-cue sauce!

He puts it all over his body. When he is done, the SHORT FIGURE takes photographs of him.

TALL FIGURE: So how does it feel to be brown?

LOU: Ha, ha, ha. Just stop this nonsense. Look, if you leave me alone now, I promise you that I will not prosecute you.

MEDIUM FIGURE: Shut the fuck up, pendejo! This isn't your racist radio show where you can say whatever bullshit comes out of your caca brain. You are our special guest, and we are going to give you the royal treatment. (*He turns to SHORT FIGURE.*) Did you get the dildo and the rope?

SHORT FIGURE: I sure did.

TALL FIGURE: Let's see how he likes it.

LOU: What are you going to do to me?

MEDIUM FIGURE: Just sit back and relax. Yeah, it's better if you relax. It will go easier for you.

LOU: No, you can't do this to me! This is not right!

LIGHTS FADE OUT. LOU screams.

SCENE FOUR:

LIGHTS FADE IN on a DETENTION CENTER. A FEMALE GUARD pulls SANDI, who is in handcuffs and wearing a light blue uniform, into an interrogation room. She looks disheveled, like she lost a fight. She has a small tissue paper stuffed into one nostril to keep the blood from dripping. She is made to sit on a chair. A spotlight shines on her. She squints, uncomfortable, still very upset.

INTERROGATOR'S VOICE: Deme su nombre y fecha de nacimiento. State your name and date of birth.

SANDI says nothing.

INTERROGATOR'S VOICE: Cual es su nombre y fecha de nacimiento?

SANDI: Fuck you!

INTERROGATOR'S VOICE: You speak English. State your name and date of birth.

SANDI remains silent.

INTERROGATOR'S VOICE: I see you not only resisted arrest, but you are not going to cooperate either.

SANDI remains silent.

INTERROGATOR'S VOICE: There are serious consequences for not cooperating. You can go to jail not only for resisting arrest, prostitution—

SANDI: I am not a prostitute!

INTERROGATOR'S VOICE: What were you doing six miles from the border?

SANDI continues her silent protest.

INTERROGATOR'S VOICE: What is your country of origin?

SANDI (*with exaggerated Canadian accent*): Canada, Aeeee….

INTERROGATOR'S VOICE: Excuse me?

SANDI (*continues with Canadian accent*): I said, Canada. That's where I'm from.

INTERROGATOR'S VOICE: What part of Canada?

SANDI (*with British accent*): No, I'm actually from England... (*With Irish accent.*) Oh, I just remembered, I'm from Ireland.

INTERROGATOR'S VOICE: Guard!

The FEMALE GUARD takes SANDI by the handcuffs and drags her to another location. LIGHTS CHANGE SLIGHTLY. The FEMALE GUARD removes her handcuffs.

SANDI: Where am I? Is this jail?

FEMALE GUARD: You're in a detention center.

SANDI: A detention center out here in the desert?

FEMALE GUARD: It's kind of like jail, but it's temporary.

SANDI: What do you mean?

FEMALE GUARD: As soon as it is determined that someone has broken the law and they have no right to be in this country, they get deported.

SANDI: What about a judge? Or a trial or—

FEMALE GUARD: You've been watching too many movies. That doesn't happen here.

SANDI: But I'm a U.S. citizen! I don't belong here. I'm not like these people.

FEMALE GUARD: Listen, I don't know about your case, so I can't help you.

SANDI: But this is not fair. I got racially profiled, so I refused to show my identification, and I refused to step outside of the car I was in—

FEMALE GUARD: Well, you broke the law, and that's why you're here.

SANDI: But this law is unfair—

FEMALE GUARD: I don't make laws, I just enforce them.

SANDI: You know there used to be laws that did not permit blacks to vote or ride at the front of a bus. Why did Rosa Parks refuse to give up her seat?

FEMALE GUARD: Don't tell me you are trying to be the Rosa Parks for Latinos?

SANDI: No! I just don't think it's fair that I have to show my papers and my Canadian boyfriend doesn't have to.

FEMALE GUARD: Honey, I want to have sympathy for you, but I hear

hundreds of people with sadder stories, so I don't have time for this.

SANDI: So, what do I do here?

FEMALE GUARD: Well, if you really are a U.S. citizen, then just chill until someone comes to get you out.

The FEMALE GUARD exits. SANDI sits down and looks all around her. Although we don't see anyone, there are several voices speaking in Spanish and other foreign languages. We may not understand some of the languages, but they are all sad voices of people in dire situations. There is also crying heard. SANDI hums, but before she realizes it, she too, is crying.

LIGHTS FADE OUT.

SCENE FIVE:

LIGHTS FADE IN at the tent. LOU is tied up again. He is sleeping. The TALL FIGURE drops a bucket of water on him, causing LOU to shake himself awake.

MEDIUM FIGURE: You don't get to sleep fascist fat boy!

As the TALL FIGURE goes to press the play back button to launch the voicemail recording, LOU yells.

LOU (*begging*): No, don't play that again! Please don't play that again!

TALL FIGURE: I won't stop playing it until you ask the right question!

LOU: What's the question? What's the question I'm supposed to ask?

MEDIUM FIGURE: Think about it!

LOU: Ah... Well.... (*Pause*) Who is getting killed? Is that the question? Am I supposed to ask about who got killed?

SHORT FIGURE: Finally figuring it out!

TALL FIGURE: So ask me!

LOU: Who is getting killed?

TALL FIGURE: My brother.

LOU: That's your brother?

TALL FIGURE: Now ask me why.

LOU: Why is he being killed?

MEDIUM FIGURE: You tell us motherfucker? Tell us why he got killed! Tell me why my brother got killed. Tell her why her brother got killed!

LOU: Why would I know that?

TALL FIGURE: And you still can't figure it out!

The TALL FIGURE slaps LOU uncontrollably. The other two FIGURES pull him away. He takes a second to recompose himself. He gets in LOU's face and unmasks himself.

TALL FIGURE: Look at my face. I want you to look at me closely. I look exactly like my brother. You killed my twin brother!!!!!

LOU (*perplexed*): How did I kill your twin brother?

SHORT FIGURE: And you still have the nerve to ask?

MEDIUM FIGURE: You tell lies about Latinos, and you teach others to hate, and you still ask?!

(BEAT)

LOU: Ah... Ah... Listen, I am not responsible for what drunk white teenage boys do to illegals—

The TALL YOUNG MAN sticks the gun in LOU's mouth. LOU tries to pull away.

TALL FIGURE: You say "illegals" one more time, and I'll put a bullet in your mouth!!!

He pulls the gun out of LOU's mouth.

LOU: I don't tell anyone to go kill Latino people. I only tell people to fight back...I mean, I only tell people to defend our country against criminals, many of whom happen to be illegal.

TALL FIGURE: Liar! Your hate spreads hate, and you may not be the person who took a bat to my brother's head, but you inspired those teenagers and gave them the words and the justification to kill my brother!

(BEAT)

LOU: Is this what this is about? Do you want an apology? Because I am truly sorry that you lost your brother, and I know nothing I say can bring him back and—

TALL FIGURE: Shut up, shut up! You are a liar! You lie about undocumented people being a third of the prison population. You know

Photo by Josefina López

Lou is threatened by his kidnappers.

that's a fuckin' lie, and you still say it! You get paid to lie, and you are doing it right here with me!

The MEDIUM FIGURE tapes up LOU's mouth.

TALL FIGURE: Let's kill him.

MEDIUM FIGURE: What?

SHORT FIGURE: This was not part of the plan! We didn't agree we were going to kill him!

TALL FIGURE: I know. I know. But now that I took off my mask, he knows what I look like. He'll know how to find me. We have to kill him.

LOU shakes his head and protests, but can't be heard.

MEDIUM FIGURE: Okay, let's kill him because, fuck, it's too hot for this mask!

He takes off the ski mask to reveal himself. He wipes the sweat off his face with the ski mask. The SHORT FIGURE takes off her mask to reveal a young woman with long hair.

LIGHTS FADE OUT.

SCENE SIX:

LIGHTS FADE IN at the Detention Center. SANDI sleeps. The FEMALE GUARD gently nudges SANDI awake.

FEMALE GUARD: You have a visitor... Looks like your Canadian boyfriend is here to get you out.

The FEMALE GUARD escorts SANDI to a desk and chair where MATT is already seated holding several papers. SANDI sits.

MATT: How are they treating you?

SANDI: It's not as bad as jail... Well, I wouldn't know the difference, but from the movies I've seen, it's not as bad... Lots of crying...

MATT: You?

SANDI: No, all the people that are getting deported...

MATT: Well, I called your mother, and I asked her to fax me your birth certificate and whatever else she could, to prove that you're a U.S. citizen. Your mother is so nice—

SANDI: I didn't ask you to do that.

MATT: Sandi, I'm going to get you out of here... I'm working on getting you a lawyer so that once I prove you're a citizen, they can drop the charges, and we can get to California.

SANDI: I don't want you to show proof. Don't you get it? What I do want is for you to go to the local paper and tell them about me so they can interview me and do a story on racial profiling and how I ended up here.

MATT: So this is what you wanted? You want publicity and fame out of this horrible experience? I could have gotten arrested and deported because of you.

SANDI: No, I don't want publicity for myself. I'm just tired of always having to prove that I am an American. It's not right!

MATT: You are nuts! I don't understand why you would put yourself and me through this just to prove a point.

SANDI: No, Matt, you will never know what it's like to be me. You don't have dark skin. Nobody ever questions your right to exist or succeed. You have no clue how hard it is to be an American when you look like me!

MATT: You want me to feel sorry for you because you're not white?

SANDI: No. I want you to understand that this is a very personal struggle that I'm going through, and I want you to be the kind of boyfriend who gets it!

MATT: Look, I get it. I know it's not fair, but it's not up to you to change the law. You can't do anything about your situation except get out of it.

SANDI: If I do nothing... No, I can't just do nothing...I don't know what else to do but this. But I can't do nothing... So will you help me out by going to the newspaper?

MATT appears to briefly consider her request before arriving at his response.

MATT: No, I just don't feel comfortable doing that. It doesn't feel right. It feels manipulative, and I can't get involved. I just can't jeopardize everything I worked for... Not for you. I can't.

(BEAT)

SANDI: I see... *(SANDI takes a deep breath.)* All right, Dylan... Well, then I'll see you later.

MATT: Just please come to your senses. Let me help you.

SANDI: No. I have to do this. You will never understand why I need to do this. This is not for anyone else, but for me.

LIGHTS FADE OUT.

SCENE SEVEN:

LIGHTS FADE IN. ERNESTO walks into the desert and is followed by a DOCUMENTARY FILMMAKER and a CAMERAMAN. ERNESTO places two full gallon containers on the ground. He assembles an orange flag and places it on a pole.

ERNESTO: I actually love the desert, especially when it rains and the monsoons make the air smell so fresh and beautiful.

DOCUMENTARY FILMMAKER: How hot does it get out here?

ERNESTO: It can get as hot as 127 degrees.

DOCUMENTARY FILMMAKER: How many people have died crossing the desert?

ERNESTO: Since Operation Gatekeeper, approximately ten thousand. Each day, one or two people die in the desert.

DOCUMENTARY FILMMAKER: Have you ever seen a dead body on your water rounds?

ERNESTO: Yes, several. No matter how many I've seen, it still shocks me to see a human being in such a state of... It's hard to describe the feeling...I guess "helplessness" would be the word. I just feel devastated that I couldn't do something to reach them in time... No matter how bad it is people will not stop coming.

DOCUMENTARY FILMMAKER: Of all the deaths you've witnessed is there one, in particular, that has made an impact on you?

ERNESTO: There are too many tragic stories that I carry in my heart... But, yes, there is one in particular. One time when I was delivering water, I saw several empty bottles of water, trash, and a burnt out fire. As I got closer, I saw a woman lying down on the ground. She looked dead, but she was not dried up or damaged. She looked like she had been dead for maybe a day. Suddenly, her body started moving, and I got happy thinking she was still alive, and I could rush her to the hospital, and possibly save her life. When I got close to her body, I quickly jumped back, startled. A black snake slithered out of her mouth, and I saw her body wiggle as a five-foot snake came out of her. She was dead...I guess the group she was with had left her behind, and the animals... Ah... Well, I started crying. What else could I do? After the snake went to hide in a hole at a distance, I took her hand, and I said a prayer for her...I think about the souls of the 10,000 who have perished wandering in the desert. I carry crosses in the desert. I carry crosses in my heart, for all these poor souls... Sometimes it's too much to bear, so I try not to think about it and keep busy. (*ERNESTO picks up empty containers.*)

DOCUMENTARY FILMMAKER: So why do you do it?

ERNESTO: Because it's the right thing to do.

DOCUMENTARY FILMMAKER: Yes, but why? What difference does it make? Like you said, two people will die in the desert whether you put water out here or not. No matter what you do or how many migrants die out here, people will not stop coming.

ERNESTO: I have to believe that what I do makes a difference... You know, I heard Ghandi's grandson, Ravi, tell a story that has always stayed with me. He said, that a father and his young son were walking along the beach, and there were thousands of tiny starfish that were on the sand, and the sun was drying them up. The small son started throwing the starfish back into the water, trying to save them. The father told him to stop because what difference did it make - there were thousands of them. His son picked up

one of the starfish and replied, "It will make a difference to this starfish." He threw it back into the water and continued picking up starfish and throwing them back into the water.

In the distance we hear trucks approaching. Some honking is heard.

ERNESTO: Hmmm. The Minutemen are here. Let's go before they start acting stupid and threatening us.

DOCUMENTARY FILMMAKER (*to her CAMERAMAN*): Make sure you zoom in on them. Ernesto, let's go confront them. I need to get this on camera. I have to capture some conflict to sell this documentary.

ERNESTO: Are you sure?

DOCUMENTARY FILMMAKER: Of course.

ERNESTO (*jokingly, light hearted*): All right. Let's wave at them and shout, "Buenos dias!" That pisses them off.

They smile and wave.

DOCUMENTARY FILMMAKER: Buenos dias. Did you hear that, Ritchie? Buenos dias.

ALL (*smiling and waving*): Buenos dias!!!

DOCUMENTARY FILMMAKER: I think he sees us. He's flipping us off.

ERNESTO: Hey, Carl!

CARL (*V.O.*): Don't talk to me, wetback lover!

LIGHTS FADE OUT.

SCENE EIGHT:

In total darkness we hear the jingle for KRZT.

GUEST DJ VOICE/CARL DUNLOP: This is Carl Dunlop sitting in for Lou Becker who is...on vacation. He's probably having a great time right now. Welcome back to Take Back America. Have you had enough? Are you thinking of joining the Tea Party? Are you a member of the Tea Party? If so, call me and tell me why you have joined. These lines are open. All righty. Our first caller is Lindsay, calling from Douglas...

The voice fades out. LIGHTS FADE IN on the tent. Still tied up in pink underwear, LOU sleeps. He is a mess. With dried barbecue sauce remaining crusted all over him, he looks like he has been through hell. The SHORT FIGURE is the only FIGURE still present. She is now unmasked and holds the gun. She browses through the photos stored on her digital camera featuring LOU posed in embarrassing and compromising positions. LOU wakes up from a nightmare and screams, "No!" He looks up at the SHORT FIGURE absorbed in looking at her photos.

LOU: How does a pretty girl like you get involved with these losers?

SHORT FIGURE: How do you know this wasn't my idea?

LOU: You don't look like you have it in you to kill.

She remains silent.

LOU: I know you don't want to kill me...I can tell by your kind eyes that you are different from the others... Why don't we make a deal? Why don't you let me go, and then I can meet you somewhere and give you some money as a reward for saving my life.

SHORT FIGURE: So, just because I'm the only female in the group, you think I'm stupid enough to believe you?

LOU: I know you are not a killer. You don't want my blood on your hands. You know you are better than that... If you think I'm wrong about Latinos being criminals, then show me I'm wrong by showing me some mercy.

SHORT FIGURE: I know what you're trying to do. If you're gonna start playing mind games with me, you better stop because I have a black belt in mind games.

LOU: Where are the other two guys?

SHORT FIGURE: They went to get gasoline.

LOU: Why?

SHORT FIGURE: They want to pour it all over you and set you on fire. That's the way they want to do it, but I don't like that.

LOU: Why not?

SHORT FIGURE: Well, we debated all the ways we wanted to kill you. We researched all the ways people have committed hate crimes against Latinos, and they thought setting you on fire was poetic. But I didn't want us to kill you to begin with. I just wanted to scare you. I agreed to help them out just to scare you and avenge my brother's death, but I never agreed to kill you.

LOU: Then don't kill me. Let me go! Please, before they return.

SHORT FIGURE: Hmm... Maybe... But you have to tell me why you do it.

LOU: Do what?

SHORT FIGURE: Why do you do your show?

LOU: It's what people want to hear.

SHORT FIGURE: Yeah, I know, but why?

LOU: Why? Because fear sells, why else?

SHORT FIGURE: Yeah, but why? Why sell fear?

(BEAT)

LOU: Because...because that's all I know how to do.

SHORT FIGURE: What do you mean? I'm sure you can do other things.

LOU: I tried... But I was no good at political commentary or serious journalism. I just couldn't cut it, so I landed this show, and I did with it the best I could...

SHORT FIGURE: But why? Why spread hate and not love?

LOU: When you get to be my age, spreading love is not that easy.

SHORT FIGURE: Do you really hate Mexicans and Latinos and illegals as much as you say you do?

LOU: No... My father did. He was so afraid of foreigners taking over. I don't hate Mexicans... My wife is Mexican-American...but like third or fourth generation...something like that.

SHORT FIGURE: For real? How come people don't know that?

LOU: I don't hide it or advertise it...

SHORT FIGURE: So when you were a little boy, what did you want to be when you grew up?

LOU (*sincerely recalling*): When I was growing up in Scotland, I wanted to be a tour guide in Edinburgh.

SHORT FIGURE: Edinburgh?

LOU: Yes, there were so many tour buses; I thought it would be nice to welcome people to my country.

SHORT FIGURE: Wait a minute. You mean you weren't born in the U.S.?

LOU: I met my wife in Canada, and I became a U.S. citizen through marriage.

SHORT FIGURE: You don't even have an accent.

LOU: I got rid of it when I knew I wanted to be in radio.

SHORT FIGURE: So you are an immigrant?

LOU: Ah... Yes....Yes, I am... You see, you and I have more in common than you thought.

SHORT FIGURE: I was born in this country... So you criticize immigrants and you—

LOU: I criticize illegal immigration! I did it through the correct channels. I had to wait in line to become a U.S. citizen.

The SHORT FIGURE yells and lunges at LOU with the butt of a gun in an attempt to strike him. LOU recoils and cowers, afraid.

LOU: Please don't kill me.

She steps back. After a few seconds, she regains her composure.

SHORT FIGURE: I don't want to kill you.... I don't want them to kill you either...but I don't want to get in trouble with them or the police.

LOU: If you let me go, I promise I won't go after you. Just them.

SHORT FIGURE: They're my brothers. I can't let them go to jail.

(BEAT)

LOU: Hmmm... All right. Let me go, and I won't go after you or your brothers.

SHORT FIGURE: You promise?

LOU: Yes. I swear. I swear on all that is holy to me...

(BEAT)

SHORT FIGURE: I have an idea... I suffer from epilepsy, so at some point I'm going to untie you without the other guys noticing. Then I'm going to pretend I am having an epileptic seizure. In all the confusion, the guys will pay attention to me and will look for my medicine, and you then gotta run like hell.

LOU: Okay. Okay... Where should I run to? Where am I?

SHORT FIGURE: We're in the desert, so just run towards wherever the sun

is setting. Go west. That will get you close to the highway.

LOU: Got it.

LIGHTS FADE OUT.

SCENE NINE:

LIGHTS FADE IN low on the Detention Center. It is very dark, and snoring is heard. A woman, MILAGROS, is crying as she lies in the cot next to SANDI's. SANDI wakes, sits up, and watches the woman cry.

SANDI: What's wrong?

MILAGROS: Que?

SANDI (*with an Anglicized accent*): ¿Qué pasa?

MILAGROS: It can't be. It can't be.

SANDI: Oh, you speak English...

MILAGROS: My children...I can't get to them. I wonder what is going to happen to them. They took me in the middle of the night while my husband was away in Texas for a job, and they left the children by themselves. I hope they are okay. I hope they are safe.

SANDI: Can you ask about them?

MILAGROS: They don't tell me anything.

SANDI: Maybe a neighbor took them in.

MILAGROS: No, no. They took everyone in that building who had no papers. They took everybody, except the children.

SANDI: Were they born in this country?

WOMAN: Yes, they were all born here.

SANDI: Well, I'm sure if they see children wandering around, social services will come get them, and they will put them in foster homes or—

The WOMAN lets out a cry.

WOMAN: They are taking them away from me, and I'll never see them again! Ay, mis hijos.... [Oh, my children....]

SANDI: Yes, you will. You will see them again.

SANDI puts her arm around her.

MILAGROS: We should have never left California. I told my husband I did not want to leave California, and he convinced me to move to Arizona, and I shouldn't have listened to him. (*She sobs.*)

SANDI rocks her. She doesn't know what to do. The silence is painful.

SANDI: Where in California did you live?

MILAGROS: San Fernando Valley.

SANDI: I lived there too.

MILAGROS: ¿Si?

SANDI: Yes. I was born there and lived there for most of my life, until I left to college four years ago, before I moved to San Diego.

MILAGROS: I liked it there. I felt right at home.

SANDI: What side did you live in?

MILAGROS: What do you mean?

SANDI: Did you live in the Mexican side of town?

MILAGROS: Oh... Yes, of course... But then later, it all became Mexican, que no? (Isn't that right?)

SANDI: Yes. Yes, it did... I was there when it was...different.

MILAGROS: Yes, I went to school in the White part of town, and I didn't like it...

SANDI: Yes. White kids would call us names.

MILAGROS: "Beaners" and "Wetbacks"... It was awful...

(BEAT)

SANDI: At my school in the valley, I was one of a few Latino children. I was in first grade, and Courtney, who was also in my class, got lice. Her mother was furious, and she threatened the school. So without informing the parents, they rounded up all the dark skinned children, and they sent us to the detention room, and the nurse looked through our hair searching for lice. I tried to explain to the nurse that I didn't have any because I had never been to Mexico or anywhere but the valley... She didn't care. She was convinced I had lice like all the rest. When we were all returned to our classes, everyone laughed at us. Nobody wanted to be our friend because they thought they would get lice from us. There was only one other Mexican

girl in my class. Milagros.... Yes, I think that was her name. One day at lunch time, some kids were picking on her and calling her a "Beaner." She looked to me for help. I saw that she needed me to say something or step in front of her and protect her. But all these White kids...well, I was scared. I couldn't stand up to all of them, and I was afraid they would hurt me... So I started calling her a "Beaner," too, and joined in the name calling... Milagros started crying, and she tried to get away, but a group of boys continued following her and cornered her. They started pulling on her hair. She pushed them back and cried out for help, but I didn't do anything. They started spitting at her, and I had to look away. Finally, a janitor intervened and told all the kids to leave her alone. The school bell rang, and I went back to class. Milagros was taken to the nurse. I thought for sure I was going to get in trouble for participating in the name calling... But Milagros went home after, and she never came back to class. After that day, I was no longer seen as one of them. I was accepted, and nobody ever called me a "Beaner" or a "Wetback." I stopped speaking Spanish and stopped calling myself Sandra and started calling myself "Sandi." As Sandi, I would fit in better. Then Courtney and Britney and Brianna made an exception for me and became my friends. I was treated like I was different...and I liked it... When I asked about Milagros, all I heard was that her mother decided to send her to a school in the Mexican part of town instead... I have never forgotten Milagros. I always wondered what happened to her.

MILAGROS: What school was this?

SANDI: Garfield Elementary.

MILAGROS: Was your teacher Ms. Johnson?

SANDI: Yes... How did you know?

MILAGROS: I am Milagros.

SANDI: Your name is Milagros, too?

MILAGROS: Yes, but I am Milagros, that little girl that got spat on.

(BEAT)

SANDI: I am so sorry. I am so sorry I stood back and did nothing. I am so sorry... I was afraid and...

MILAGROS: ...and you were a little girl and you didn't know any better....

SANDI breaks down crying. MILAGROS puts her arm around her.

SANDI: Yes. I am so ashamed of myself, and I have never forgotten you or that awful day, and I am haunted by you and...

MILAGROS (*compassionately*): I forgive you. You don't have to cry anymore...

SANDI buries her face in MILAGRO's chest.

MILAGROS: Sandi, listen to me. Tomorrow night when they are taking us on the bus back to Nogales, something is going to happen. You need to stay awake the whole trip.

SANDI: What's going to happen?

MILAGROS: You just need to be awake. Promise me you will stay awake.

SANDI: Ok. I promise. I'll drink lots of coffee.

MILAGROS: Yes, and lots of water... Lots of water...

SANDI: Okay.

(BEAT)

MILAGROS: I feel better now. Good night. *(MILAGROS lies down on her cot.)*

SANDI: Good night.

SANDI watches her and then lies down on her cot and goes back to sleep. LIGHTS FADE OUT. Seconds later LIGHTS FADE IN. SANDI is asleep on her cot. SANDI wakes up, sees that the cot next to her is empty, and then looks around for MILAGROS.

SANDI: Milagros?

SANDI gets up and looks around. The FEMALE SECURITY GUARD enters.

SANDI: Where is the woman who slept next to me? Was she deported?

FEMALE SECURITY GUARD: There was no woman sleeping next to you.

SANDI: Yes, there was a woman next to me. She woke me up with her crying, and I spoke to her.

FEMALE SECURITY GUARD: Maybe it was a dream. You must have imagined it, because nobody gets out of here without me knowing about it.

SANDI: I put my arm around her. She was real.

FEMALE SECURITY GUARD: Hey, you won't be the first person to have seen a ghost around here.

SANDI: I don't believe in ghosts... She was real. Her name was Milagros.

FEMALE SECURITY GUARD: We don't have any Milagros booked here today.

SANDI sits down and takes it in. She clutches her stomach.

FEMALE SECURITY GUARD: Are you all right?

SANDI: I want to throw up.

FEMALE SECURITY GUARD: Maybe you're pregnant.

SANDI (*with attitude*): Just because I'm a Latina, you automatically assume I was put here to procreate.

FEMALE SECURITY GUARD: Honey, let me tell you something. If Latinas don't die in the desert, they get raped by coyotes – you know, the human traffickers, or bandits, or maybe even the Border Patrol officers, if you ask me. Pregnancy is so common that sometimes I think contraceptive pills should be handed out at the Mexican side of the border. These women end up vomiting all over my detention center. I feel for them, but I didn't sign up for this job to be cleaning up vomit from morning sickness.

SANDI: Well, I'm certain I'm not pregnant.

FEMALE SECURITY GUARD: Good. (*Pause.*) You will be happy we got the order to deport you and you'll be leaving this wonderful place this evening.

SANDI: I don't want to be deported.

FEMALE SECURITY GUARD: What? I thought you wanted—

SANDI: I want to produce proof that I am a U.S. citizen and call my mother to come get me.

FEMALE SECURITY GUARD: Well your mother can go get you in Nogales, then. It's too late. You should have presented your paperwork yesterday.

SANDI: But I'm a U.S. citizen.

FEMALE SECURITY GUARD: Well, then, you'll have no trouble getting back in.

LIGHTS FADE OUT.

SCENE TEN:

LIGHTS FADE IN on the tent where the three FIGURES, all unmasked, are still keeping LOU. The male TALL and MEDIUM FIGURES talk about their murder plan, while the female SHORT FIGURE guards LOU, who is gagged and tied up.

MEDIUM FIGURE: So let me get this straight, we shoot him first, and then we set him on fire?

TALL FIGURE: No. We set him on fire first, and then when he's in so much pain that he wants to die, and he's begging us to shoot him, we won't shoot him. I want him to suffer and scream like my brother did, and then I'll shoot him.

MEDIUM FIGURE: Oh, and you know what we should also do? We should first cut out his tongue!

BOTH (*in unison*): Yeah!

MEDIUM FIGURE: That way, he'll never talk shit again!

They both get very excited about this and huddle closer to continue working on the details of the murder.

SHORT FIGURE (*to the guys*): Hey, we need to put more barbeque sauce on him.

TALL FIGURE: So what's stopping you?

She rolls her eyes and throws him a look of annoyance. She picks up the brush and puts barbeque sauce on LOU. She then stands behind him.

SHORT FIGURE (*whispers to LOU*): Wait. (*She puts down the brush and bucket.*) Hey, should we feed him before we kill him? Give him his last meal?

MEDIUM FIGURE (*bothered, with attitude*): Do whatever the hell you want.

The SHORT FIGURE sticks an apple in LOU's mouth and takes his photograph.

SHORT FIGURE: Doesn't he look like a pig now?

The three FIGURES look at LOU and laugh out loud. The SHORT FIGURE laughs the hardest, but then begins to choke and shake as she goes into convulsions. Her brothers run to her aid; one holds her jaw open and the other pins down her legs. She slithers and hisses, moving her tongue like a snake. LOU takes the opportunity to flee. After a few seconds the SHORT FIGURE stops moving. (BEAT) She stands, and the FIGURES break out in hysterical laughter. Their laughter increases, becomes outrageous, and finally dies down.

MEDIUM FIGURE: You are one evil bitch.

SHORT FIGURE: No, I can't take all the credit.

TALL FIGURE: That was some plan of yours.

MEDIUM FIGURE: But what if he... What if he survives in the desert?

SHORT FIGURE: If the barbecue sauce don't roast him to death, the wrong directions will. That pendejo won't discover he went the wrong way until he's out of breath, and it's too late. He ain't gonna make it.

MEDIUM FIGURE: I just don't want to go to jail for this...

TALL FIGURE: We won't.

MEDIUM FIGURE: But how do you know?

SHORT FIGURE (*grabbing MEDIUM FIGURE by his collar and getting in his face with the meanest look*): Stick with the fucking plan!

MEDIUM FIGURE: But how about if he does survive?

SHORT FIGURE: He's as good as dead! Now grow some balls and help me pack up this place so we can get the hell out of town.

MEDIUM FIGURE: I'm starting to feel bad about this.

SHORT FIGURE: Feel bad about those white teenage boys getting away with killing our brother. Feel bad about that!

MEDIUM FIGURE: Yeah, but what did we accomplish? We humiliated the guy, and then he goes to the desert to die. That doesn't change anything. He's just one of many who keep spreading hate talk and—

TALL FIGURE: Hey, let's go kidnap another one. I really enjoyed this.

SHORT FIGURE: Me too. It won't bring our brother back, but it keeps me from going insane.

MEDIUM FIGURE: You are insane. We are all insane for doing this.

LIGHTS FADE OUT.

SCENE ELEVEN:

LIGHTS FADE IN on a stretch of desert. SANDI appears, drenched in sweat. She runs out of breath, and lies on the sand. She fans herself and looks all around her.

SANDI: Where the hell am I? Where is the road? I'm burning up! (*SANDI takes off her blue uniform. She is left in her underwear. Her shoes are disheveled, and it's evident that she has been through hell.*) God, please take me now! I can't stand another minute of this. Please save me, or kill me, but I can't take it anymore! (*SANDI rests on the sand.*)

LIGHTS CHANGE and LIGHTS FADE UP on another patch of desert. LOU stumbles in and falls on the sand. He is bright pink and looks like a roasted pig ready to eat.

LOU: I run and run and I can't find the highway. (*LOU cries. After a few seconds, he spots something in the distance.*) An orange flag? What's that?

LIGHTS FADE A LITTLE and RISE again. LOU approaches the orange flag, which is a marker for water. There are several jugs of water at the bottom of the flag. SANDI also approaches. Both she and LOU run toward the orange flag, which is surrounded by jugs of water. They each take a jug and drink from it only to discover it is empty. To their horror, they find all the jugs have been punctured (probably by a vigilante group). They desperately lick the jugs for any drops of water they might still contain. They both cry. (BEAT)

LOU: Who are you?

SANDI: Sandi...

LOU (*incredulous, half laughing*): Your name is Sandi, and I'm out here in the desert... What a sick joke. (*LOU laughs to himself, somewhat out of his mind, at such a big cosmic joke. He stops laughing. After he touches SANDI and realizes she's not a hallucination, he seriously asks:*) What are you doing here?

SANDI: I don't know....I don't know why this happened to me. I can't explain what has happened....I was on a bus to Nogales last night when the driver lost control of the bus, and then I heard gun shots, and people ran. It was so dark I couldn't see what was happening.... I just ran as far as I could from the gunshots and the screams, and I don't know.... Am I alive? Am I in hell? Where am I?

LOU: I was hoping you could tell me. I've been running all day and I don't know where I am...

SANDI: You think the Border Patrol will find us?

LOU: I hope so.

(*BEAT*)

SANDI: My feet are all swollen, and my skin is torn. I can't move anymore.

LOU: We have to keep moving or this sun will eat us up.

LOU gets up and takes SANDI's hand. Each step is a monumental achievement, but they can't go any further.

LOU: Here, let's rest by this rock. This little tree gives a little bit of shade.

They move towards a skinny tree that resembles a charred human skeleton. It has few leaves and gives hope more than shade. LOU and SANDI sit beneath the tree, practically naked.

SANDI: Please sun, go down, go away.

LOU tries to scratch off the barbeque sauce.

SANDI: What's on you?

LOU: It's barbecue sauce... It's a long story that I don't care to tell. *(LOU shouts in pain. His skin comes off. SANDI looks away, horrified.)* We're going to die...I deserve to die... *(BEAT)* The sun is getting brighter... It's so bright... too bright...

LIGHTS GROW VERY BRIGHT and then FADE A BIT to show the passage of time. Seconds later they FADE DOWN A BIT. The desert is dark and silent except for the wind howling... They both shake, freezing, hugging each other for warmth, huddling together to cover each other from the wind. Footsteps are heard. LOU and SANDI stop moving and shaking. Gunshots are heard and then a yell. It's as if it's all happening right in front of them, but no one is there.

LOU: Did you hear that?

SANDI: Yes.

LOU: What is going on?

ARTEMIO HERNANDEZ appears and walks towards them. He is wearing dirty clothes and carrying a small backpack. Startled, LOU and SANDI yell in unison.

ARTEMIO: ¿Me puedes ayudar? [Can you help me?]

LOU: What's he saying?

SANDI: I don't speak Spanish.

LOU gives her a look.

SANDI: Well, I don't, all right. Why didn't you learn Spanish?

ARTEMIO: ¿Me puedes ayudar? [Can you help me?]

SANDI: Sí.

ARTEMIO: Por favor, ¿dile a mi esposa que estoy detenido? [Can you please tell my wife I have been detained?]

SANDI: Sí.

LOU: Ask him if he knows how to get to the highway.

SANDI shushes him.

ARTEMIO: Por favor, dile a mi esposa que no la tracione. Dile que me detenieron en el desierto y todavía estoy aquí esperando. [Please tell my wife I did not betray her. Tell her I was detained in the desert and that I'm still here waiting.]

SANDI: He says that he was detained in the desert and that he is still waiting here.

LOU: What does that mean?

SANDI: I can barely make sense of it. Let me figure this out.

ARTEMIO: Por favor, llévenme con ustedes. [Please take me with you.]

SANDI: I think he said he wants us to take him with us.

LOU: Take him where? He's asking us for help, when he's in better shape than us?

Photo by Josefina López

*Lou and Sandi see a man who has been
"Detained" in the desert as a ghost.*

59

ARTEMIO disappears. SANDI and LOU look around and can't find him.

LOU: Where did he go? He does know the way out. Let's follow him.

LOU trips over something. SANDI goes to help him up. She looks at the ground and finds a bone.

SANDI: It's a bone! *(BEAT)* These are human bones! *(SANDI digs in the sand.)*

LOU: What are you doing?

SANDI finds a wallet with bills and an I.D.

SANDI: I found a wallet...and there is an I.D. *(SANDI looks at it.)* Oh, my God! My God!

LOU: What? Who was he?

SANDI shows LOU the I.D. He takes it and studies it. She remains silent. He doesn't know what to say.

SANDI: These are his bones. That's what he meant. He wants us to take him with us.

LOU: You mean, he's a.... No, we must be hallucinating. Maybe we're asleep, and this is just a dream or a nightmare...we're going to die. *(LOU sobs.)* I don't want to die this way. I'm not proud of my life.... I just can't die this way. No. It's just not the way I....

SANDI: We're not going to die.

LOU: What chance do we have of making it out of here? Look at this guy. He probably rested and fell asleep and got baked in the sun...

SANDI: No, he was murdered. Those gun shots... He was murdered... probably by some bandits who robbed him and left him here to die...Wait! There's money in this wallet....

SANDI studies the wallet. LOU gets caught up feeling sorry for himself.

LOU: My wife...my children... I should have been a better person... I should have...

SANDI *(suddenly realizing)*: We're going to live!

LOU: How do you know?

SANDI: Because... Because...something like this happened to me before, and I know that some force or something has brought you and me here... It's meant to be.

LOU: I want to die. I just want to get this over with.

SANDI: No. We can't die. We have to live to return the bones to his wife and find out who murdered this man.

LOU: He was murdered?

SANDI shows him the piece of fabric that indicates the violence.

SANDI: His wife is still waiting for him. She needs to know what happened to him.

(BEAT)

LOU: Yes. If I were to die here, I would want my wife to find me.

SANDI: And if you were murdered she would want your killer brought to justice.

LOU nods. (BEAT)

SANDI: Let's pray for a miracle. Let's pray somebody find us before...

LOU: God and me aren't on good terms right now. I don't think prayers are going to do anything.

SANDI: We have nothing left.

They look at one another and begin to pray together.

SANDI: Dear God, please do not leave us to die here. I am sorry for whatever I have done to put myself in this situation.

LOU: Yes. I am sorry for what I have said that has caused me to be in this situation.

SANDI: Please forgive me for my wrongs against others, against myself, and against you.

LOU: Yes. Please forgive me.

SANDI: Thank you for sending me this person next to me to keep me company in this hour of need.

LOU: Yes, thank you. Thank you for sending me someone to keep me company so that I don't die alone.

SANDI: Despite what is happening to me, now I know...it is the right thing, and whatever happens to me, I still love you.

LOU *(to GOD)*: Love? I don't even love myself, much less you, so I'm not going to lie now just because I really need you... *(BEAT)* But whatever

happens... *(BEAT)* I love you. I do.

LIGHTS FADE OUT. A few seconds later, LIGHTS FADE IN. It is bright, hot, and sunny. SANDI and LOU are lying on the sand, still as corpses. Several seconds pass, and there is no movement coming from them. (We should be convinced they are dead.) Footsteps are heard. ERNESTO, who is carrying two gallons of water, enters by himself, singing a song. He puts water by the orange flag and notices the vandalized water containers... He turns and sees SANDI and LOU. He walks up to them and puts his fingers on LOU's neck. He studies his face and recognizes him.

ERNESTO: Lou? Lou Becker? Lou, what are you doing here?

LOU wakes up.

LOU: You? What are you doing here?

ERNESTO: I'm doing my usual rounds. Why are you wearing pink underwear? Who is this next to you?

SANDI wakes up. She sees ERNESTO and practically jumps for joy. He hands them water, and they quickly drink it.

SANDI: Thank you. Thank you! *(She hugs ERNESTO.)*

ERNESTO: Come on, I have a first aid kit in my SUV. I'll get you to the hospital. *(ERNESTO picks up LOU and walks with him.)*

LOU: Wait. We can't go yet. We have to take someone with us.

ERNESTO: What? There's someone else with you?

SANDI: Yes. We found the bones of a man named Artemio Hernandez. Can you help us collect his remains?

ERNESTO: I'll come back and get him.

(They exit.)

ERNESTO returns and pulls out a large plastic bag. He respectfully picks up the bones and places them in the bag. As he does, the voice of MRS. ARTEMIO HERNANDEZ fills the theater.)

MRS. ARTEMIO HERNANDEZ *(voice over)*: Querido Ernesto, I am writing this letter to thank you for letting me know how Artemio died and for returning his bones to me. I cannot thank you enough for the work you have done. I cried for two years, convinced he had betrayed me and abandoned me and my children, until the day I got your letter. Although I was crushed to discover that he was murdered and left alone in the desert to die, I was relieved to know that he was now in God's embrace. My family can now stop wondering what happened. We can begin to mourn him and come together to pray for him. I pray that you never give up doing what you do and that God will always provide for you so that you can help other families like mine who want to escape poverty and misery. Sinceramente... Florencia Hernandez.

LIGHTS FADE OUT.

A song of mourning plays in the background until it blends in with the KRZT jingle.

SCENE TWELVE:

LIGHTS FADE IN on LOU at the DJ booth. LOU is tanned, but not fully recovered. He has a few bandages on his forehead and arms. The KRZT jingle plays.

LOU (*with discomfort*): I am Lou Becker, and I want to welcome you to *Take Back America*...I am back from my vacation...in Palm Springs, and I forgot to wear sun block one day when I fell asleep by the pool... You can never forget to wear sun block, folks... And you can never have enough water.... (*He picks up a piece of paper and reads.*) Today in the news... Ten illegal aliens.... (*BEAT*) Ten migrants were caught at the... Ah...I'm going to deviate today from my normal show... You know I don't think I've ever shared with you the real reasons why I love this country. Not many of you know that I was born in Scotland and my parents moved to Canada, and that's where I met my wife and became a U.S. citizen through marriage. I am so lucky that this great country is truly the land of opportunity where a poor boy from Scotland with lots of hopes and dreams can end up having his own radio show and living well reaping all the benefits of this great country... I love this country... (*BEAT*) You know, I want to play a song for you that always inspired me when I was just starting out in radio. Let's start the day right with some inspiring music.

KEN BEAVERS, the show's producer, walks into the sound book with a smirk, bothered.

KEN BEAVERS (*whispering*): Lou, what the fuck are you doing?

LOU plays Woody Guthrie's version of "This Land is Your Land." He stands still in contemplation. (BEAT) LOU throws the day's script into the trash. The song keeps playing as he gathers his coat.

KEN BEAVERS: Hey, Lou, where you going? The song is going to end soon.

LOU exits the sound booth without turning back to give an explanation.

KEN BEABERS: Commercial! Go to commercial!

A radio commercial plays for Arizona Bar-be-cue Sauce.

LIGHTS FADE OUT.

SCENE THIRTEEN:

LIGHTS FADE IN on SANDI sitting in ERNESTO'S SUV.

SANDI: Thank you so much for the ride to California... My boyfriend...I mean ex-boyfriend, took off with my car. He hasn't returned my calls, so I don't know where the hell he is... Probably drove off to Vancouver... It was an old car ready to break down. I hope it breaks down on him... Sorry, don't mean to throw all my crap on you... I'm just really grateful for the ride back to California.

ERNESTO: Oh, no, thank you. I love company on my trips. Most of the time it's always just me... Although, you're not going to believe this, but sometimes I swear I see spirits sitting in the backseat.

SANDI: Oh, I believe you. I know the mind can play tricks on us, but I also believe in ghosts, spirits, whatever you want to call them... So what can we do to find out who killed Artemio?

ERNESTO: Unfortunately Artemio's body was so deteriorated...there is no evidence left...

SANDI: But there was money in his wallet. Who would leave money in a wallet next to the body?

ERNESTO: Maybe it was a Border Patrol officer. There have been so many killings at the Border... It just gets worse.

SANDI: Ernesto, I want to help. Next time you go deliver water, I want to join you.

ERNESTO: That would be great. We're all volunteers, and no matter what the law says, we have to do what is right.

SANDI nods. ERNESTO turns on the radio. The jingle for KRZT comes in.

CARL (*V.O.*): This is Carl Dunlop the new host of *Take Back America*. In the news today, more protestors have put graffiti on the state capital. Augh!!! It just disgusts me when I hear this! When are these illegals gonna get it. We don't want you in our state, and we will do whatever it takes to exter – I mean expatriate – or whatever – send you back to your country. Go back to your countries and—

SANDI: Do you mind if I use your cell phone to call in?

ERNESTO: No, go right ahead. I have it on speed dial.

ERNESTO presses a few buttons and hands her the cell phone. SANDI dials.

SANDI: Hmm, I got their voicemail... This is Sandra Sanchez. Why do you spread all this hate? Why? Well, we're not going to take it anymore! We are not going back to our countries. We are already in our country! We are Americans with the same rights as you, and we're not going to let you get away with this.

ERNESTO (*whispers*): Immigration reform - tell him about that.

SANDI: Ernesto Martinez wants me to remind you...that if you create laws that are unfair, we will protest, and we will stop them, and we will continue to fight! Immigration reform now! (*SANDI hangs up.*)

ERNESTO: Well said!

SANDI returns his cell phone back to him.

SANDI: Ernesto, I have a question for you—

ERNESTO: (*joking*) Yes, I'm single.

They both laugh and after a few seconds they smile.

ERNESTO: You like Rancheras?

SANDI: Ah.... Well... (*BEAT*) Yeah... I love Rancheras, sure.

ERNESTO adjusts his radio, and a Ranchera song comes on. They sing together at the top of their lungs.

LIGHTS FADE OUT.

The End

CASA 0101 *presents*

TRIO *Los* MACHOS

Cantamos porque no podemos llorar

We sing because we cannot cry

A Special Presentation of a New Play
by Josefina Lopez
with songs made famous by Trio Los Panchos

Directed by Edward Padilla
Musical Director: Jose "Pepe" Rodriguez

September 26 - October 12, 2008

TRIO LOS MACHOS

PLAYWRIGHT'S NOTES

My father was a "Bracero" and this was his music. He played the music every evening and I grew to love Los Panchos. I wrote this play as an homage to my father and Los Panchos. I also wanted to bring attention to a part of history Latinos should know about. When politicians use immigrants as scapegoats and talk about how we immigrants rob this country I like to remind them of our contributions. This is one way I do it; through my writing. Although I am not a man and had so many conflicts with my father for his macho views, I felt that as a feminist I wanted to reconcile with my father's machismo through this play. I recognize the value of his sacrifices and how sometimes machismo is the way a man survives when he is being dehumanized. I hope you enjoy this play and fall in love with the music of Los Panchos. I invite you to learn more about the "Bracero" history by going online and viewing the many websites on the Braceros and their present plight...

Josefina López

November 2008

*All the songs mentioned in my script are merely suggestions and can be substituted for others if the rights are not available.

**"Corrido del Bracero" is an original song.

TRIO LOS MACHOS

ACT ONE

SETTING

In darkness, PERFIDIA, a beautiful romantic ballad plays by Trio Los Panchos. After a few seconds the same song is sung by TRIO LOS MACHOS, made up of LALO, NACHO, and PACO, all in their eighties. LALO is large and rotund, and NACHO still has his good looks.

SCENE ONE

LIGHTS FADE IN on a MEXICAN RESTAURANT in OLVERA STREET where our trio plays in front of an ANGLO COUPLE. The beautiful song is slowly degraded and the men now sing off key. Their singing is a little sloppy and the joy they used to bring to couples is now a thing of the past.

ANGLO WOMAN (*whispers to husband*): Give them a dollar so they will go away.

The ANGLO MAN gives them three dollars and shoos them away.

They finish singing, ending the torture.

The ANGLO COUPLE exits, restaurant closes, and the RESTAURANT OWNER approaches them and hands them cash.

LALO: Why are you paying us today?

RESTAURANT OWNER: Muchachos (young men), it's time to call it quits.

NACHO: ¿Qué, qué? (Say what?) What are you saying?

68

RESTAURANT OWNER: I don't want to be disrespectful, but you lost your "mojo".

PACO (*to LALO and NACHO*): ¿Qué chingados es mojo? (What the hell is mojo?)

NACHO (*aside to PACO and LALO*): Did he call us Jotos? ("fags")

RESTAURANT OWNER: The magic is gone. You're not the same group my father hired years ago... I think one of you has lost your hearing, I ain't gonna say who, and one of you could lay off the tequila.

NACHO: Are you calling me a drunk?

RESTAURANT OWNER: I'm not calling you anything, but I can't have you scaring away my customers with your singing.

NACHO: Okay, now you really insulted us!

NACHO advances toward him.

LALO: Nacho, ¡párale! (Stop it!) Señor Estrada, give us an opportunity to show you we can "clean up our act".

RESTAURANT OWNER: Lalo, this was your second chance. Retirement would be good for all three of you.

PACO: Retirement? Who the hell is going to pay for our retirement? If I don't sing, I don't eat. What else are we supposed to do?

RESTAURANT OWNER: I wish I knew... Maybe you can teach guitar lessons... I don't know. I have to close, my wife is expecting me at home. Excuse me muchachos. (Excuse me young men.) Buena suerte. (Good luck.)

He exits.

The three men scratch their heads and look down ashamed, then:

PACO: Nacho, didn't I tell you not to bring your tequila bottle? He probably saw it in the locker room.

NACHO: It's not my fault. It's your singing that made the gringos leave.

PACO: Pinche Nacho, ¡tu eres un desgraciado! (Damn you Nacho, you're a bastard!)

They are about to throw blows when LALO steps in.

LALO: ¡Párenle! (Stop it!) Have some respect. Today is our fifty year anniversary.

They stop fighting and swallow their tears.

PACO: Why did you have to remind me? Now I feel even worse.

NACHO: Que gacho (that sucks), today of all days, ya ni la friegan...(this really sucks)

(BEAT)

LALO: So what are we going to do?

(BEAT)

PACO: I'm going to go on my own.

LALO: We're a trio. You can't do anything without us.

PACO: I'm tired of...all this...this... I'll figure it out and make it on my own. I'm glad this happen because for a while I've been feeling like an unhappily married man and...ya no puedo más (I can't go on). I'm glad it's over.

LALO: What else can you do? This is all you know.

PACO: I'm finally going to sing my songs and see if I can put out an album and--

NACHO laughs.

NACHO: Have you taken a good look at yourself lately? Ya estas viejo. (You're old.) Who is going to want to hear your songs, hombre (man)? They want young chavalos (kids) with sexy looks; it's not about your music but about shaking la nalga (ass) and wink wink. You're not cut out for that life--

PACO: Pues (well) I'll never know unless I try... I don't want to die with my music still left inside me!

LALO: That's a nice saying, Paco, but be reasonable...we shared our music with a lot of people, our life was good--

PACO: No, ya basta. (That's enough.) I don't want to hear anymore. I know you can't teach a dog new tricks and all those stupid expressions that are supposed to remind me to roll over and die, so I don't want you to talk me out of it. Ya me voy. (I'm leaving.) Buena suerte. (Good luck.) Thanks for everything.

PACO picks up his guitar and walks off. NACHO attempts to stop him. LALO holds NACHO from interfering with PACO.

LALO: Let him go. He needs to do what he has to do.

LIGHTS FADE OUT.

SCENE TWO

LIGHTS FADE IN on a COWBOY BAR. NACHO is at the bar, drunk out of his mind. He downs another tequila shot and sings TU RECUERDO Y YO. LALO walks in towards the end of the song and sits next to him.

LALO: Nacho, it's time to go home.

NACHO turns to the WAITER and orders another round.

NACHO: Another tequila shot and one for my great amigo (friend) Lalo!

LALO: Nachito, they're waiting for you to leave.

NACHO: But the bar is--

LALO: They're closed...but the owner is a friend and he didn't want to throw you out. He called me to come get you. I know this hurts, but we have to take it like men and move on.

NACHO: Move on? And where do we move to? The grave?

LALO: Look, I usually have something wise to say that will make a borracho (drunk) like you listen up, pero (but) even I don't know. I've been at home wondering what to do next. If Paco was still with us then we'd just go look for work someplace else. Now that he's not with us, I can't even imagine bringing in someone new... It's just too depressing to think about life without Paco.

NACHO: You're not going to believe me, but I actually miss the cabrón (jerk)... I didn't think I would, and then it hit me and I just had to visit my favorite cantina to forget about him. I don't think I've ever been close to a vieja (a dame) the way I am close with you and Paco. I feel so betrayed; like he cheated on us. I thought he loved us—*(BEAT)* Ay, I'm really drunk... Let's go home.

LIGHTS FADE OUT.

SCENE THREE

LIGHTS FADE IN on MARIACHI PLAZA at NIGHT. SEVERAL MARIACHIS and MUSICIANS wait around for clients to hire their services. PACO stands at a corner along with others waiting to get picked up for the night. LIGHTS FADE close by on SANTA CECILIA TACO SHOP where LALO and NACHO converse as they finish their tacos.

LALO: Just let me do all the talking, because tu eres cabezón (you are

stubborn) and any little thing will make your stubborn pride sabotage you, ya te conosco (I know you)...

NACHO: Fine, fine. You do all the talking. As long as I don't have to apologize that's fine...

LALO pours a lot of salsa on his tacos. He eats, more like swallows, his greasy tacos, quickly.

NACHO (CONT'D): No se mande, compa' (don't over do it, buddy), remember what the doctor said to you about your cholesterol.

LALO: Mira (look), I'm going to tell you a little story. Escúchame bien (listen up). There was this man who went to the doctor one day and he told the doctor, "I don't drink, I don't smoke, I don't over eat, and I'm celibate. I feel so healthy I could live to be a 100!" So the doctor told him, "With that lifestyle why would you want to?"

NACHO laughs.

LALO (CONT'D): Besides this is my only bad habit.

LALO finishes his tacos.

NACHO: Let's go before someone hires him and we have to wait another night to do this.

LALO: Patience, patience.

NACHO: At this age, who has patience.

They walk over to PACO. PACO sees them and makes every effort to ignore NACHO.

LALO: Buenas noches. (Good night.)

PACO does not reply. NACHO turns away.

LALO (CONT'D): Somebody say something besides me.

PACO: What do you want me to say?

LALO: What do you say we get back together?

LALO looks to both of them. A "CAR" is heard driving up. PACO runs to catch up to it. The car drives away. PACO returns disappointed.

LALO (CONT'D): So what do you say? Should we get back together?

(BEAT)

NACHO and LALO look at each other, then look away.

LALO (CONT'D): You want to get back together? If you do, speak now or forever hold your pride, because I'm not going to beg either one of you!

(BEAT)

They nod slightly.

LALO (CONT'D): Pues entonces, a huevo, tienen que hablar! (Then damn it, we have to talk.)

LALO pulls out a bag of tortilla chips from under his coat and occupies his mouth crunching them and eating. The men are forced to talk.

PACO: Hmmm. Let's start by admitting that we need a leader.

PACO waits for LALO and NACHO to jump in.

PACO (CONT'D): I think I should be the leader.

NACHO: ¡Ni madre! (No way!) Why should you be the leader?

PACO: Because I have the best voice and I want us to sing my original songs--

NACHO: You sing like a vieja (dame); una voz de maricon...(a "fag's" voice)

PACO: And you sing like a drunk even when you're sober.

LALO: ¡Compañeros! (Comrades!) Let me remind you we're in public.

NACHO: I started the trio, it's because of me that we even got together.

PACO: It's because of you that we got fired.

NACHO: It's because of your stupid songs. Nobody likes them. You think you're Julio Iglesias or what?

PACO: ¡Te parto la madre, cabrón! (I'll kick your ass, jerk!)

NACHO: Órale pues. ¡Vente! Come on! Let's settle this once and for all. I'm tired of you whining like a maricon.

PACO throws a blow, barely missing NACHO. LALO gets in the middle of them to stop their fists. Suddenly, LALO chokes on the chips. NACHO wraps his arms around him and does the Heimlich Maneuver. LALO spits out the chips. They land on PACO's nice jacket.

LALO (*barely able to speak*): ¡Basta! Both of you are going to give me a heart attack with all your fighting!

LALO wipes his mouth and forehead with his handkerchief. After a few seconds he regains his composure. The other two men relax a bit. LALO clears his throat.

LALO (CONT'D): I propose that I be the leader.

Both men look at him, they roll their eyes, sway their heads, but can't disagree.

LALO (CONT'D): This way we avoid fights. Well, what do you think?

NACHO nods in agreement, PACO also nods.

LALO (CONT'D): Okay, pues. I'm the leader.

LALO digs into his pocket and takes out two pieces of paper. He gives them the paper.

LALO (CONT'D): Here is a list of changes I propose as our new leader.

PACO and NACHO hesitantly take the paper and read down the list.

PACO: No! We agreed. No. No women!

LALO shakes his head. He gives back the paper to LALO.

LALO: If we are going to continue working, this is what we need to do to give us a chance.

PACO: Don't you remember we agreed years ago no women?

NACHO and LALO make an effort to remember. They shake their heads, they can't remember.

LALO: I was watching cable last night and I saw this movie about these two gringos who hire a female singer and they get more jobs that way.

NACHO: I like the idea. So how do we do it?

PACO: I haven't agreed.

LALO: Paco, let us try. If it doesn't work out then it'll just be just us.

They wait on PACO for a decision. He nods.

LALO (CONT'D): Good. I'm glad we're all in agreement. The auditions are tomorrow morning.

LIGHTS FADE OUT.

SCENE FOUR

LIGHTS FADE IN on LALO's STUDIO APARTMENT, crowded with knick-knacks everywhere and lots of junk. It's a cozy apartment with a sofa and a TV, but definitely the home of a pack-rat.

DOOR BELL rings O.S.

LALO answers the door.

ROSARIO, 18, tall, pretty, with long hair, enters. LALO stares at ROSARIO. She waits for him to say something.

ROSARIO: Buenas tardes. (Good evening.) I'm here for the audition.

LALO: You came to the right place. We are ready for you.

ROSARIO: ¿Aquí? (Here.) You want me to sing...right here?

LALO: Yes, no tengas pena. (don't be shy.)

NACHO: What song would you like to sing?

ROSARIO: I'm going to sing "Contigo en la Distancia."

ROSARIO clears her throat and sings PIEL CANELA. Her voice is angelic, exceptional. LALO and NACHO stare at her. They nod to the music. ROSARIO finishes. She waits for them to say something.

PACO: Could you wait outside just a minute?

ROSARIO nods and exits.

NACHO: Who could have thought that from such a pretty little mouth--

PACO: She's too young.

LALO: Who cares, as long as she can sing.

PACO: It's going to look like she's our granddaughter.

NACHO: We're not going to marry her, she's just going to sing. She was prettier than the rest of the other old women.

LALO hits NACHO gently on his chest.

LALO: "Calmado venado, sereno moreno." (Down boy, down boy.) You don't even know if she's eighteen.

NACHO: You know I'm just kidding.

PACO/LALO: Yeah right.

LIGHTS FADE OUT.

SCENE FIVE

LIGHTS FADE IN on LALO's LIVING ROOM. No one is present.

The door bell rings. NACHO opens the door.

ROSARIO's face is red from crying. She quickly covers her cheek.

NACHO: ¿Qué te pasa? (What's wrong?)

ROSARIO: Nothing. No es nada. (It's nothing.)

She breaks into tears. NACHO holds her.

NACHO: Rosarito, what's wrong?

ROSARIO (*crying*): Selena...

NACHO: Yes, what a shame...

ROSARIO: I want to be like her, but my boyfriend won't let me! He's a macho!

NACHO: No. He's worse than a macho. I'm a macho and I would let you. He's a nobody who is scared to lose you because you Rosarito, are so pretty and talented.

ROSARIO: You really mean that?

NACHO: What's important is if you believe it.

ROSARIO: You're so wise.

NACHO: It comes with age. Are you hungry? I was making lunch.

ROSARIO: You cook?

NACHO: But of course. I'm a modern macho.

ROSARIO laughs.

NACHO (CONT'D): Don't laugh. I'm trying.

ROSARIO: I'm not laughing at you. I just think you're...cool.

NACHO stares at her. ROSARIO swallows, eyes widen.

NACHO: Cool?

He gives her a flirtatious smile with his macho charm. She returns his smile with a coquettish giggle.

ROSARIO: Yeah... Real cool.

LIGHTS FADE OUT.

SCENE SIX

LIGHTS FADE IN on LALO's APARTMENT. The rehearsal has ended. LALO and NACHO arrange the living room back to order. LALO collects the music. ROSARIO collects her belongings.

LALO: You're doing a great job.

ROSARIO's face turns red.

ROSARIO: Thank you. Buenas noches. (Good night.)

ROSARIO walks to the door.

NACHO: Are you walking home again?

LALO stops in his tracks and turns to look at them.

ROSARIO: I'm taking the bus.

NACHO: The bus? Oh, no, it's too dangerous for a young señorita to be walking by herself in this neighborhood. I'll give you a ride.

ROSARIO: Thank you.

NACHO: Lalo, where are your car keys?

LALO: On the table.

ROSARIO follows NACHO out the door.

PACO looks out the window and after a few seconds sits next to LALO.

PACO: We have to talk.

LALO: Is this going to take long because the novela (soap opera) is going to be starting in five minutes and it's getting really good...

PACO (*embarrassed*): It's none of my business, but since I think it will affect us all and... Since you are the leader.

LALO: I don't have a whole life time to live, get to the point.

PACO: I don't know how to tell you, because I'm not completely certain--

LALO: Then don't tell me until you are.

PACO: But I have to tell you before it's too late. I don't want to tell you because I hate chisme (gossip).

LALO: Gossip? Tell me.

PACO: I think la niña (our little girl) Rosario is involved with Nacho.

Lalo breaks out laughing.

LALO: ¡No me digas! (You don't say.)

PACO: I saw them!

LALO: You were there? He can still get it up? I don't believe you! What could she possibly see in him? He's like a mango, en lo amarillo y chupado. (in that he's yellow and all mushy.)

PACO: I'll prove it to you. Come with me.

LALO: Right now? ¿Y la novela? (And the soap opera?)

PACO: Just come with me... It will be better than a novela.

LALO: You better be right about Nacho or I'm going to miss the best episode and I'll never forgive you for it.

PACO: Trust me...

LIGHTS FADE OUT.

A "MOTEL" sign LIGHTS UP.

LALO and PACO talk under the sign, hiding out.

LALO: Macho 'till the day he dies.

PACO: Didn't I tell you?

LALO: Let's go. Whatever they do is their business.

PACO: Poor girl. It's not right.

LALO: Paco, vámonos (let's go). So now we know.

PACO: How can he take advantage of her like that?

LALO: She's old enough to know what she's doing... Paco, are you jealous? Is that why it bothers you so much?

PACO: How could you accuse me of that? Yo soy un hombre decente! (I'm a decent man!) And that's why I have to put a stop to this!

PACO pulls up his sleeves and walks off.

LALO: ¡No seas pendejo!!! ¡Vámonos! (Don't be an idiot!!! Let's get out of here.)

LALO waddles after him.

LIGHTS FADE OUT.

SCENE SEVEN

LIGHTS FADE IN on the MOTEL ROOM in which ROSARIO is seducing NACHO. ROSARIO sings PIEL CANELA as she undresses seductively. She takes his chin and kisses him.

PACO runs in to "rescue" ROSARIO.

ROSARIO screams. NACHO covers himself. He is wearing big colorful trunks.

PACO: ¡Viejo rabo verde! (Dirty old man!)

PACO punches NACHO's face. NACHO falls on the bed. He quickly bounces back up.

ROSARIO takes the blankets with her as she makes a run for the bathroom.

NACHO grabs PACO and gets him in a wrestling headlock. PACO struggles to free himself.

NACHO: ¡Pinche cabrón! (Godamn jerk!) What the hell are you doing? I was about to get --

LALO runs in.

LALO: ¡Quietos hijos de la chingada! (Stop fighting sons of bitches.) Stop fighting or they're going to call the police and throw you crazy old men into the pinta (jail).

LALO continues to try to get them apart. PACO releases himself. They throw punches at each other a la "Three Stooges" and end up hitting LALO. LALO falls like a ton of bricks.

NACHO: ¡Cabrón! (Jerk!) Look at what you did!

PACO: I did? You did!

They go at each other again like rams and pay no attention to LALO lying unconscious.

ROSARIO (*yelling*): ¡Miren! (Look!) Lalo hasn't gotten up!

PACO and NACHO go to LALO's aid.

ROSARIO (CONT'D): I'll call an ambulance!

LIGHTS FADE OUT.

The loud sound of an ambulance becomes the sound of an emergency siren heard during World War II.

In the darkness we hear Patriotic American music from the 1940s era.

RADIO ANNOUNCER (*V.O.*): In times of need we must request the assistance of our Mexican neighbor. While our men are at war we will form a work program called the Bracero Program which will allow Mexican laborers to work in the fields to ensure our economy prospers even in times of war.

SCENE EIGHT

LIGHTS FADE IN on a POST IN THE FIELDS. An ANGLO RANCHER wearing a white hat passes out checks to BRACERO MEN in line. YOUNG NACHO, 25, YOUNG PACO, 25, and YOUNG LALO, 27, wait in line. YOUNG NACHO and YOUNG PACO get their check and get out of the line. YOUNG LALO anxiously takes his check and inspect it. He shakes his head perplexed. He walks up to the ANGLO RANCHER.

YOUNG LALO: Why did you take ten percent out of my check?

ANGLO RANCHER: Everyone knows you'll get it back when you retire.

The ANGLO RANCHER continues handing out checks dismissing YOUNG LALO.

YOUNG LALO: But what if I die before I retire?

ANGLO RANCHER: Then your wife will get it.

YOUNG LALO: What if I never marry or have kids?

ANGLO RANCHER: I don't know, it's for health care.

YOUNG LALO: I need that ten percent now. I can't wait until I'm old and dying. Give me my money.

ANGLO RANCHER: Well you can't have it now. You'll get it later!

YOUNG LALO: Liar!

ANGLO RANCHER: Are you calling me a liar, you greaser?

YOUNG LALO: Liar! (*To the other BRACEROS:*) They're never going to give us that money back! He's a liar!

The ANGLO RANCHER slaps YOUNG LALO. YOUNG LALO punches him. The ANGLO RANCHER punches him back. YOUNG LALO falls to the floor. The ANGLO RANCHER is about to strike him with a two by four when YOUNG PACO and YOUNG NACHO step in and defend YOUNG LALO. The ANGLO RANCHER steps back outnumbered.

ANGLO RANCHER: Call Immigration! I need some greasers deported right now!

YOUNG NACHO: ¡Vámonos! (Let's go!)

The THREE MEN make a run for it.

LIGHTS FADE OUT.

SCENE NINE

LIGHTS FADE IN on YOUNG LALO, YOUNG NACHO, and YOUNG PACO on an immigration bus.

YOUNG NACHO: ¿Porqué no me escuchastes? (Why didn't you listen to me?) Why didn't you run in the direction I told you to?

YOUNG LALO: Because I didn't think the migra (border patrol) was going to show up that minute.

YOUNG NACHO: We could have gotten away.

YOUNG PACO: No we couldn't. The migra is always around and it was useless to try; we couldn't have gotten far.

YOUNG NACHO: Why didn't you just take the check and not complained? Look where this got us?

YOUNG LALO: I know this is my first time doing this kind of work in this country, but they pay us so little it didn't seem fair for them to take any more money away.

YOUNG PACO: It's a lot more than what we would have made back in Mexico.

YOUNG LALO: Yes, but...you know they are not going to give us back that money.

YOUNG NACHO: Just be grateful you have a job.

YOUNG LALO : Sí, sí, but they treated us like animals when we signed up.

They need us as much as we need them. We are their men while their men are away, but they treated us like we weren't. If we let ourselves be taken advantage of then we deserve it.

YOUNG PACO: All that sounds good, but it seems that you have never gone hungry.

YOUNG LALO: Yes, I have. I know hunger. I know it very well, but I am a man and no matter how hungry I am, they can't treat me like I'm not one.

YOUNG NACHO: Si, si, Señor Filósofo (Mr. Philosopher), after many months and many contracts you'll see it won't be so easy to say that.

YOUNG LALO: Sí, bueno, (well then), maybe after I've done this long enough I will have learned my place...but I'm still young and until they break my back and my spirit, I won't let myself be treated--

YOUNG NACHO: You sound educated, why are you doing this kind of work?

YOUNG LALO: What do you mean?

YOUNG NACHO: Let me see your hands.

YOUNG NACHO takes YOUNG LALO's hands and inspects them.

YOUNG NACHO: You've never done this kind of work before, have you? How did you get past the inspection?

YOUNG LALO: I put bandages on them and told them I had burnt them in a fire that broke out in my stable.

YOUNG NACHO: You're not from the rancho. (farm) You went to school and tried to make something of yourself, but what happened?

(BEAT)

YOUNG LALO: Yes, you're right. I was studying to be a priest, but then I decided it wasn't for me and since I couldn't earn a living I came here to help out my mother and my brothers and sisters.

YOUNG PACO: No wonder you complain a lot. You're not used to hard work.

YOUNG LALO: I'm not afraid to work... I've just been used to using my mind instead of my hands.

They remain silent.

YOUNG LALO extends his hand out to YOUNG NACHO and YOUNG PACO.

YOUNG LALO: My name is Gonzalo, but you can call me Lalo...

YOUNG PACO: I'm Francisco, but you can call me Paco.

YOUNG NACHO: I'm Narciso, call me Nacho.

YOUNG LALO: I want to say thank you for stepping in and...saving my life.

YOUNG NACHO: He wasn't going to kill you. He was just going to teach you a lesson you'd never forget.

YOUNG LALO: And what lesson is that?

YOUNG NACHO: To be afraid of the gringo and keep your eyes down... But you'll get to learn it some other time.

YOUNG LALO: Did someone already teach you that lesson?

YOUNG NACHO: Hey, we're not friends, don't talk to me like that.

YOUNG LALO: Sorry... Thank you for trying to help me. I'm sorry you lost your jobs because of me.

YOUNG PACO: Don't mention it. It was nothing. Life is hard and you just take the punches.

YOUNG NACHO: Pos sí. (Well yeah.)

They remain silent.

YOUNG LALO: So are you going to go back to Calexico for another contract?

YOUNG PACO/YOUNG NACHO: Pos ni modo, no nos queda otra. (Of course, what else can we do.)

YOUNG LALO: I hear picking avocados is not as hard, won't kill you as much.

YOUNG PACO: Yeah, I think I'm going to get a contract picking anything from a tree and not from the ground. I always get backaches with the strawberry.

They remain silent.

Spotlight on YOUNG LALO.

YOUNG LALO: My poor mother, I better not tell her I got deported or she will be worried. She will spend too much money buying candles and ofrendas (offerings) to the Virgen so I will be safe and married soon. I better not tell her so she can save her money...my money.

Spotlight on YOUNG PACO.

YOUNG PACO: I better not tell Elena I got deported. She will probably cry and wonder if it is worth it for her to keep waiting for me. If I tell her I got deported and lost a contract she might give up hope and marry the next guy who asks... I'll have to tell my mother to lie to her and tell her I am doing very well so she'll keep waiting for me... Sometimes I think the price is too high for this kind of work.

YOUNG NACHO: Shit, I got deported... So what. Won't be my first, won't be my last.

LIGHTS FADE OUT.

A VOICE in the darkness yells out orders.

MAN'S HARSH VOICE (O.S.): Braceros! Everyone in line. We are going to disinfect you and make sure you're clean. Now everyone undress!

YOUNG PACO, YOUNG LALO, YOUNG NACHO all slowly undress with a blank expression on their faces. They know the routine and submit themselves to the humiliation of being treated like animals for the sake of a job. They are naked holding their contracts at their pelvis to hide their privates.

A DOCTOR, passes by, asks LALO to open his mouth. LALO does as he

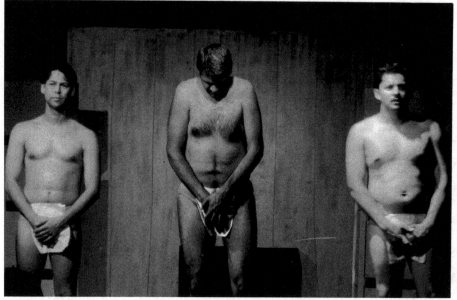

Nacho, Paco and Lalo go through a medical check up and are sprayed with poison. They sing "Corrido del Bracero."

is told. The DOCTOR sticks a wooden stick in his mouth and inspects him without caring to treat him with respect. The DOCTOR performs the same procedure on YOUNG PACO and YOUNG NACHO. A MAN sprays powdered poison for lice on the heads of the Braceros. He sprays a heavy dose on YOUNG NACHO.

YOUNG NACHO: Do you have to put so much?

MAN WITH POISON: If you don't like it go back to your country to find work!

Spotlight on NACHO.

YOUNG NACHO: As if I could say anything. As if we could go back to our beloved Mexico because we didn't like this treatment. With hunger who has a mouth? With hunger who speaks up? You think I don't want to tell you to take your lousy job and shove it up your ass? You think I would ever let another man touch my ass if I didn't have to take it? Ya ni la friegan, pinchis gringos. (Damn you fricking gringos.)

YOUNG NACHO hums.

Another spotlight on YOUNG LALO.

YOUNG LALO (*furiously*): ¡A la chingada! (To hell with them.) I wish I could tell them I didn't need their job and I could walk away... But then I think about my mother and what if I just walk away with my pride intact and she and the rest of my younger brothers starve. Me caga que no puedo hacer nada (It hurts that I can't do anything about it) and that's why I remain silent, like a lifeless tree.

YOUNG LALO hums.

Spotlight on PACO.

YOUNG PACO: Not this again. One day I will not have to go through this again. And one day I will go back to my country and I can send all these gringos to hell. But then I think of Elena and poor girl she waits for me... Maybe I'm not worth it. Maybe I should let her go. I'll never be the man she deserves and I can't give her the life that other men with more money will promise her... I can't say a thing and my heart aches... Yo canto porque me aguanto. (I sing so I can bare it.)

The three men talk/sing a song acappella:

YOUNG PACO/YOUNG NACHO/YOUNG LALO:

Cantamos el corrido del bracero. (We sing the ballad of the bracero.)

Somos más que brazos,

somos corazón. (We are more than arms, we are heart.)

Cantamos el corrido del bracero. (We sing the ballad of the bracero.)

Somos más que brazos,

somos corazón. (We are more than arms, we are heart.)

Tanto desprecio, tanta humillación. (So much indignity, so much humiliation.)

Siendo simientos (Being seedlings)

De esta nación (Of this nation)

Cantamos el corrido del bracero. (We sing the ballad of the bracero.)

Somos más que brazos,

somos un corazán. (We are more than arms, we are heart.)

Cuando canto yo me aguanto. (When I sing I can bare it.)

Para no expresar mi llanto. (I sing so I don't cry.)

Canto, canto, canto, ¿por qué no? (I sing, I sing, I sing, why not?)

Cuando canto yo me aguanto. (When I sing I can bare it.)

Para no expresar mi llanto. (I sing so I don't cry.)

Canto, canto, canto, ¿por qué no? (I sing, I sing, I sing, why not?)

MAN'S HARSH VOICE: Put your clothes on and get to work!

The BRACEROS get dressed. YOUNG NACHO and YOUNG LALO, and YOUNG PACO turn to one another, but say nothing. They lower their heads and walk off to work.

LIGHTS FADE OUT.

SCENE TEN

LIGHTS FADE IN on the three young men picking avocados from a tree.

YOUNG NACHO: Last night on the radio I heard the most beautiful song sung by a trio named Los Panchos. I'll see if I remember some of the words, but it went like this.

YOUNG NACHO sings AMORCITO CORAZÓN. YOUNG PACO sings when YOUNG NACHO doesn't remember the lyrics. YOUNG LALO sings when the other two can't remember the lyrics.

YOUNG LALO: Hey, we don't sound too bad.

YOUNG NACHO: This way the silence doesn't kill you. My arms and shoulders burn, with music it makes me forget the pain.

YOUNG PACO: Maybe the three of us could put money aside and buy a radio...

YOUNG NACHO: But what happens if we all get in a fight? Who keeps the radio then?

YOUNG LALO: It sure would be nice to have a radio in our bunker. A little radio to make this long prison sentence go faster. The nights are so long without music.

YOUNG NACHO: Or women... I'll sing you another one.

YOUNG LALO: Aver, échate otra. (Go ahead.)

LIGHTS FADE OUT.

SCENE ELEVEN

LIGHTS FADE IN on the young men dressed in their best clean clothes. They gather in a circle counting their money.

YOUNG LALO: I think we almost have enough for a radio now.

They all dig in their pockets and find loose change.

YOUNG PACO: Yes, this should be enough. Let's go to the store now before it closes.

They approach a STORE next to a BAR. They stop in front of the store. A WHITE STORE CLERK switches a sign that says: OPEN to CLOSE when they are about to go in.

YOUNG PACO: ¡Chingado! (Damn it!) The store just closed.

YOUNG LALO: There go our plans.

YOUNG NACHO: Look, there's a bar. Let's go in and get a beer.

YOUNG LALO: But look at the sign.

Spotlight on a sign that reads: "NO DOGS, NO NEGROES, NO MEXICANS".

YOUNG NACHO: Let's go in anyway.

YOUNG LALO: They'll kick you out.

YOUNG PACO: They'll kill you.

YOUNG NACHO: I don't have anybody waiting for me back home. Just bury me here.

YOUNG LALO grabs YOUNG NACHO by the hand and stops him from going in.

YOUNG LALO: No, don't go in there. Maybe nobody will miss you back home, but we'll miss you. Let's go back to our bunker and call it a night.

YOUNG NACHO: So much work all day and no place to at least get a beer. We're not just brazos (we're not just arms), soy hombre! (I'm a man.) ¿Qué no somos machos? (Aren't we men?)

YOUNG LALO: Si, somos hombres, pero no pendejos. (Yes, we are men, but not idiots.)

A MEXICAN MAN gets thrown out of the bar by a WHITE BARTENDER with a rifle pointed at him.

WHITE BARTENDER: And don't you come back here you greaser!

The MEXICAN MAN runs for his life. The WHITE BARTENDER laughs and goes back into the bar.

(BEAT)

YOUNG NACHO sings PARESE QUE VA A LLOVER and the other men join him. People passing by throw change at them. YOUNG NACHO picks up the money.

YOUNG NACHO: They gave us money! They actually thought we sang good enough to pay us money.

YOUNG LALO: We sound pretty good.

YOUNG PACO: They liked us.

YOUNG NACHO: We should buy a guitar instead of a radio and sing to all the bunkers. Don't you play guitar Lalo?

YOUNG LALO: Yes, I used to play it in church... Maybe we can make some money entertaining all the men who don't have radios.

The THREE MEN look at one another. They nod their heads in unison.

LIGHTS FADE OUT.

SCENE TWELVE

LIGHTS FADE IN on the YOUNG MEN now with LALO playing the guitar and NACHO playing maracas. They sing RELOJ. There is loud applause.

YOUNG NACHO: *Muchas gracias. Somos Trio Los Machos para servirles.* (We are Trio Los Machos here to entertain you.)

The TRIO takes a bow.

Spotlight on the YOUNG MEN counting their money.

YOUNG LALO: This is the best performance. We got a good amount tonight.

YOUNG NACHO: Too bad this will soon be over. The gringos are returning home from the war and we have to go home.

YOUNG PACO: Why don't we stay here? Maybe we can escape next week after they pay us and take off to Fresno or some small town where there are lots of bars.

YOUNG NACHO: You think we could do it?

YOUNG PACO: What about the migra? Aren't they everywhere?

YOUNG LALO: I have an uncle who will come pick us up. He can help us and maybe we can live off our music.

YOUNG NACHO: That would be amazing not to have to work in the hot sun everyday.

YOUNG PACO : Yes, wouldn't it be great to do something besides manual labor.

LIGHTS FADE OUT.

SCENE THIRTEEN

LIGHTS FADE IN on a hospital room.

DR. MEDINA, 40's, passes by. LALO and NACHO run to him.

PACO: Dr. Medina, what's wrong with Gonzalo Cervantez?

DOCTOR: Are you related?

They shake their heads.

NACHO: No, he doesn't have any family in this country and he never married. We're the only family he has.

DOCTOR: Mr. Cervantez suffered a mild stroke... He'll live, but his life will be limited. Half of his body is paralyzed.

NACHO: Is he going to be all right?

DOCTOR: Yes, in a few weeks he'll be better, but he's going to need a full time nurse.

PACO: A nurse?

DOCTOR: Yes, full time care. Excuse me I have to check on another patient.

NACHO/PACO: Sí, sí. Thank you doctor.

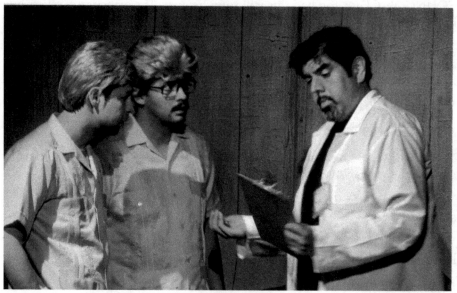

Photo by Josefina López

Nacho and Paco consult with the doctor about Lalo's condition.

They approach LALO who is helplessly tied to a machine and with an IV. The sight of LALO makes them want to cry.

PACO: Perdón. (I'm sorry.)

NACHO: Sorry, compadre.

LIGHTS FADE OUT.

RELOJ plays in the background.

END OF ACT ONE

TRIO LOS MACHOS

ACT TWO

SCENE ONE

LIGHTS FADE IN on LALO's APARTMENT. NACHO and PACO enter pushing a sleeping LALO in a wheelchair. They struggle to get him in. PACO who carries the medical supplies looks around for an empty space to put down the supplies, but every inch is taken up by some memento.

NACHO: Lets put him on the sofa. Dame una manita. (Give me a hand.)

NACHO and PACO move LALO onto the sofa. It takes them a great deal of effort to lift him and not drop him. Once they have propped him up on the sofa they don't know what to do next. They remain silent waiting for the other to take charge.

NACHO: Let's turn on the TV.

PACO: We're not going to turn on the TV and treat him like a child by having the TV baby sit him.

NACHO: Well what ideas do you have?

PACO: I don't know... Ah, did he eat?

NACHO: No, but we have to buy groceries. I'll go out and get groceries.

NACHO gets up and makes for the door.

PACO: No, you're not going to leave me alone with him.

NACHO: I'll take me less than half an hour.

PACO: I know you, fifteen minutes turn to fifty at a bar and then I will be responsible for Lalo from then on... Te conosco mosco miserable. (I know you.)

NACHO is about to contradict him, but he can't, so he mumbles and quiets down.

They remain silent. NACHOS speaks because he is unable to remain silent.

NACHO: Say something! It's so quiet. I can't stand it this quiet. We've never been this quiet together...

PACO: Maybe that's why we sing because we can't stand to be quiet.

They don't say anything.

NACHO: Okay, well ah... What's that smell? Did you? Did you?

PACO: No. It's him.

NACHO: No me digas (don't tell me) Lalo did number two?

PACO: I think it's time to change his diaper.

They look at one another.

PACO/NACHO: Are you going to do it?

They stare at each other.

PACO/NACHO: Why don't you do it?

NACHO: You do it!

PACO: Nah, you do it!

NACHO: ¡Tu haslo! (You do it!)

PACO: Why do I always get stuck with this shit? Look, I've been wiping down his saliva since we left the hospital. It's your time to wipe.

NACHO: What do you mean? I'm always the one doing what you say--

PACO: That's a lie - you're always giving orders.

NACHO: No, you're the one always acting like you're the pinche jefe-- (damn chief)

PACO: ¡Mira pinche cabrón tu eres el mandón! (Look you bastard you are the bossy one!)

NACHO: No me digas cabrón o te la parto pa que sepas respetar-- (Don't call me a bastard or I'll kick your ass so that you learn to respect me.)

Their arguing escalates into almost a fist fight, then LALO snores loudly and interrupts them.

They stop arguing. They remain quiet, then look at one another.

PACO: Well, who is going to clean him up?

NACHO: Why don't we flip a coin?

PACO: This is horrible that neither one of us wants to do it; he's our best friend!

(BEAT)

NACHO: There's love and then there's love.

PACO: What's that supposed to mean?

NACHO: I love him like a compadre, pero no como vieja... Only women can love men enough to wipe their asses... Yo no soy vieja (I'm not a dame), I wasn't made for those things.

PACO: Y que, ¿yo soy la vieja? (What, and I'm the bitch?) You think God put me on this earth to wipe ass?

NACHO: No, but I just can't do it.

PACO: Pues I'm not going to do it!

NACHO: No, I'm not doing it!

They continue arguing.

PACO: All right, give me a coin!

NACHO takes out a coin.

PACO (CONT'D): Aguila. (Eagle.)

NACHO: Come on heads.

NACHO tosses the coin and covers it. He uncovers it.

NACHO (CONT'D): ¡Pinche...! (Damn!)

PACO: Look, Lalo would wipe your ass in a second if you were in his situation.

NACHO: Easy for you to say since you're not going to do it... Bueno (well then), why don't you help me? I'll wipe, but you hold him up and that will make it go faster.

PACO: Okay, okay, ya, para que te calles. (Okay, so you'll shut up already!)

NACHO: There has got to be an easier way.

PACO: Maybe he has a savings account and we can get a hold of it so we can get him a nurse.

NACHO: Do you have a savings account?

PACO: No.

NACHO: Then what makes you think he would have one since we made the same lousy money?

PACO: Yes, but Lalo always saved everything, maybe he was smarter than both of us, you know.

NACHO: Maybe he has an illegitimate daughter out there who might be willing to take care of him.

They think about it.

PACO: Lalo, no. He was a saint.

NACHO: ¿Pero tiene verga, no? (Yeah, but he has a penis, no?)

PACO: No, he was... I mean he's such a decent man--

NACHO: Maybe, we can get social security and some services for him.

PACO: You know about that stuff? We always got paid cash and I know Lalo never applied for a "greencard". Asi es que I don't think he's eligible for anything.

NACHO: Why didn't he apply?

PACO: Lalo hates the U.S. government and said if he died in the U.S. to ship him back to Mexico.

(BEAT)

NACHO: Where do you want to be buried? In Mexico or here?

PACO: Me? I want to be cremated and liberated to the wind... Hey, that rhymes... That would make a good lyric. I should write that down. Where's a pencil?

PACO searches for a pencil and finds one. He takes out a tiny paper pad from his back pocket.

NACHO: I want to be buried here, in the U.S.

PACO: Maybe you and I can pay for a nurse... No, we have to do this for him. He has done so much for us, it's the least we can do for him... We wouldn't be who we are without him.

NACHO: A pair of "has-beens"?

PACO: No, a trio who has made so many people fall in love.

NACHO: ¿Qué, qué? (Come again.) You think we did that? Is that why so many borrachos (drunks) fought at our concerts?

PACO: You make jokes, but I know Lalo brought us together for a reason, and I'm proud to say we made people fall in love with our music and we brought joy to the lives of a lot of miserable people.

NACHO: Don't be staring at me when you say "miserable."

PACO: I wasn't staring, I was just trying to look at you to make a point.

They take a deep breath.

NACHO: Who would have thought trying to save a man from getting beaten up would have landed me having to wipe his ass too. If you would have told me I wouldn't have believed it.

PACO: Me neither, ¡asi es que chíngate! (so screw you) Lets get this over with before its stinks up the whole house!

They carry LALO onto the wheelchair and take him on it to the bathroom.

LIGHTS FADE OUT.

LIGHTS FADE IN.

LALO sleeps on the sofa, NACHO and PACO sit next to him still traumatized from the bathroom experience. They have a frightened expression on their faces.

NACHO: I just can't... I just can't... He's going to do number two in a few hours and I don't think I can go through it again. He must have an illegitimate daughter out there or someone who will take responsibility, por que yo no puedo (because I can't).

PACO: Why didn't he get married?

NACHO: You know what, I don't know. I mean, I never thought about it before, but yeah, now that you mention it that's pretty strange...

PACO: So what are we going to do? Are we going to live here?

NACHO: Someone has to live here, but it's not going to be me. It should be you. You're better at these things.

PACO: No, you should do it because you've never done anything for anybody. You owe it to him, you're the one who punched him.

NACHO: But it was your fault. If you hadn't run in and interrupted us--

PACO: But it was your punch that did the damage.

They continue to complain.

PACO: Look, we're both going to live here.

NACHO: But where are we going to sleep? This house is so full of cochinero (junk) and there is no room.

PACO: We'll find a place to sleep. Why don't we pick up and find someplace to set up our beds.

NACHO: So now I have to clean up. So I have to be his nurse and now his cleaning lady--

PACO: Nacho, no seas un pinche macho-- (Nacho, don't be a damn macho--)

NACHO: Pero what's wrong with being a macho, I'm proud of it. Que, ¿tu no eres macho? (Aren't you a macho?) What are you, a vieja (woman)?

PACO: You know what I mean. Stop it! Stop acting like you're el rey (the king), this isn't a corrido (ballad), this is Lalo's life.

NACHO: Look, what if you do the cleaning and I do the cooking. ¿Sale-vale? (How about it?)

PACO: No, it's too much work just for me to do. Help me clean up now, and afterwards I'll maintain it clean and you do the cooking.

NACHO: Why don't we make a list and then we can split the chores, para que sea justo (so that it's fair) and you can't bitch later about how you always do all the work and nobody appreciates you. I think it's because of you I never married.

PACO: What do you mean?

NACHO: You nagged like a vieja (hag) all the time, it was like I was already married.

PACO stares at LALO and almost loses it.

NACHO: You're gonna start crying?

PACO: No, no... It's just that look at him... It won't be long before we end up looking just like that and who is going to take care of us?

NACHO: I don't want to think about it. Why do you have to start talking about that? Lalo, is going to recover, he's not going to die.

PACO: Yes, maybe he won't die now, but he will.

NACHO: Yes, we're all going to die, but before that happens I'm going to live it up and I'm not going to think about it until we get there. You know, I thought I'd be dead by now. I was convinced someone was going to kill me at a cantina when I was drunk... Some jealous husband or--

PACO: Yeah, me too.

NACHO: You too? You thought you were going to go like me?

PACO: No! I mean with your big mouth someone would have made you shut it forever.

NACHO: I know... You know I don't like getting old. It's not for me. Machos should die at a young age, pero con nuestras botas puestas (with our boots still on) and bien proud.

PACO (*mockingly*): ¿Y qué pasó? (And what happened?) I thought you were going to shoot yourself at sixty. Weren't you bragging at fifty que tu eras bien macho (that you were so manly) and you weren't scared of death?

NACHO: Yeah, I'm going to do it. Pues (Well) I'll do it right now! I'm not scared. I'm going to go get my gun right now!

NACHO makes for the door. PACO stops him.

PACO: You'll do anything to keep from wiping ass... Pues, you better not kill yourself and leave me all alone to wipe it.

NACHO shoots PACO a look and goes back to sit.

NACHO: It should have happened to me.

PACO: No, it should have happened to me.

NACHO: I shouldn't have punched him. I practically killed him.

PACO: No, it wasn't your fault.

NACHO: Go, ahead, punch me. Punch me.

PACO: No, don't blame yourself.

NACHO: Go ahead, punch me.

PACO: No, I'm not going to punch you.

NACHO: Punch me!

PACO: No, I'm not going to punch you in front of Lalo.

NACHO: We can do it behind him.

PACO: No!

NACHO: I said PUNCH ME! Punch me so that at least I can feel something and maybe that way I can finally cry because I haven't in a long time that I've forgotten how.

PACO: You really want me to punch you?

NACHO nods gently. PACO punches him viciously. NACHO yelps in pain.

NACHO: Cabrón (Jerk), why did you punch me?

PACO: You said to do it!

NACHO: Okay, but I didn't really mean it. I didn't think you were going to do it... You hate me that much?

PACO: I don't hate you-- No-- Yes! I really do hate you.

NACHO: Why do you hate me so much?

PACO: You know, I don't remember, but I know I hate you for something.

NACHO: Well if you remember, let me know. And if I remember that I hate you, you better watch out.

PACO: ¡Ya! (Enough!) We're not getting anywhere. Let's start cleaning up. And after we clean up we'll make food and feed him and then we can... (*realizing*) La telenovela! We'll make him watch his telenovelas and maybe he'll...

NACHO: ¿Telenovelas?

PACO: Yes, that should make him happy. We should try to make him happy; we don't know how long he has.

NACHO: Don't say that compadre. Don't say that.

PACO: I know, but he's here, and he's not really here... No se que decir. (I don't know what to say.) Bueno, after the telenovelas we'll put him in bed and then we'll figure it out.

(BEAT)

NACHO: So what do you want me to do? Where should I clean?

PACO: Why don't I start on this side and you take that side?

NACHO and PACO bend down and clean all around them.

NACHO hums a song and PACO hums along until they sing the lyrics and continue cleaning.

LIGHTS FADE OUT.

LIGHTS FADE IN.

LALO's APARTMENT is now almost clean.

PACO: ¡La telenovela! Turn on the TV.

NACHO: You think this will work? You think it will inspire him?

NACHO turns on the TV and then sits next to LALO. They watch the TELENOVELA. PACO continues cleaning, going through a pile of unopened letters.

Telenovela (*V.O.*): ¡Pero tus jemelos son bastardos! ¡Yo me casaré contingo y te daré toda la felicidad de mundo! (Your twins are bastards, but I will marry you and give you all the happiness in the world.)

LALO wakes up and opens an eye. He tries to smile, but only half of his mouth moves. NACHO puts his arm around him LALO's head falls on NACHO's shoulder.

NACHO: No se preocupe (don't worry) Lalito, we'll take good care of you.

TELENOVELA (*V.O.*): I can't marry you because I'm your sister!

PACO: Mira! Look at this. This letter says something about Braceros. There was a civil law suit against the U.S. and the Mexican government. They reached a settlement and if we can prove we were Braceros we will be given 38,000 pesos... That's like $3,500 in dollars -- something like that!

NACHO: ¿Pero por qué¿ (But why?)

PACO: They kept our money. Remember? They kep ten percent que pa que cuando (so that when) we retired? LALO always said they were just stealing it. Pos I guess they're giving us something.

NACHO: Maybe with that money we can gt him a nurse!

NACHO: Aver (Let's see), and what do we have to do?

PACO: Ay, no. They want proof, they want documents...our contracts...

NACHO: That was 50 years ago, no one kept records.

PACO: Lalo probably did.

PACO sits next to LALO who watches his telenovela.

PACO: Lalito, mira.... (look)

PACO grabs LALO's face gently and makes him look at him.

PACO: Lalo, do you have your contracts?

LALO just stares back blankly.

PACO: Lalito, can you point or move your eyes to show me where they might be?

LALO does not respond. PACO releases his face, it falls back on NACHO's shoulder.

PACO stands up and paces back and forth.

PACO: I know they're here. After we put him to bed we'll look for them.

TELENOVELA (*V.O.*): Pero esto no se acaba así, traidora! (This is not the end of this, traitor.)

LIGHTS FADE OUT.

LIGHTS FADE IN.

PACO and NACHO are on the floor digging through piles of old things and boxes.

PACO: Look what I found. There are photos here. I think it's a scrapbook.

NACHO: I didn't know he did scrap booking. Is that an announcement for our first concert?

PACO: Sí. He kept this? Fifty years?

NACHO: That's a long time. Fifty years.

PACO sniffles and cries.

NACHO: Are you crying?

PACO is too emotional to respond.

PACO: No, no.

NACHO: Párale, párale (stop, stop) or you're going to take me with you.

PACO: We have to find those documents!

NACHO: Do you remember our first performance?

PACO: Yes, that I'll never forget. I remember thinking how happy I was knowing I could make money with my voice and not just with my hands. That I was not put on this earth to just live a hand to mouth existence, but that it could be something more. I remember thinking how easy it was to get women by singing. Por eso cantamos. (That's why we sing.)

NACHO: ¡Por las viejas! (For the women.)

PACO: Pos sí, cantamos pa no sentirnos viejos. (We sing so we don't feel old.)

NACHO: Tu recuerdas...our first song? (Do you remember our first song?)

NACHO and PACO sing their first song.

LIGHTS FADE OUT.

SCENE TWO

LIGHTS FADE IN on a CANTINA. An ANNOUNCER appears on stage.

ANNOUNCER: Give another round of applause to Los Traileros del Norte... Now for the first time at La Jornada, we are proud to present Trio Los Machos! Let's give a round of applause to welcome them!

Applause is heard.

NACHO, LALO, and PACO, now in their 30s, play guitars and sing AMANECI EN TUS BRAZOS (the same song). AURELIA, 21, steps forward and sticks out her hand to NACHO.

AURELIA: Hola, my name is Aurelia. I sing too.

She shakes all of their hands.

PACO: Sí, what do you sing?

AURELIA: I can sing boleros (romantic ballads) like you. You need someone like me?

NACHO: We're a trio. I don't think we need a woman.

LALO: Well, maybe we do. Sing a song and maybe we'll see.

AURELIA sings SIN TI in a spotlight.

Photo by Josefina López

Trio Los Machos performing as young men.

The LIGHTS FADE IN and the song becomes a duet between AURELIA and PACO.

They kiss.

LIGHTS FADE OUT.

LIGHTS FADE IN back to NACHO and PACO going through the scrapbook in LALO's apartment.

NACHO: What a beautiful girl.

PACO: I know... I married her so you wouldn't beat me to it. Ah, ya se! Now I remember why I hate you!

LIGHTS FADE OUT.

LIGHTS FADE IN.

The YOUNG TRIO finish a song.

PACO and AURELIA talk.

PACO: I have to go out tonight again.

AURELIA: But you go out every night. Why don't you spend time with me?

PACO: Aurelia, let's not go through this again. I have to go talk to all the bar

owners so I can convince them to let us play. You know I have to do this so we get work.

AURELIA: I know, but have you forgotten what day this is?

PACO: No, why?

AURELIA: You don't remember?

PACO: No, tell me.

AURELIA: If I have to remind you than it's obviously not important to you.

PACO: Aurelia, I don't have time for games like this, tell me or stop bothering me with it.

AURELIA: It's nothing. Go. Be careful la migra doesn't get you.

PACO: I'm always careful.

PACO kisses her on the forehead and exits.

AURELIA cries, sings SOLAMENTE UNA VEZ.

NACHO approaches her.

NACHO: ¿Porqué lloras¿ (Why do you cry?)

AURELIA: I wasn't crying.

NACHO: You don't have to be embarrassed in front of me. You can tell me.

AURELIA: Paco, doesn't love me anymore... He forgot our anniversary...again.

NACHO: Of course he loves you. He tells me all the time.

AURELIA: He should tell me. Why doesn't he tell me?

NACHO: He writes songs about you. He sings them to you.

AURELIA: No, he's in love with his music. He doesn't know how to love me. When he's with me he is always thinking of his songs. I'm his mistress. His music is his wife. He doesn't love me anymore.

NACHO: That's not true.

AURELIA: Then why does it feel so...

NACHO: Maybe he is afraid to lose you and that's why he doesn't tell you... so you never feel like you're good enough and you don't ever leave him.

AURELIA: You think so?

NACHO: I know if I had a woman like you I would do whatever I needed to keep her...but I would treat her like a rose.

NACHO sings SABOR A Mi to AURELIA. They kiss. She then turns away as if ashamed. He exits.

LIGHTS FADE OUT.

LIGHTS FADE IN.

AURELIA is at the same place where NACHO kissed her and she is singing SABOR A MI. PACO enters.

PACO: Why do you sing that song every night by the door?

AURELIA: I love this song.

PACO: Who do you sing that song to?

AURELIA: What are you talking about?

PACO: You sing that song every night like a nightingale.

AURELIA: What are you insinuating?

PACO: I better not catch you-- You know what I mean.

AURELIA: Paco, estás loco. (you are crazy) You are the only man I love... When are we going to have children?

(BEAT)

YOUNG PACO: Not now.

AURELIA: When?

YOUNG PACO: When things are better for us.

AURELIA: Us? Do you mean us or do you mean the trio?

YOUNG PACO: I don't want to talk about this.

AURELIA: I want to talk about this now... I don't want to keep waiting... Make me a woman... I love singing with you, but I want to have your children--

YOUNG PACO: I said I did not want to talk about it! We can't afford them and they can't get in the way of what I'm trying to build here.

AURELIA: And what are you trying to build...with us?

YOUNG PACO: Ya me voy. (I have to go.)

LIGHTS FADE OUT.

SCENE THREE

LIGHTS FADE IN on LALO's APARTMENT with NACHO and PACO buried in junk.

PACO: Cabrón (Jerk), you cheated with her!

PACO jumps on NACHO and goes for the throat.

NACHO: No, I didn't betray you... Yes, yes, I did kiss her, but I didn't do it... She cheated on you with another man.

PACO (*suspiciously*): ¿Con quién? (With whom?) Don't tell me Lalo--

NACHO: No, Lalo would never do that to you.

PACO: Who was it?

NACHO: I don't remember... I didn't want to tell you because I knew it would hurt you.

PACO: But you knew I suspected you.

NACHO: Yes, but I didn't care if you hated me... I didn't want you to hate her. I didn't want you to find her with the other man and mistreat her.

PACO: I would never have hurt her.

(BEAT)

NACHO: So if you suspected me, why didn't you confront me? Were you too scared of me?

PACO: No... I loved you and Lalo so much that I was willing to tolerate the humiliation... I didn't want us to break up...I guess I loved my music and us more than I loved her.

NACHO: Yes, I think she knew it... I loved Aurelia. I would have left us for her, but I never touched her. I loved her so much...

PACO: So all these years...why didn't you tell me after she died?

NACHO: Because I wanted you to remember her with loving thoughts.

PACO: It killed her that I never confronted her. I think she wanted me to confront her and show her that I still loved her, but I didn't.

NACHO: The truth ate her up just like the cancer.

PACO: Aurelia... Aurelia...

PACO breaks down crying.

NACHO: Sí, viejo, cry your heart out. I also miss her. I never married because I was a borracho (drunk), but I was in love with her... When I'm drunk she visits me and sings.

PACO: Me too.

LIGHTS FADE and AURELIA's SPIRIT sings PIENSA EN MI in a spotlight.

LIGHTS FADE IN and AURELIA disappears.

PACO and NACHO cry some more.

NACHO: I never took her away from you because I never wanted to lose her...but we both ended up losing her.

PACO: We both lost her and now we're going to lose Lalo.

NACHO: Don't say that.

PACO: Well look at him. Look at what is left of him.

NACHO: Who would have thought it would be Lalo... It should have been me. I'm the alcoholic son of a bitch who deserves to die first. God, take me instead of Lalo.

PACO: No, take me.

NACHO: No, take me.

PACO: No, take me!

NACHO: No, take me!

PACO: Why are we always fighting?

NACHO: That's right. It's tiring.

PACO: All of our lives we've been competing to see who is the best. The best what? Macho? Idiot?

NACHO: Yes, we're the best idiots. Yes, that's what we are.

PACO: All the time we wasted fighting and for what? We've lost all that ever meant anything to us. And for what?

NACHO: Pinche orgullo. (Fucking pride.) Doesn't do anything. Doesn't take away death. (*NACHO wails.*) This is the first time I really cry. It feels real good to finally do it.

PACO: Me too.

NACHO: So many years that we couldn't cry. Tantos años que no pudimos

llorar... How beautiful life is... One day we're here and the next we're gone.

PACO: You know what, I don't know how much time I have and you don't know how much time you have, so from this day forward, this stupid pride ends.

NACHO: Yes, from now on let's not waste our time with those pendejadas.

(BEAT)

NACHO: So do we begin again? And do we begin without Lalo if...

PACO: Do you think we should go on without Lalo?

NACHO: No se... Let's sleep on it.

PACO: Maybe tomorrow will be a different day.

NACHO and PACO lie on the floor and fall asleep.

LIGHTS FADE OUT.

After a few minutes LALO slips out of bed and tip toes to a secret location and takes out a shoebox. He places it close to NACHO and PACO.

He sings RELOJ almost as a lullaby to them. He tip toes back into bed.

LIGHTS FADE OUT.

LIGHTS FADE IN.

NACHO wakes up. He sees the shoebox and opens it. His eyes widen in excitement.

NACHO: Paco, wake up. Look what I found!

PACO wakes up.

NACHO: It has letters and the documents!

NACHO pulls out a stack of photos. They go through them.

PACO: Look, there are also lots of photos of Lalo and a man...and who is that man?

NACHO: Ay, no, ¡mira! (Oh, no, look!) Who is this man and why are they hugging like that?

PACO: No, no me digas (No, don't tell me.) God, please don't tell me!

NACHO: No, men don't hug like that!

PACO: Ay, no! Do you think--?

NACHO: No... No!

PACO: He never married.

NACHO: No!

PACO: Well, but what if he were? So what, no?

NACHO: Pos sí, ¿qué no? (Well, yeah, no?) Ay, no. Don't tell me he was a "fag" all this time.

PACO: Don't call him that.

NACHO: So what do I call him? Maricón? (Queer?) Homosexual?

PACO: No, don't use those words, I don't like those words.

NACHO: It doesn't change what he is.

PACO: All those years, how could he--?

NACHO: But how could it be that we didn't know? Fifty years and not know this?

PACO: How could he tell us? We were pinches machos (damn men).

NACHO: But in fifty years?

PACO: But how can it be? No.

NACHO: Well I did notice he had a good eye for design and things like that, but who would have thought. No.

PACO: He liked telenovelas!

NACHO: So? (then:) Ay, you're right. Now that I think about it there were all these little things about him that now I notice.

PACO: You're right. It's starting to make sense.

NACHO: Well, yeah, after our performances he would leave the bars early because he had to wake up early and we would think nothing of it because we were too caught up chasing women and...

PACO: De veras (That's true), I never saw him with a woman and I never asked him because I figured he liked to be discreet, tu sabes (you know).

NACHO: Yeah, we thought that since he was close to being a priest that maybe he didn't care for women that much, but it never would have occurred to me, pos que (you know).

PACO: Why are you crying?

NACHO: I'm not crying... I'm just sad. Look at him. He's a jotito (a fairy) and he never told us.

PACO: Don't call him a joto! ("Fag!")

NACHO: Well what do I call him?

PACO: Our friend, our compadre (buddy), our compañero (our companion), he's just our Lalo.

NACHO: It's sad that he never told us.

PACO: Oh, yeah, what if he had told us. What would you have done? Do you think if he would have told us that we would have accepted it?

NACHO: You're right. I would have slapped him and felt betrayed.

PACO: Why betrayed?

NACHO: Because that's how I would have felt back then. We wouldn't be able to continue as a trio if he were gay. You like that better? Gay?

PACO: Sounds a little better, but still doesn't make it easy... I guess Lalo kept his secret so we could stay together.

NACHO: You think that's why he did it?

PACO: Lalo did everything to keep us together, even putting up with us fighting all the time.

NACHO looks at the photos. He examines them closer.

NACHO: You know, I know this man. He was our biggest fan. *(BEAT)* He already died...a few years ago.

PACO: You think that was his...his? He was in all the photos.

NACHO: Que triste (how sad), his "special friend" died and he never told us about it. He had to keep the grief all to himself... Why didn't he trust us?

PACO: Because we were always fighting and acting like children and we never stopped to ask Lalo how he was doing and if he ever needed anything.

(BEAT)

NACHO: Good. I'm glad we found out this way. He is who he is and that's how God made him and that's the way it is.

PACO: Who cares. He's our friend however he is. He was always a good person, y ya (and that's the end of it).

NACHO: Pos sí (Well yeah)... He should have told us.

PACO: Look, here are the Bracero contracts! Now all we have to do is fill out the form and mail all this and maybe we can get a nurse!

LIGHTS FADE OUT.

LIGHTS FADE IN.

PACO is by himself tuning his guitar. He plays and begins singing EL CORRIDO DEL BRACERO, a song he wrote. NACHO walks in. PACO stops singing and pretends to be tuning his guitar.

NACHO: Go ahead, continue with your song. It sounds beautiful.

PACO: Nah, you think so? I wrote this song for Lalo.

NACHO: Why don't you play it for Lalo?

PACO: He's sleeping.

NACHO: Play it for him, maybe he'll have nice dreams.

PACO and NACHO go over to the bed where LALO is sleeping. PACO sings the song for LALO.

Half way through the song LALO opens his eyes and smiles.

LALO: Que bonita canción. (What a pretty song.)

PACO/NACHO: Lalo! Es un milagro. It's a miracle!

PACO and NACHO hug and kiss LALO.

PACO/NACHO: How do you feel?

LALO: I feel like I just woke up from a well deserved sleep.

PACO/NACHO: Can you move your body?

LALO: Yes, I think I can.

LALO moves his body.

NACHO: I'm sorry I punched you.

LALO: You did?

PACO: I'm sorry I didn't listen to you. It was none of my business... I'm sorry Nacho for ruining...your action. I know how hard it can get to, you know...

NACHO: No, I should have stayed away from her. Poor girl doesn't know any better about staying away from men like me.

PACO: No, it was all right, I was just jealous you still got it and I don't--

NACHO: No, all this mess was my fault

PACO: No, it was really my fault.

NACHO: No, it was my fault!

LALO: Are you going to start fighting again? Because next time you fight, I'm staying out of it or you're finally going to kill me.

PACO: No. Nacho and I have called a truce. No more fighting.

NACHO: No more nonsense. We promise to act our age and I'm promising to give up tequila... Beers yes, tequila no... One step at a time, que no?

LALO and PACO nod approvingly.

(BEAT)

PACO (*uncomfortable*): Lalo, we were going through your things looking for your Bracero contracts and we found--

NACHO: Is there anything you need or want to tell us that you've never told us?

LALO: Like what?

PACO: Anything... You can tell us anything.

NACHO: We would understand anything, especially now that we're all grown up...

(BEAT)

LALO: Yes. I have something I want to tell you... I've been thinking that we should change our name. What about calling ourselves Trio Los Braceros?

PACO and NACHO look to one another and chuckle.

PACO/NACHO: I like it. Yes, why not? Let's do it!

They ad lib all the changes for their new name.

LIGHTS FADE OUT.

SCENE FOUR

LIGHTS FADE IN at ANOTHER RESTAURANT in OLVERA STREET.

LALO, PACO, and NACHO, dressed in their new trio outfits, come out to make their debut as a trio and sing SIN TI.

LALO steps forward and introduces his trio.

LALO: We are Trio Los Braceros.

ROSARIO, who is a patron at the restaurant, applauds.

They take a bow and are about to exit. NACHO pinches PACO's butt cheek and PACO slugs him playfully.

LALO: ¡Calmados muchachos! (Calm down boys.) Let's be serious or they'll send us back to retirement.

The End

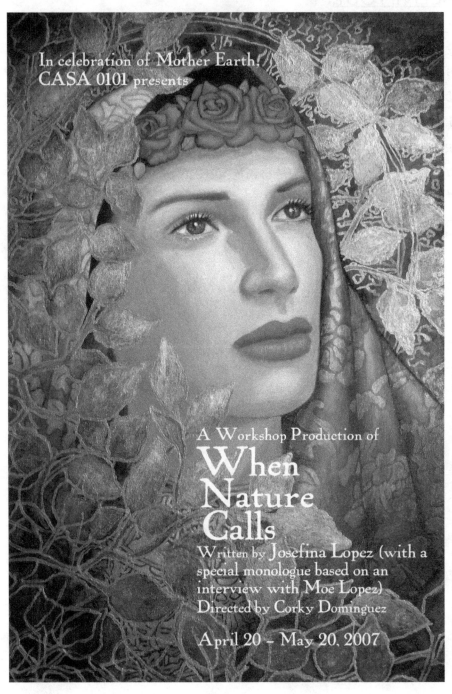

In celebration of Mother Earth!
CASA 0101 presents

A Workshop Production of

When Nature Calls

Written by Josefina Lopez (with a
special monologue based on an
interview with Moe Lopez)
Directed by Corky Dominguez

April 20 – May 20, 2007

Graphic design by Gaby López - Painting by Juan Soliz

WHEN NATURE CALLS

PLAYWRIGHT'S NOTES

I was so inspired by an article in the *Los Angeles Times* by Ching-Ching Ni about a woman in China nick-named "The Battery Queen" that I cried after I read the article. I immediately wanted to write something about her. She stayed with me for many years until I realized that I had personally come across so many women who had courageously fought for a cause at their personal expense. The cause was not just for social justice, but also for environmental justice. In doing research about the murders in Ciudad Juarez, Mexico, I came across women who were valiant warriors. The monologue in the piece about Juarez was actually inspired by a dream/visitation that Cynthia Huerta described to me claiming that perhaps the spirit wanted me to know this... The monologue about Katrina is based on a real woman who I just happened to meet and had to include her story in this show.

Long before Al Gore's *An Inconvenient Truth,* I've been wanting to write a piece that made people especially, women and Latinos, aware of the fact that being environmentally conscious and caring for the earth and la tierra is part of our heritage and our being. My father taught me to always pick up trash and be considerate of others; to recycle cans and anything else that could have a new life... I didn't realize that made me an environmentalist until I looked back and made the connection that my father was a campesino; and proud of it.

Josefina López

April 2007

WHEN NATURE CALLS

Lights fade in. A CHINESE WOMAN, late 40s, dressed simply, welcomes us.
Her house is filled with batteries of all sorts.

"THE BATTERY QUEEN"

Ni-hao. Hello, you're the reporter from the *L.A. Times*? Yes, you found me; I'm 'The Battery Queen"... Welcome and come in. Thank you for your interest in my cause... But I'm sorry I have no furniture or a place to sit... You didn't think my apartment would look like this, did you? Yes, it's a mess, but it's what I must do. Until China, who produces 15 billion batteries a year, more than any other country, and not just regular ones, but cheap ones with mercury still in them; until this country has a recycling program for batteries, this is what I must do... Look at them, all these batteries... They are like unmarriageable daughters. I worry about them night and day. They are so many I can line them up from here to the Great Wall. But these are only some of them. My mother's house is also filled with them and my brother's balcony, and a factory close by. I've collected approximately 40 tons. When I found out that 150,000 gallons of water could be poisoned by a single battery, I just had to do something. 150,000 gallons of water, that's one person's entire lifetime supply. It's like killing a person... I am a simple woman, we have very little money, so this is the only thing I can do for now. It's for my conscience too... I can sleep a little better at night knowing these batteries are not out there...

Now I really appreciate you doing a story on me, but I don't want you to write about me as though I am a saint for doing what I am doing. I want you to know the truth, all of it... You see we were cotton farmers in the countryside and we came to Xinxiang for a better life. I created a job for myself selling batteries on the sidewalk. That was the only job I could get that was profitable. I saved enough money and opened a counter at a farmer's market where I sold cheap batteries. Then I opened another and

Photo by Hector Rodríguez

"The Battery Queen."

pretty soon people started calling me "The Battery Queen." So I supported my family selling batteries... Honestly, I feel somewhat responsible... I didn't know how dangerous they were. I wouldn't have sold them had I known... I had to make a living, but not this way... People think I'm crazy that I've spent over 25,000 Yuan Renminbi, that's a lot of money for people like us who only make 4,000 Yuan Renminbi a year, to buy back used batteries... My husband, he's been approached by metal scrappers offering him a lot of money to retrieve the usable metal. He's tried to convince me to sell them, make back some of our money and forget this whole thing... But I know they'll just get the metal and toss out all the poison. They don't care... My husband didn't understand before. He would tell me that he would support me if we were millionaires and we could afford to do humanitarian work... But a conscience isn't something you buy or something that comes when you can afford to have one. He asked me, "Where's the profit in what you are doing? We live in a market economy now!" We had so many fights over this. He even threatened to divorce me. When he told me I remember running to the balcony and crying my heart out. I overheard other families joyfully playing Mah-jong down below. I didn't want to tear my family apart, but I knew I had to keep doing what I was doing. So I told my husband. "Fine, let's divorce. You can go back to being a farmer and I'll keep doing what I'm doing." You see I fell in love with my husband when I spotted him doing laundry in the river. We lived in a small village called, "the place where two rivers merge". The water was clear, the air was fresh, and there was a huge willow tree next to him and purple mountains behind them. He was such a nice boy. It was picture perfect. But now we're old, the river is either black or dry, the air is dirty, and the mountains disappeared behind all the pollution. "Don't you remember how beautiful it was?" I asked my husband. "Don't you want our son and his children to have the same beautiful sights?" He thought about it for a long time and he finally understood that this meant so much to me that I was willing to sacrifice my love for him to do what I know is right. Now he's my biggest supporter. Now he takes care of the house so I can travel. I lecture at universities and community centers about the dangers of battery poison and how to temporarily recycle batteries.

It's nice that even though I have no more money to buy back used batteries; people drop off their used batteries at my door. Slowly I'll change the minds of people... Now my son, that's another story. He can't propose to his girlfriend until we own an apartment and some decent furniture. The way things are he'll never bring her home. He's embarrassed of me... My son doesn't understand me now...but his children will. For now, only Mother Earth understands me. Unfortunately she can't talk. But I'm a soldier for her. China is a long way from making the environment a priority because she's too worried about feeding the population first. But the land, the water, these are the essentials of life. People may call me a mad woman, but fighting to preserve the land and water, is the sanest thing I can do as a human being.

Lights fade out.

Lights fade in on a doctor's examination room. ALMA, a Mexican-American woman, 30s, undresses. She reveals a gun in a holster under her blouse. She puts the gun away in her purse and puts on a paper hospital gown. ALMA sits on the examining table and waits for her doctor for a few seconds. She turns to talk to her doctor, an empty chair besides her.

ALMA

Doctor, I don't remember the last time I slept the whole night... I've been following the story of all the missing women in Ciudad Juárez since 1993 back when there were only a few women missing... That's when I started investigating and writing articles for an El Paso newspaper... So I guess back in early 1993 I slept through the whole night...after that the weight of the 450 murdered women has kept me up at night.

The first time I had a nightmare was after I saw the first body... I saw the "V" carved on the back of a headless female corpse in the desert of Lomas De Poleo. She was one of eight women found in the mountains of that desert. It was then that I felt them... It must have been at that time that they followed me home. Now, Doctor, I know you are probably thinking I'm exaggerating, and if I'm not you're wondering if I should be talking to a psychiatrist and not a gastro-enterologist. But that was the first time I felt their presence...

Doctor, can I confide in you? You see I'm not Catholic so going to a priest is out of the question and going to a therapist would make my editor worry about me and take me off the story. He already told me it's too dangerous the last time my life was threatened by the police and the narcos in Juarez, so I don't want to give him a reason. If he finds out about my health he'll definitely kick me off the story. So can I confide in you? I can't even confide in my fiancé because he's ready to call off the wedding. He's sick of hearing about the murdered and the missing women. He's been my only source of support, but he can't take it anymore... Why is it that men can't take so much pain? Why is it that all the fathers of the missing women become alcoholics while the mothers who cry their hearts out continue to fight tirelessly for justice, but not give up hope? Sorry, I was trying to--- So can I confide in you? *(BEAT)* Thanks.

Last night I had a visit. Maybe, it was a dream and we can dismiss it as

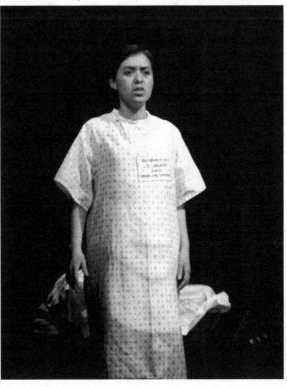

Photo by Hector Rodríguez

Alma recalls her "nightmare" in which the ghost of Esmeralda visited her.

119

that... But one of the nameless young women came to me and she asked me to follow her. I touched her hand and I became her. Instantly I was she, working at a maquiladora assembling a television. My feet hurt after standing for 12 hours. My schedule had been changed last minute to a night schedule. I asked them to please keep me on the day schedule but the manager said it was either the night schedule or no job at all. I, as the young woman, walked out of the factory at night, tired and sleepy. I got on two buses that would take me to the desert Lomas De Poleo. It was strange because although I was the young woman, my spirit or my mind could also see that an older White man with salt and pepper hair who worked at the factory had convinced the manager to change my schedule... Later, in a white pick up truck with a hatchback this man would wait for me in the desert. He already knew my stop. Then I, as the young woman, walked home in the dark. My house was a shack somewhere in the desert and there is no electricity. I heard footsteps and I walked faster... And then suddenly I felt a rock hit my head and I fainted... I woke up and felt a massive pain on my head. My body is naked and I feel a burning sensation in my anus. I'm being penetrated anally and the salt and peppered haired man humps me and he chants "Nomed! Nomed! Nomed!" He takes out a large knife and carves a "V" on my back. The pain is unbearable and I faint. That's when I stop being the young woman but I remain there like an invisible witness and can see the man carrying the body of the young woman and dumping it on a hill in the desert. Before he leaves he sets the body on fire and watches it burn. I can't stand to look... I get in his white pick up truck and he then drives across the border to El Paso and he goes home to his big house... In his living room he has a large grandfather clock and he opens it. In it are several notches carved by a knife. He takes the large knife that still has blood on it and he carves another notch. He hides the knife in the grandfather clock and goes to sleep... It was as if the young woman wanted me to see her life and she told me, "Mi nombre es Esmeralda" and she also said "Adios." That's when I wake up and I start investigating. El Paso is the drop off for sexual offenders who have just gotten out of jail. It would be a simple theory, but it would make sense that an American sexual offender would cross the border to Ciudad Juárez, do his crimes and then drive back to the U.S. So I try to find out if any of these sexual offenders on file match the man I dreamt of...but no match...

Okay, maybe I should be talking to a psychiatrist, maybe that's what I really need... Doctor of course I've tried sleeping pills, but they don't work... They don't work because things aren't getting better... I've read reports that wherever there are maquiladoras throughout third world countries like Sri Lanka, Bangladesh, and Guatemala, that the violence against women increases because they displace men out of work and it creates and environment of hatred towards women... This isn't just about one or two or three serial killers, copy cat criminals, corrupt government officials and police officers and narco-traficantes, but about the exploitation of women, a third world country's resources, and the earth's resources... The trees are dying in Juarez...you can't kill so many women without it affecting the land... The land has memory, it has a pulse, and it feels the absence of these nameless women...

Doctor, I know I have an ulcer, and the fire in my gut isn't just a yearning for justice. I know I can die from it, I'm not stupid...I know.... I know that in trying to save the lives of these women I am ending my own. But you have to believe me, at night they come to me. They come to my bed and ask, "When Alma, when?" And I look at them with shame and sorrow, and say, "Soon... Soon there will be justice in Juárez. Soon they will apprehend the killers. Soon it will be safe for women in Ciudad Juárez to walk the streets wearing mini-skirts without being called whores who deserve violence perpetrated upon them." But their sad faces don't change. I look at them all...this army of dead blue women, assembly line workers, maquiladora workers, women who assembled pieces and ended up in pieces...and I can't convince them... They will not stop visiting me...and each time more and more women appear. They know I care. They know I will carry the torch for them. They know they are not just nameless women whose cheap labor did not make their lives cheap in my eyes... But I want them to go home; to cross over and go home to their families; to God. Do you have a pill that can do that? Do you have a prescription for that kind of peace?... I didn't think so... Someday Ciudad Juárez will be safe for women. Someday this world will be safe for women. I have to live as though it is possible; I have to believe that even if it kills me.

Lights fade out.

Lights fade in on YOLANDA, early 20s, she's wearing a black shirt with the Virgen De Guadalupe image on the back. On stage there is only a chair and a silhouette of a tree.

"TREE WOMAN"/YOLANDA

Do I miss that tree? Yes, and no... The first thing I want to clear up is that I am not an activist. I wish I were that conscious and selfless, but I'm not... That still doesn't explain why a perfectly sane woman would climb up a tree and live there for two months.... I was simply running away from my fiancé-- ex-fiancé. One night after dinner at a fancy restaurant in Beverly Hills he got upset with me for correcting him in public. So when we were in private he slapped me. After he did that I just ran... I knew he would say he was sorry and he would never do it again and he would buy me flowers and like a love-starved idiot I would go back to him and he would do it again. So I ran, but something about this tree... It begged me to climb it. And I didn't

want to go home and I didn't want to go back with him... You see I ran and I knew there was no future with this man, but I didn't want to have a future without him. So I stopped the world; my world. That's why I climbed that tree.

YOLANDA climbs on the chair.

When I was on that tree... The moon kept me company while I contemplated my life... It only got lonely when I let myself feel sorry for

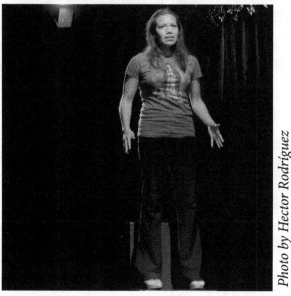

Photo by Hector Rodríguez

Yolanda explains feeling "rooted" by her connection to the tree.

myself... The next morning after I climbed the tree I was awakened by an argument. A police officer was arguing with an environmental activist about my right to be up there on the tree. So I was about to get off, but the young man ordered me to "Stay up there sister. You don't have to get off. We pay taxes. You enjoy that tree!" So I stayed up. Quickly the activists started comparing me to "The Butterfly Woman" and other women who have climbed and lived on trees... Coincidentally they were building yet another Starbucks right next to that tree... So the activists took the opportunity to make me a symbol of anti-globalization and anti-capitalism... I mean I don't mind Starbucks, but do they have to be at every corner? Okay... So the environmentalists would feed me and I wouldn't say anything, I wouldn't disagree or agree with them, I'd just take their food and blankets and toilet paper... I liked being on that tree, with my thoughts...

At night when all the activists and police officers and TV Crews would go home, I would pee...and it was like making rain. I howled and it felt good to be part of the wind. I rubbed my hands and made fire. I stretched out and I felt connected to the earth. I became the four elements. Earth, fire, water, and wind... I envied that tree. It had roots... I had none... I felt so disconnected to everyone...

Things really got serious when the manager from Starbucks wanted the whole fiasco to end before they opened the coffeehouse, so he hired a private detective to investigate my life and he dug up my fiancé and convinced him to come plead for me to get off. My fiancé said he would take me back and forget the whole thing. Basically forgiving me for being temporarily insane... After he was done begging and making a fool of himself I assured him that I would not be getting off and I would make the tree my permanent home. The activist cheered...but I didn't really mean it. I was just pissed off at him thinking he was coming to rescue me...

After two months of being up on that tree, I begged God for a miracle... I didn't want to get off and disappoint all those wonderful people who devoted their lives to saving trees and the earth. I also didn't want to get off and face my life, but I couldn't go on pretending I was an environmental activist. I couldn't go on pretending I wasn't a coward running away from my life. Of course I loved the attention, but I desperately wanted to go to the bathroom on a regular toilet. So one night one of the Spanish networks was filming me and the tree started to glow... We all looked around for the source of the light and there was no explanation. Then one of the crewmembers crossed himself. The camera crew gasped and some even got on their knees. They pointed the cameras up and I couldn't see what they were looking at. (*Yolanda turns around and shows the image of the Virgen.*) Pretty soon more people gathered. The news quickly got out that the Virgen De Guadalupe was appearing on a tree in Beverly Hills. The tree was surrounded by hundreds of Mexican and Latin American gardeners, nannies, cleaning ladies, valets, and cooks on their way home. This was the miracle I was waiting for. No one paid attention to me. They were too busy looking at the Goddess, the Goddess of Latino immigrants, the Goddess of the earth, the true Goddess of that tree... I climbed down and I let Guadalupe take my place...

YOLANDA gets off the chair.

So you see I am not an activist. Instead I made things worse for that poor tree. With so much traffic and Latino immigrants gathering in Beverly Hills to pay homage to the Virgen De Guadalupe they had to close down that particular Starbucks and cut down that tree... I managed to save some of the wood from that tree. I made a chair from it.

YOLANDA sits on the chair.

I sit on it when I start to feel sorry for myself, and then I imagine the moon next to me and feel connected to that tree, connected to all the beautiful things I often take for granted like the earth, water, fire, and wind. (*She howls.*)

Lights fade out.

Lights fade in on a little to show a jail cell shadow. A blonde woman with a white blouse with black stripes, very Parisian looking, is escorted on stage in handcuffs.

SALLY

(dramatically, with a French accent)

Je suis innocente! I am innocent. Innocent. (*She stops the drama and looks at the audience.*) Oh, who are you? Where's my lawyer? Oh, they sent you from the American embassy... No, it is not true I am not a terrorist! Je suis innocente! I am an American and an activist. (*They remove her handcuffs.*) I'll explain... Okay, fine I'll take off the phony French accent. (*She speaks with a slight American southern twang.*) It's all a mistake. I suppose you want me to start from the beginning otherwise none of this will make sense...I came to Paris a few years ago because I was in love with French culture, French literature, French Art, French pastries, everything French, except their condescending French arrogance, but that's not my point...or maybe it is about arrogance...maybe mine... Anyway, when I arrived in Paris I happened to get a small room in a fancy building. A chambre de bonne, a maid's room in the 16th arrondissment... You know, the neighborhood where you have skinny women dressed in Chanel and Dior, holding Louie Vuitton bags and Gucci sunglasses, old women wearing mink coats while walking their poodle. You know I don't get how anyone who loves animals could wear a mink coat. Does that make sense? Okay, okay, I'll get to my whole story... So every day on my way to French class I would observe what a beautiful city Paris is, except for the fact that there is dog shit and cigarette butts littered all over the streets. Especially in the 16th where you would think people with money and education and supposedly class, would know better than to let their dogs take poops on the streets and especially in people's front doors. I guess being a considerate human being has nothing to do with class... So one day I was dressed in my finest clothes on my way to a job interview and I take my first step and I was distracted by my neighbor who complimented me on my outfit and I take a step outside my front door and I slip and slid on red colored merde. The reason I remember it was red-dog feces was because it didn't go well with my outfit. I not only ruined my outfit for the day, lost my job interview, but my neighbor had to call a taxi and rush me to the hospital with a broken ankle. Well you can imagine how annoyed I got every time I saw a dog owner letting his dog take a poop in the middle of the street. I would kindly go up to the dog owners and remind them that it was dangerous because someone could slip and slide and get hurt. But their response was that only an idiot would do that. I quickly would remind them that people get distracted and anyone could have an accident. They would shrug their shoulders in that annoying French way and say, "Ce n'est pas mon problème", it's not my problem and walk away. The same thing would happen every time a smoker was waiting for the bus and the bus would arrive they would just throw their lit cigarette on the floor no matter who was passing. It didn't even occur to them that they could hurt someone or start a fire aside from just plain littering. I hate smokers because they don't care. Or maybe they care too much about themselves to remember there are other people on the planet breathing the same air. If people want to kill themselves smoking, let them. I say, "Go ahead and kill yourself, just don't take me with you." No, I'm not saying smokers are the most selfish inconsiderate people in the world, no, that's not what I'm saying. No, smokers who have dogs and who litter their cigarettes and let their dogs take a shit are the most selfish and inconsiderate human beings on the planet. —Oh, you're a smoker? And you have a Terrier... Yes, I know dogs have to take a shit too, but if there are so many dog lovers in Paris why don't you guys get together and create little patches of land – yeah- public dog toilets. Maybe if it was organized well enough the city could use the dog feces as fertilizer for the grass and bushes in public parks? Why aren't dog lovers in Paris people and environment lovers too? (*She waits for his response, but takes a deep breath instead.*) (*Aside*) I see you don't agree with me so on with my story. After many months of being burnt by lit cigarettes being smoked on the street by would be fashion models trying to stay anorexic and stepping on dog shit once a week, I had enough... So one day when I saw a little old lady smoking her cigarette, polluting the air, while her dog took a shit on the street like every other day, I noticed that when she was done with her cigarette she just threw it on the floor and it landed on the poop... Poop is fertilizer... Hmmm... That moment I had an idea. You see I studied chemistry in college and had considered pursuing it, but my love for the arts won me over. However, my knowledge of chemistry and creativity devised a plan in my head so delicious I couldn't pass it up. I created a liquid combining every day household cleaners in addition to other easy to get chemicals to create a small…a small…a small…a tiny…a very little…bomb…I guess you could call it that... Cocktail sounds better... Okay a cross between a little bomb and a cocktail. So that night I walked around the 16th and sprayed all the dog shit I came across with the chemical concoction. The plan was that any time a smoker dropped a careless cigarette on the street close to dog shit, the dog shit would explode on them. Didn't that seem fair? All the smokers who had taken innocent second hand smoker's lives that had gone unpunished! Wasn't this poetic justice? Okay,

fine don't agree with me... But I bet you want to prove me wrong just because you're a smoker. I bet you think you're the exception. You're the one good smoker who doesn't litter and is always considerate of other people... Let me ask you... Can you honestly tell me you put out your cigarette and disposed of it in the garbage can each and every time for the many thousands of times you smoked a cigarette? (*She gets real close to the imaginary US Embassy representative as if looking in his eyes.*) Yeah? Really? You have? Ah! Your pupils dilated, you lied, Mr. Litterbug! Yeah, yeah, I know I'm the one being interrogated not you... The next day the plan worked beautifully. Little old ladies in mink and fur coats were sprayed with dog shit... See how they like wearing it... It worked so well I stayed up a few nights without sleep so I could spray all the dog shit in my neighborhood. The many explosions quickly caught the attention of the press and pretty soon it wasn't just a trick being played on lazy dog lovers, but the authorities thought it might be terrorist related. I stopped as soon as that connection was made, but then it was too late. I had considered picking up all the dog shit to ensure no one would come across it, but there was so much dog shit everywhere it would be impossible... Then finally one day when the little green men assigned by the city to pick up dog shit, to think our taxes go to this... They collected a lot of it, one of the collectors threw his cigarette close by and the whole thing blew up like a real bomb. No one died, but even non-smokers got sprayed...I'm sure you read about it in the papers...I think even ZETA or some other liberation front or terrorist group took credit for it. (*Pleads and begs.*) So you see I'm just a stupid American with a little too much knowledge of chemistry, but I'm not part of any cell or network or anything like that. I just wanted people to pay attention; to give a shit about others... Do you think the judge will understand? What do you think they are going to do to me? (*She pauses and waits for an answer.*) 50 years to life?! What? Are you serious? I could die in prison! But they can't prove I'm a terrorist... Is that French law or American? Oh, you're extraditing me to the US where this stuff is taken very seriously... (*She sits down and does everything she can to calm down and not cry.*) Give me a cigarette! (*She is given a cigarette and lights it. She smokes it and calms down. Her whole personality changes and is transformed into a smoker before our eyes.*) Wow, when I take short puffs it calms me down. Oh, I've forgotten how great they tasted... Yes, I used to smoke, that's why I hate it so much.... I used to have Asthma, but that didn't stop me. I'd swear it would cure it temporarily. No, I wasn't an addict, addict...I wouldn't smoke like five packs a day, but I did love each and every cigarette...a lot. Wow, when I take long drags it wakes me up, when I take short drags it relaxes me. Wow this is better than any anti-depressant or speed. Wow, a magical little stick. I guess it's sexier to smoke this than to take Prozac or some other pill that makes people think you're a loser. Who needs to go to a psychiatrist to check for chemical imbalances when all you have to do is go to the Tabac or pass by the vending machines in the metro and get a "magic stick"? Life is sweet and easy this way. (*Realizing*) I've forgotten all my problems... Wow! No wonder knowing that it can kill you isn't so scary; smoking cigarettes makes you feel alive! (*BEAT*) (*She stops smoking.*) Okay, I've officially gone insane. (*BEAT*) Hey, can we plead insanity? No... How about...? No... There's nothing I can say or do to...? Hey, do you have another cigarette? (*She throws the used up one at the audience. To the audience:*) What? It's just a cigarette butt. It's no big deal. What are you complaining about? Yeah, I bet you're an American. What, you want me to pick it up? Look I've got more important things to think about... No, I'm not going to pick it up. It's not my problem. Ce n'est pas mon problème.

She takes another cigarette and lights up.

Lights fade out.

SPOTLIGHT

MOE, 40s, short, tough, but jovial, walks up to a spotlight wearing a Red Cross vest.

MOE

We were sitting at Wal-Mart in circles and everybody was being sent out to the different shelters and I was assigned to the Cajun Dome. I was like, wait a minute. The first was the Super Dome in Louisiana and the second was the Cajun Dome in Lafayette. And they assigned me there. I was like, "Is this the Super Dome?" And they said, "No it's the Cajun Dome," so I was like, "Oh, ok." I got my suitcase and my backpack.

They gave us a briefing about what color our pee should be. They didn't want us to faint and pass out. So they said, "If it's this color, please drink more water". They wanted to make sure they took care of us. We were told that our pee shouldn't be dark yellow or we'll be dehydrated. Just regular yellow; so that's how we had to monitor ourselves.

There was a huge bus of volunteers. There were 43 of us. I remember I was the only Latina. I noticed that right away. So when we arrived at the location it was a dome. That's when I got intimidated because I had seen the news about all the awful things that had happened in the Super Dome. I stopped for a minute to think about how just three days ago I had volunteered for the Red Cross thinking I was going to collect blankets and food, but here I was on my way into a dome...

When the volunteer coordinators read my volunteer application they were very impressed by my resume. They told me I was perfect for this job. They

saw that I was an ex-gang member who worked with gang members in prison trying to get them to turn their life around. I thought they needed people with medical experience to go into New Orleans, but they said, "We need people like you, because there is a criminal element that you understand."

There were army tanks parked outside the dome. It really intimidated me. Why all this? But then one of the girls on the bus told me, "Did you know that this is Super Dome part 2." What do you mean? The same things are happening here? She said, "Well it's the biggest shelter and the roughest." I was like...okay. I thought to myself, I must be here for a reason. So as soon as we got out, I acted like nothing was wrong. All the other volunteers didn't hide the fact they were scared.

So we went in to get our assignments and they told us we would be sleeping upstairs in the skyboxes. We went to take our suitcases and I came downstairs because I wanted to walk through the dome. The MP guarding the door advised me not to walk through there. I asked why. "Well, if the power goes out you'll be in the middle of it." The middle of what... He goes, "In the middle by your self." I replied, "In the middle of the people I'm supposed to be helping?" He continued, "Well, yeah Ma'am. I don't think you understand what I'm saying. You know what happened in the Super Dome. When the power went out, people died, people were raped." "Ok, I understand, but I think I'll be all right". And he goes, "All right suit yourself." I started walking through there, I could not believe that what I had seen on TV at home and what I heard and what I read in the newspaper didn't compare to what I was about to see.

I walked in and the first thing I see was twenty five little kids from the age of 3 to 9 sitting around a little TV, like 4 by 4 inch TV, all trying to watch cartoons. That broke my heart because I have kids and they were that little at one point. I remember thinking "Oh my God." I felt faint because I couldn't believe what I was seeing. Then when I looked around there were 3,000 people in there. The cots were touching each other. I mean people didn't know each other. They were predominantly Cajun folks, light skinned with green eyes and there were a few Anglo families and like 4 Honduran families. I even saw a family of 6 Koreans that were cooks at the French quarters. I knew a little bit of Korean and I tried talking to them. The more I walked in the middle, I didn't feel fear at all, but I felt overwhelmed and it was almost as if I could feel so many spirits crying out. Broken spirits and the heaviness was almost too much. You know because I'm a spiritual person and I go by that and it was almost too much for me to bear. I felt like falling to my knees and start crying but I didn't want to do that because I was supposed to be the muscle there; the strong and the help that had just arrived.

The people began to ask me what my name was. My real name is Ramona Guadalupe Camacho de la Paz Lopez, but I said just call me "Moe." People began calling me Mrs. Moe. "Hey Mrs. Moe. Hey red jacket. Hey red vest. Ain't no one walking through here like you do. You ain't scared?" I said, "No, I ain't scared. Why should I be scared, I'm here to help you?" But inside I just felt like grabbing them, hugging them and crying. I felt they're trying to keep their spirits up so I better keep it up too. But I seriously could not fight the tears so I walked through there and I walked out and when I started to walk towards the door I heard a familiar song from church called, "I feel Jesus." I arrived in Lafayette on a Sunday so when I started to hear the song I started to walk towards the music and when I walked out to the quad of that place they were having church service and there was the other part of the 3,000 people and it was packed out.

There was a woman preacher and they were singing, "I feel Jesus." I didn't even look at the people, I just went straight towards the front and I was just looking at her because I felt at the point I needed to feel something because I was overwhelmed. So when I walked up there she pointed at me and she called me up to the platform so I just walked up there and she hugged me. I put my head on her shoulder and I started crying because I could not believe where I was. I could not believe that there were so many people and I felt that God chose me. When I started walking out of the crowd, the evacuees were tugging on me saying, "Mrs. Moe you blessed. Mrs. Moe God knows you, and you're blessed." Because she called me up there at that point in time I knew it was a divine moment because that day the people accepted me because a preacher just accepted me. And that day I knew that that's where I was supposed to be even though it was the roughest shelter. That night I went to sleep feeling like everything was going to be all right.

Well, the next day they appointed us our job and right away, I don't know why someone asked if I wanted to be in the kitchen. Are all Latins in the kitchen all the time? And I just started laughing and I said "No, I don't want to be in the kitchen; I'm needed out here and they were like "Well we need you in the kitchen." But there are people who love to cook and I'll find them for you. So then I saw the manager of the dome and I wasn't jockeying for a position but I saw she was overwhelmed and I asked Juanita, the Dome Manager if I could assist her and she said, "Oh, yeah. I need assistance because there's a lot of people coming in." She was in charge of giving the Red Cross assignments, jobs, and walk through the dome and seeing what the needs were of all the evacuees. So I became her assistant and walked the dome with her for hours. I was like, "Juanita, I have to walk with you. I have to learn what you're doing." And she said, "Moe this is what you do. Learn the people." She goes, "I've already seen you make friends with the roughest crowd, that crowd of boys out there; that was smart. Well that's where I come from. "That was smart because you always have to stay close to them. If anything happens they're the first ones to nut up." I walked around with her for a couple of more hours and then she left and when she came back I could tell that she was crying and she goes, "Moe, I've been here a full week, I'm gone. I can't take this, I've been here a week and I'm going crazy." One of the people she was trying to help left the dome and tried going home and literally died, died getting there. She got wind of it and it broke her and she goes, "Could you handle this by yourself? I showed you what to do." Not only am I the only Latin at the time I'm younger than all the doctors I got sent with. She goes, "You can do it, you're a rough girl. I can tell you're a thug." I said, "I used to be." She said, "You can do it. You're one of them." She meant this as a compliment. That day I became the Cajun Dome Manager, Mrs. Moe, the Cajun Dome Manager. So I started assigning jobs and I didn't let it become overwhelming to me, when it would get fast I ran faster. There were some things I was not prepared for.

One night I was in the middle of the dome and the lights went out. People screamed expecting the worst. The lights maybe went out for a minute, but a minute in darkness. You see there were a lot of criminals from the prisons who escaped and had no place to go, but the dome. There was no way to identify them. So the lights went out…

Lights fade out, it's pitch black.

I just froze. I could feel the presence of something evil in my face. I heard a man or the devil whisper "Aren't you afraid?" I was certain I was going to be raped because I could feel a hand reaching for me…then it disappeared… The lights came back up…

Then the lights come back on.

And a nurse behind me had her uniform torn and almost raped. I looked around and saw one of the boys from a Honduran gang I had befriended and he looked at me as if to say, "Don't worry about it, we took care of him for you."

Then hurricane Rita hit and we had to be evacuated from the dome and go to Shreveport six hours away in a convoy of fifty-four buses. The dome could not take the size of Rita; it was going to take the top off. I ran back to the dome and started lining the people up with the bullhorn in Spanish, English and some Korean. I was trying not to lose it. We got on the road and we were going fast. It was weird because we were on the freeway but we could see that here comes Rita. All of a sudden I felt overwhelmed when people started screaming. "Mrs. Moe the water will turn this bus around!" and I was like, "We're OK. We're leaving the water." And they said, "Look at the trees!" The trees were breaking on the side of us and in front of us and the buses were trying to dodge them. All of a sudden the bus in front of us, the back tire got hit and it fishtailed and almost flipped. Everybody started screaming even our bus driver. The bus rocked and stopped again and took off. We just kept going. The bus driver turned to me. She was a tough black lady. She asked me, "Mrs. Moe, do you know God?" And I said, "Yeah. Yeah, I know God." She said, "You better start talking to him." "All right," I said. I could see the fear in her face when she told me that.

So I grabbed my phone and I couldn't call home. I called my sister in Florida and I said please put me in a three way to my family and she goes, "Moe, what are you doing out there? You're going to get killed. Save yourself! Get out of there! Rita is hitting right now. I heard it on the news it's blowing roofs off of things and the water's hitting." I was like, "Mary, please call my family." I felt like when 9/11 happened people on the plane were making their last call. I thought that was my last call because of the way the bus was rocking and how it was rushing and the hurricane was going to get us. There were so many people and they were screaming on the side of the road. Wanting us to pick them up and we could not stop and that broke me, it broke my heart. My sister called my family on three ways and I talked. And my husband, he's trying to be very calm. The first thing he says, "Yeah, you'll be all right." See, I was trying to calm down and he goes, "I'm sure you're all right. I'm proud of you. It's all right. I love you." I told him, "I always love you, and if I wasn't there I wouldn't mind you having a nice "jaina" just as long as she was good to the kids. It's OK." He laughed and said, "All right, I'll talk to you later." "I'll call you when I arrive." I said out loud. He reassured me, "Yeah, you call me when you arrive." So as soon as I hung up I closed my eyes and started to pray. A stillness came all over me.

I was 6 years and I was picking string beans and I looked at my mom and asked her, "¿Tenemos que estar aqui?" Do we have to be here? And then I saw the vision God wanted me to see to have hope. I remember the farmer who owned the land where we were working. He was in a blue '64 station wagon with a cowboy hat. Legs crossed up on the window and he was just listening to Billie Holiday and I got peaceful because I remember I said, "One day I'm going to sing like her. Sing like a black girl." I looked at that moment and my life. That's what popped in my head; when I was little. You see that was the moment when I had told my mother I wanted to be a singer and she hit me on the head and said, "¿Estás pendeja?" Are you an idiot? After she did that I decided that I was not going to end up like my parents who were poor campesinos... So I joined a gang and became a drug-dealer. I've never done drugs, believe it or not, I just needed the power and the money so I wouldn't be treated like my parents were treated all their life. God wanted me to see that moment, because that's when I lost hope... But

it showed me that all the horrible things I did and went through prepared me for this moment. I knew that I had to be here and I knew that I was not going to die because I had to sing.

MOE sings.

So when I opened my eyes I looked at everyone with a calming smile and I knew we were going to make it. I told everyone we were going to live and people calmed down... The bus continued moving forward and we were out of harms way. We took everyone we could to a safe place. I look back on this and I realized that my young life had been a waste, but when I decided to use my life to give back to people, my life was recycled and my hope was renewed.

Lights fade out.

Lights fade in. SOLEDAD, 30s, rushes on stage. She is wearing a red silk scarf around her neck.

SOLEDAD

Hi, sorry I'm late. I hate to be late. I'm usually never late, but I just couldn't find your office... I've never done this before. My friend told me, "Soledad, you have to do something about that neck pain." I went to the doctor and he says it's just my imagination. I've tried getting massaged and the pain doesn't go away... So my friend finally gave me your number and I figured what do I have to lose-- Are you sure it's perfectly safe? Okay, I'll lie there. But could you please place a blanket over my body while I'm being hypnotized. I promise I won't fall asleep, I just have bad circulation and my feet get cold...

SOFT FEMALE VOICE (*V.O.*)

Close your eyes and relax. At the count of five you will be completely relaxed as though you are floating...weightless...1...2...3...4...5... There is a river. There is a bridge in front of you ... Now take off all your clothes and all your worries and put them in the bag that appears in front of your feet. (*She mimes removing her clothes and puts them in a bag.*) When you are completely done, letting go of all your fears and your worries and your chatter, then toss that bag into the river. Walk across that bridge to the other side. (*She tosses the bag and crosses the river.*) There is a lavender mist. Walk into the lavender mist... At the count of three, step out of the mist...1...2...3... Step out... What do you see?

SOLEDAD steps forward and as she describes herself she becomes the person.

Photo by Hector Rodríguez

Soledad walks into the mist into another lifetime.

SOLEDAD

I see leather sandals on my feet. I am running up a castle. I must get there quickly. I am late. I am late and it's my fault... What year is it? It's...1300s... I get to a tower and I look out the window... I think I am a man...or perhaps a woman disguised as a man with short black hair... It's Italy, before it was Italy... The king knows who I am... I am his prophet... I look at the stars and I am afraid tonight is the night the king will be assassinated, but if I hurry I can tell him to flee before they make the attempt on his life... I turn away from the stars and head to the wooden door, but there are men with swords and I know who they are. They are the king's assassins. A sword goes into my left side and it burns... (*She mimes getting stabbed by a sword. Her red silk scarf becomes the blood gushing out of her stomach.*) But the pain is not as bad as knowing that I was late and the king will die... It's my fault the king will die...among other regrets was the fact that I loved a man, but never told him... I was late, because I hesitated... (*CRIES*)... But I step away from the body, I float and I am no longer trapped by that body or lifetime... I walk into the mist again... (*She steps away from the body and is pain free.*) At the count of three I step out.

SOLEDAD steps forward and as she describes the person she becomes that person.

....1...2...3. I walk out and I am wearing fancy little black boots with a heel... Where am I? France 1800's. I look in the mirror and I am an elegant woman with white hair and a beautiful face. For an older woman I am attractive. I fix my cameo around my neck and I smile. I walk past a room full of young women dressed in corsets. Some of them half naked... They are like my daughters. I am like their mother... We are happy and we laugh... But it is now time for work and I make sure they are ready... I open the doors and many French gentlemen in suits and proper attire come in. It's Montmartre, Paris... I welcome them "Bonsoir messieurs et bienvenue." I know their tastes. I know which girl will be perfect for them... I am the madam and I am well liked and respected.... My life flashes forward... I look in the mirror again, but this time I look old and beaten, hopeless... They are taking away my business... A man I loved, the only man I trusted...is taking away my business and I can't do anything about it and I am a woman and they are taking away my business... I am about to put my cameo back on, but instead I take a shaving razor and I slash my throat... (*She stands before a mirror and slits her throat. The red silk scarf becomes the blood gushing out of her neck.*) I fall forward on the porcelain sink and then I fall back and land on the floor... I quickly drown in a pool of blood... I step away from the body and I am no longer hurting... (*She steps away from the body.*) I am free from that body and lifetime... I walk into the mist... At the count of three I walk out.

SOLEDAD steps forward and dances flamenco.

... 1...2...3...My feet are moving so fast I am dancing. I tap, tap, tap... I am in a tavern... Where am I? I think it's Spain, Sevilla. What year? 1600s... It's dark. Just candles light up the place. I dance beautifully. I am beautiful. My skin is dark, very dark. I'm a gypsy. I'm 17. I dance flamenco around tables... I dance next to a man and I flirt with him as I dance... But he grabs me forcefully. He's drunk and he wants to kiss me. (*She mimes pushing the drunk man away.*) The man playing the guitar, he tries to stop him. He is my husband. He gets killed... (*She mimes seeing her dead husband get stabbed and fall to the ground. She falls to the floor to hold him in her arms as he dies.*) They blame me. They kick me out of the clan... I run away to Granada... I don't dance anymore... I don't dare... My life flashes forward... I work in a small house, like a hen house in the mountains somewhere... I have a small bed and I have sex with men to survive. There are many other gypsy women in that tiny house. There are only curtains separating us. I am beautiful, and they desire me, but they don't love me. One man loves me. He sees me every week and I love him... After ten years of working there... I beg him, please take me away... But he is white, a Spaniard... He cannot marry me... He is already married and is part of the royal family and he cannot risk losing everything for me. I beg him with all my heart, "Please take me out of here"... But he won't. He insists if I continue to make such demands he will never return... He leaves... I am broken, devastated... I am disgusted with myself... I am beautiful, men desire me, but no one can love me... I grab a knife and slash my face. I cut away at all the beautiful features of my face... (*She mimes slashing her face. The red silk scarf becomes the knife and blood.*) My face. My face?!!! I stop cutting and feel the wounds. I look in the mirror and I realize what I have done... I am ugly. I am a monster... Who will have sex with me? How will I survive? I grab a rope and I hang myself... (*She uses the red silk scarf to hang herself.*) I step away from the body...

SOLEDAD steps away from the body.

In seconds...many other lives flash before my eyes... My soul is like the wind traveling all over, forever... I have been so many people, so many races and colors. I have been a man and I have broken hearts too... I have been the oppressed and the oppressor, slave and master, a traitor, brave and courageous, cowardly and meek. I have been everyone and experienced rejection. I have been the light and I have been the darkness... So much tragedy...so much regret...so much pain, so much change, and yet, I'm indestructible... My soul continues to exist... Suddenly 12 figures, Masters, they call themselves, appear before me and through telepathy they tell me, "Soledad, your soul is indestructible, but the earth is not. Don't be a coward by ending your life again... Raise your head and the pain will go away, heal yourself and you can heal the earth. Heal yourself and you can heal the earth." I ask them, "Why does our soul exist?" They answer, "Your soul exists...for the journey, for the experience...for the evolution of your soul..."

SOFT FEMALE VOICE (*V.O.*)

At the count of five you will come out of hypnosis...1...2...3...4...5. What year is this?

SOLEDAD

It's 2009... I feel so peaceful, the pain is gone, but I wonder... (*She touches her neck and the pain has gone away. She smiles, satisfied, and stands up.*) Did I imagine everything? Did I make up all those stories or do all those stories make up me?

Lights fade out.

Lights fade in. THELMA, 60s, old hippie, stands in front of a podium with a clipboard. She is dressed in a very colorful robe with large ethnic jewelry looking very much like a modern day Goddess herself. On a bulletin board it reads "INNER GODDESS WORKSHOP".

THELMA

Ladies welcome. I hope you are all in the right place. This is the "Getting in Touch with your Inner Goddess Workshop". If anyone is not interested in finding her Inner Goddess I suggest you get out. Now, I want to assure you that we will not be exploring our vaginas - that's the "Getting in Touch with your Inner-Inner Self Workshop" just down the hall... Good. Now, let's get started. My name is Thelma Johnson, and I have a Ph.D. in socio-anthropology with an emphasis on the history of the Goddess. I used to teach a previous workshop called "How to Be a Super Woman" and the "You can have it all workshop", but it finally evolved into this workshop... Now, what is a Goddess? I know many of you are taking this workshop because you read the Da Vinci Code and got pissed off about the role of the Catholic Church in the suppression of the Goddess and the Sacred Feminine. We're glad to have you. But for some of you you've probably been called a "Diva" or a "Bitch" too long and now you want to know how to assert your power without forcing it, or losing your femininity... And there are those of you who've never done any spiritual self-exploration work but are curious because you've looked in the mirror and something special smiled back at you and you thought, "Hey, who was that woman that sometimes shows up when I'm feeling great?" For some of you who are older you decided against the Botox and the expensive miracle creams and opted for dignity in aging and you are ready to own your Goddess especially now that you have a young lover. Am I right? Am I right? Yeah, after teaching these workshops for so long I know my audience...I can tell by the way some of you are dressed that you look and act like Goddesses, but that's just half the battle. All right, well, all you women are in the right place because I am going to teach you how to be absolutely divine on a daily basis... So what is a Goddess? Hmm, it's hard to define because as soon as you define her you rob her of her beauty and power. You can't just say what she is; you just know when you see her. A Goddess lives inside of us, each and every one of us has a Goddess, but we rarely let her out. She was locked away in all of us a long time ago. So I am not going to teach you how to be a Goddess, because you are already one... I'm simply going to illuminate for you the many ways in which you sell out the Goddess... Here's my list: You sell out the Goddess when you put everyone else's needs ahead of yours. You sell out the Goddess when you don't speak up to injustice because you're afraid to be called a "bitch". By the way, did you notice that when Hilary Clinton was running for President they called her a "Bitch" to try to murder her presidential career, but if she were back in the 1700s she would be called a "witch" and burnt at the stake... "Bitch" is simply "a high tech/modern day" burning at the stake-- Okay, back to the list. You sell out the Goddess when you put other women down to make yourself feel better and more beautiful. You sell out the Goddess when you accept designer merchandise like Louie

Vuitton bags, Tiffany jewelry, Gucci sunglasses from a man who abuses you. Or stay in a job that abuses you so you can afford designer things. You sell out the Goddess when you don't listen to your inner voice telling you to stop consuming. You know what constant consuming is? It's about feeling like you're not enough. It's about the lack of self-love "Ms. Shop-a-holic." You sell out the Goddess when you give up your best girlfriend for the love of a man. You sell out the Goddess when you call an older woman with a young lover a "Cougar"--

Her cell phone rings.

THELMA

Who could be calling me? They know not to disturb me when I'm teaching this workshop. (*She looks at the caller ID on her cell phone.*) (*excitedly*) I can't believe she's calling! Just like her to be so spontaneous. (*She answers.*) Well, hello Katie. I know, sorry, you don't like the nickname, yes, but I know how much "Supreme Force" bothers you even more, okay. "Mother". How are you "Mother"? (*She listens.*) Yes, "Mother". (*She listens.*) Yes, "Mother." (*She listens.*) Thank you! Thank you! I'll get them ready! See you in a second! (*She hangs up and does a little dance full of joy.*) You are not going to believe this, but Mother Nature just called. I had begged her to attend my workshop as a special guest, but she told me she was busy designing a special hurricane to end all hurricanes and couldn't make it, but because she saw many acts of compassion in a third world country a few days ago she thought she'd spare us one less hurricane and decided to come by... So you're in for a real treat. Oh, by the way, she says she's sorry about Katrina, but we deserved it. So she won't be answering questions concerning Katrina, so please don't ask... Oh, she's here! I haven't seen her since I did a rain dance in Berkley so long ago... Okay, everyone, give it up to the lady, known as Guadalupe, Azna, Sofia, Gaia, Tonantzin, the O.G. Goddess herself-Mother Nature!

Loud applause is heard along with drums and music befitting a queen... A few seconds later a 12 year-old girl in pigtails walks in wearing a bright lime green dress with white daisies.

MOTHER NATURE

This is the easiest way to clear security at the airport... (*The applause dwindles down.*) Thank you... Reduce, reuse, recycle... What else can I tell you that I haven't already told you? All you do is produce waste and you don't give back. You take and you take and sometimes I just want to swallow you up and get a belly full of you and then turn you into waste to fertilize all that you have damaged on my body...but I will survive. Don't worry about me. I will survive...I've already done everything I can to warn you about

your survival. I've called upon your soul, but you are not listening... I've called upon your conscience, but you are not listening... Next time I call; listen.

The End

Breath of Fire Latina Theater Ensemble

When Nature Calls

written by
Josefina Lopez

Painting by Josefina López, Graphic design by Carla Zarate of Sol Gallery and Design

CASA 0101 presents

Boyle Heights

written by **Josefina Lopez**
directed by **Hector Rodriguez**

Back by popular demand!
Aug 22-Sept 14, 2008

*Poetry is being... Being here...
Being home... Boyle Heights...
My beautiful little Barrio.*

Graphic design by Gaby López

BOYLE HEIGHTS

PLAYWRIGHT'S NOTES

I was 27 and heart broken by my screenwriting career in Hollywood and by a man I loved beyond myself...whom I could never be with because destiny had other plans for me. I moved out of my expensive West Hollywood apartment and moved back to Boyle Heights, the neighborhood where I grew up. I lived in my parent's garage and gave up writing for film and television. I was also depressed and somewhat hopeless. As a way of lifting up my spirits I took floral design classes and wrote poetry...I had returned to my neighborhood and saw that it was becoming more dangerous. I knew that there were gang shootings because I had heard them often as well as the helicopters lighting our backyard. It wasn't until my sister told me that someone got shot at the corner of our block that it really dawned on me how dangerous Boyle Heights could be. (She told me she had to give a police report because she saw the car that took off after the drive-by shooting. The family that lost their son planted a small tree in his honor.) Perhaps there was a lot of denial on my part or because I came from an intact family that I was oblivious to all the gang violence Boyle Heights is known for, but I finally opened my eyes. I realized that to me my neighborhood was a wonderful place, but it also needed people like me to return to give something back. When I wrote this play, I didn't know that I would someday be the Artistic Director of CASA 0101, my theater in Boyle Heights, and that thirteen years later I would be opening a cultural center as my contribution to my community with the help of my wonderful husband Emmanuel, the man I was destined to marry.

This play captures the sadness and hope I was feeling back when I was 28. Every time I read it or see it on stage I cry and laugh, what a terrible time in my life, but what great material for a play.

Josefina López
March 1, 2011

BOYLE HEIGHTS

ACT ONE

SETTING

The front yard/porch and roof of the Rosales' four-bedroom house on Mariposa Street in Boyle Heights.

TIME: The play begins when Dalia is 19, then when she is 28. She arrives in January and the play ends in March. We flash back to the past 35 years and then again another 15 years.

CHARACTERS

THE ROSALES FAMILY:

DALIA   is 28, an actress/poet who comes to live with the family every time she breaks up with a boyfriend. She is a dreamer, an activist, and a bohemian.

ROSANA   is 35, an attractive woman with two children who is impeccably dressed. She's been married to Jaime for 15 years.

CARMELA   is 55, mother of Rosana, Margie, Dalia, and Ernie. She is a great complainer, a metiche, a gossiper, and a martyr.

RUBEN   is turning 62, the father of the family. A big macho who always keeps his word. He has a green thumb and dresses like a cowboy.

MARGIE   is 20, a cashier at a grocery store who wants to be a teacher.

She has a boyfriend who she loves, but doesn't want to get married until she can save up enough money to buy a house.

ERNIE   is 18, a high school student who is searching for his manhood. He dresses like a gangster, because it's cool to dress like that.

JAIME   is 42, Rosana's husband. He has an opinion on everything and lets everyone know it. He is a social alcoholic.

JUAN   is 23, Margie's boyfriend, a security guard who wants to marry Margie, but is afraid of her father.

<u>OTHERS:</u>

CHAVA   is 26, handsome, the next-door neighbor, who is a "tagger" and an artist. He sells Marijuana on the side.

As the audience sits the following poem is played:

DALIA (*V.O.*):

My father came to the U.S., he entered not by

the island where the lady stands tall,

but by the dark and cold borders,

divided by rivers, fences, and wild mountains,

filled with rats, snakes, coyotes, and border

patrol officers waiting for you to fall.

It wasn't until the fourth attempt did he manage to

find work and not get caught.

The money he earned he sent back.

Back to the little pueblo where we remained.

On an unexpected night my mother came to my

bedside and said:

"We're going."

"Going where?" I curiously asked.

"To join your father en la ciudad de

Los Angeles!"

"Angels?"

We left at night trying to stay out of sight.

We took a bus, then a train, then a bus again.

The journey took three days and a lot of hours

of dreaming, of my father, and the clouds, the

angels, the music, and the golden gates.

I kept staring at the wheels of the bus waiting

for them to lift us up to the sky.

I truly believed we were going to heaven.

We had reached Los Angeles, but we were still

on earth.

This isn't heaven, but it is my home.

SCENE ONE

Lights fade in. The Rosales' house is a quaint red brick house with a comfortable porch. The porch is not just a place where the Rosales family often sits to relax and talk, but it's a front row seat to the many activities on Mariposa Street. It's the best view you can get of the whole street. There is no fence or gate separating the house from the rest. A young woman with a suitcase comes out of the house tiptoeing. She puts her suitcase down and walks to the center of the room. She is DALIA, at 19. Spotlight on Dalia.

DALIA: My two sisters and I were braiding each other's hair. We were in the courtyard of our high school and we were peacefully being sisters. Then suddenly a storm approached and there was thunder and lightning. I looked up to see the lightning coming toward us. Before I could warn my sisters, they had already run off without me. I ran after them, screaming, "Wait for me! Wait for me!" But they kept running, running, running home. Ahead

was a metal gate and there were a pack of wolves waiting for us at the gate. As soon as my sisters passed the gate, the wolves got ready. I ran past the gate and they chased after me. I screamed louder to my sisters, "Wait! Wait!" But they kept running home. There was a second gate and more wolves waiting. They passed the second gate, and more wolves waited for us to pass the second gate. After I passed it, more wolves chased after me. My sisters made it past the gate, the gate in front of our house, I saw it. Then as I passed the gate the black and gray wolves snapped their jaws as they gained on me. I ran up the stairs. (*DALIA climbs the stairs to her house.*) As I was about to go in the house, I froze, a beautiful man with curly hair and deep dark eyes stuck out his hand. For a second, we danced together. If I took his hand I would be saved and he would let me in through the door, if I didn't, the wolves would get me. The prince or the wolf? I hesitated, I didn't take his hand. I didn't need his help. I fell back and a wolf bit my leg and I tried fighting them off, but then I woke up.

DALIA picks up her suitcase, takes a few steps and puts the suitcase down.)

DALIA (CONT'D): If you leave now, you can never come back to the same place, stay... What you take with you is more than enough, go!

Dalia looks all around her neighborhood as everyone sleeps.

DALIA (CONT'D): Boyle Heights, thank you for the stories. Thank you for the memories. I will return when I have something to give back to you. Goodbye.

DALIA picks up her suitcase and walks off the stage. Lights fade.

SCENE TWO

Lights fade In. The lamplight is on. A couple, ROSANA and JAIME, come through the gate, arguing.

ROSANA: I wanted to go to Paris!

JAIME: But we have to fix up the kitchen.

ROSANA: You promised we would go to Paris for our 15th anniversary.

JAIME: Yes, about five years ago. That's before you wanted a bigger house. We can't sell our house unless we fix the kitchen. So it's either Paris or the kitchen.

ROSANA seriously considers her decision.

ROSANA: Paris... I want to go to Paris.

JAIME: You do? I don't want to go to Paris... I'm tired of traveling.

ROSANA: Well, I haven't gone anywhere.

JAIME: Maybe after we get a new house we'll go to Paris.

ROSANA: Yeah... You're right. Tu siempre tienes la razón.

JAIME: Now, don't go complaining to your Mamá.

ROSANA: No, I never get a chance to. She's always busy complaining about my father.

JAIME: They always fight, but they're still together. Your mother is a saint. I don't know how she put up with him for 35 years.

ROSANA (*mutters*): I do.

JAIME: I hope your parents brought us some of those Mexican candies they brought us last year.

ROSANA: Of course they will. Every year they bring the same stuff and pumpkin seeds that give you the runs.

They arrive at the front door and ring the doorbell. CARMELA comes out and hugs them.

CARMELA: Pásense. (Come on in.) I didn't think you were coming. Where is April and Marcos?

ROSANA: They stayed home con mi suegra (with my mother-in-law).

JAIME: How was your trip back?

CARMELA: The way my viejo (old man) drives made me repent all the bad things I did to my mother. He's a little upset because he got a speeding ticket, but what else is new. Pero (but) come on in. I'll make some dinner.

They enter the house. A few seconds later DALIA, enters through the gate quietly carrying a small suitcase and a backpack. She gets to the porch and hides her suitcase behind a plant. She takes out a notebook and writes.)

DALIA (*reading*):

"He'll remember me on lonely nights,

or when the moon is full,

or when he swears he's in love again.

I'll remember him on happy warm nights,

or when I see the coliseum,

or when my heart is broken again.

We'll remember that night and swear

it never happened.

On paper perhaps.

In our hearts perhaps,

but there are no more traces."

ERNIE, was by the door as she recited this. He comes out and stares at her for a second.

ERNIE: You're weird.

DALIA: I was just writing a poem.

ERNIE: So you got a job yet?

DALIA: ...No...

ERNIE: I did... But I can't lend you money because they haven't paid me yet.

DALIA: I don't want your money.

ERNIE: So who told you my parents returned today?

DALIA: They did? They're here?! Oh, shit! Oh, man! Oh, no!!

ERNIE: I guess you're anxious to see them.

DALIA: Don't tell anybody, all right. I broke up with Craig. Well, it was coming, but anyway I moved out.

ERNIE: No you didn't. Where are you moving?

DALIA: Where else? Here. I don't have money to get a new place.

ERNIE: So where is your stuff?

DALIA: Behind there. I gotta go pick up my other stuff tomorrow... I thought they were coming in three days.

ERNIE: My Dad got in a fight with his brother again over my grandpa's land and left early.

DALIA: Don't tell them anything, all right? I'll tell them when they're rested and happy.

DALIA enters with ERNIE. A few seconds later MARGIE enters through the gate wearing her cashier outfit. Her boyfriend JUAN, stops behind the gate.

MARGIE: You want to come in through the back?

JUAN: I don't like sneaking around. I love you, why shouldn't I be able to go through the front door?

MARGIE: Because we're not married.

JUAN: Pos I'll marry you right now.

MARGIE laughs.

MARGIE : You're crazy. It takes more than you just asking.

JUAN: Well we could just rent.

MARGIE: I don't want to rent. Look if my parents could work two jobs each and raise money to buy their house having no education, you and I can do it.

JUAN: Yeah, but I can't wait. Man, it could take us five years.

MARGIE: Well, then we'll wait until we save the money. You want to come inside the house?

JUAN: Yeah, but through the front.

MARGIE and JUAN approach the door. As they are about to go in they stop.

MARGIE: Hey, I think my parents are back from Mexico!

JUAN: No way!

MARGIE: Just go! I'll call you later.

They kiss on the lips quickly and he runs off as the door opens. DALIA comes out fuming. She sees MARGIE and can barely utter a word.

MARGIE (CONT'D): What's wrong with you?

DALIA holds back from crying.

DALIA: I broke up with Craig.

MARGIE: Is that all?

DALIA chuckles a bit.

MARGIE (CONT'D): So, you're moving back?

DALIA: I have to.

MARGIE: Ayyy, Dalia. What number was Craig?

DALIA: I lost track.

MARGIE: Well, sleep with me until you get back on your feet.

DALIA: Thank you.

MARGIE: I'll see you inside.

DALIA reaches into her suitcase and takes out another notebook. She writes another poem.

DALIA (*reading*):

"When will my mother understand?

She thinks I can't live without

a man.

She says I can't keep one,

much less feed one.

"Un hombre, solo uno" she

claims with pride and righteousness.

I tell her, "I'm sorry for you.

You didn't have a choice.

Let me pick and choose,

enough already, let me have

a voice,

in the way I live my life."

Oh, my mother,

when will she understand?

That I love her and that she

didn't screw up.

"Then why did you turn up

this way?"

Oh, my mother,

when will she understand

that with the life I live

I celebrate hers too.

Where did I get this lust

for life?

"It must be from your father."

"No, from you...

All that lust you couldn't

express, all those flavors

you couldn't taste. I will,

for you."

JAIME, who is a little tipsy walks in on DALIA as she is reading her poem. He holds a glass of wine in one hand.

JAIME: Dalia, why do you talk to yourself?

DALIA: Because there's no one to talk to.

JAIME: People are gonna think you're crazy. When I first met you I seriously thought my wife had a crazy sister but I figured if I was marrying her I had to take her family as they were. Man, I'll tell you. You can take the girl out of the barrio, but you can't take the barrio out of the girl.

DALIA: Rosana didn't grow up in this barrio. She came from Mexico and then you married her.

JAIME: Okay, so you can take the girl out of the rancho, but you can't take the rancho out of the girl... So, why are you out here by yourself?

DALIA: Just thinking.

JAIME: Hey, so what if your boyfriend dumped you.

DALIA: He did not dump me. We just decided that...

JAIME: Listen, Dalia, you're a pretty girl, you'll catch another man (*snaps*

his fingers) like that. You've got big breasts and you're sexy so you'll have no problem catching another guy.

DALIA: It's not like I have to have a man... I just would like somebody who is not intimidated by me.

JAIME: It's cause you speak your mind.

DALIA: That's true.

JAIME: So stop it.

DALIA: What?

JAIME: Just let guys think they're in charge and pretend to obey them and then just tease them. Don't have sex with them until you are in control of them. They'll think they're in charge, but you'll be really in charge.

DALIA: Whatever... But who told you I broke up...?

JAIME: Your mother.

DALIA: Dang! I told her not to tell anybody—she is such a chismosa! (gossiper) I can't trust her with any secrets.

CARMELA comes out of the house. RUBEN, dressed in cowboy boots and a nice shirt, follows her out.

Photo by Hector Rodríguez

The Rosales sit on the porch where all the chisme happens.

CARMELA: Que refresco está aquí. (How refreshing it is out here.) It's nicer out here. : And those "Santa Ana Winds" que bonito se siente... (They feel so nice.) Ernie, bring us some more chairs!

RUBEN: I'm going to miss this old house.

JAIME: Why? You're going to sell it?

RUBEN: Of course.

DALIA: Why?

RUBEN: I'm turning 62 in three months. I've had enough of this life in the U.S... Work to pay taxes. The property taxes are killing me and that's it. 27 years is enough. I kept my word, I paid my dues, but as soon as I turn 62 I'm buying a truck and going back to mi tierra (my country). As soon as my birthday comes that's it; we're going.

ERNIE brings out three chairs.

CARMELA: I thought we were going to leave a few years after you retired.

RUBEN: No. Now I see how my brothers have had it easy in Mexico. Here I've been breaking my back and sending money to my parents only so they can give it to my lazy brothers. I risked my life coming to this country and for what?! To feed those leaches.

CARMELA: I don't want to leave in three months.

RUBEN: But I told you we would.

CARMELA: You also told me you'd shoot yourself the day you would turn 50 rather than get old, but you didn't do it.

RUBEN: Mujer, what have we been talking about for the past years? Since we got here I told you we were returning to Mexico when I retired.

CARMELA: Yes, but I didn't think you meant in three months.

RUBEN: Whatever I say I keep to my word.

CARMELA: Ruben, I'm not going back.

RUBEN: ¿Cómo que no? (What do you mean, no?) You gave me your word. I kept mine.

CARMELA: I would rather have you shoot me than go back to that little pueblo to live there again. Tanto que sufri, para llegar a morir allí. (I suffered so much to end up dying there.) Don't you remember why we left?

RUBEN: So we could give our children a better life.

CARMELA: Yes, that's what I would tell you, but I won't go back, you can't make me.

CARMELA goes inside the house. RUBEN is stunned. He looks at them and looks away.

RUBEN: Excuse me. I'm going to get a gun.

DALIA and JAIME gasp.

RUBEN (CONT'D): I'm joking…I'm just going to go talk some sense into her.

DALIA and JAIME gasp again.

RUBEN (CONT'D): She's just being dramatic. She doesn't mean it.

RUBEN goes inside too. JAIME and DALIA stare at each other.

JAIME: As I was saying, a lot of guys would love to go out with you. You won't have trouble getting married. I don't know why your parents worry about you ending up an old maid.

DALIA: I'm not an old maid! I'm only 28.

JAIME: Uuuff! If you were in Mexico, you'd be married with five kids and pregnant with another. Dalia, it's time to settle down, stop fucking around…

ROSANA comes out of the house.

ROSANA: Let's go. You told me you weren't going to drink. Give me the keys, I'm driving. Bye!

ROSANA and JAIME exit. Lights fade out. End of Scene 2.

SCENE 3

(MEXICO: 35 YEARS EARLIER)

At Rise: The moon is out. RUBEN, at 26, enters dragging a bicycle. He is a young handsome man, pre-cowboy. He whistles. After a few seconds, CARMELA, at 19, with braids in her hair and a white dress comes out with her few belongings wrapped in a shawl.

CARMELA: Ruben, ¿eres tu? (Is that you?)

RUBEN: Sí, are you ready?

CARMELA: Ruben, I'm scared…

RUBEN: Come with me.

He reaches for her lips with his hand. He caresses her chin.

CARMELA: My parents will never talk to me again. All my brothers and sisters will think I'm a whore. Everyone in this village will talk about me.

RUBEN: We'll go far.

CARMELA: Far? Far enough to escape the gossip? Far enough that my parents will forgive me someday?

RUBEN: We'll go to el norte. (the U.S.)

CARMELA: ¿El norte? You promise?

RUBEN: Sí, I give you my word. We'll live in Los Angeles if you come with me.

CARMELA considers her options. She looks at her house and looks at her few belongings.

CARMELA: I'm going to miss my parents. Mi mamacita (my dear mother) prayed so much that I'd get married properly to a hard working man. Why don't we wait?

RUBEN: Because she won't give me a divorce and—

CARMELA: Maybe you should go back to her.

RUBEN: But I love you!

CARMELA: Yo también te amo. (I love you too.)

He grabs her hand and pulls her toward him. He kisses her, melting her resistance.

RUBEN: Let's go.

CARMELA looks at her house painfully.

CARMELA

Adiós Mamá. Adiós Papá. (Goodbye Mother. Goodbye Father.)

CARMELA extends her hand to RUBEN. He leads her away.

Lights fade out.

End of Scene 3.

SCENE 4

(MEXICO: 35 YEARS EARLIER)

Lights fade in. CARMELA, at 19, is outside in the field wearing an apron. She is carrying beans on her apron and is cleaning them. CARMELA looks out as if searching, impatiently waiting for RUBEN. She cleans the beans and starts crying. Her tears land on the beans. RUBEN, at 26, enters and sees her crying.

RUBEN: ¿Porqué lloras? Why do you cry?

CARMELA is startled. She stands up and drops all the beans on the ground. She quickly gets on her knees and picks them up.

CARMELA: Ayyy, no! Your mother is going to scream at me. She already thinks I'm good for nothing.

CARMELA has to pick up every single bean.

RUBEN: Déjalos. (Leave them.) Just leave them on the dirt. When it rains they'll sprout and we'll grow beans.

CARMELA: No. These are our beans. When you go away for days and you're not here she doesn't give me anything to eat. She makes me work for everything and gives me the bad beans.

RUBEN: You're lying. Mi Amá (my mother) wouldn't do that.

CARMELA: ¿Porqué no me crees? (Why don't you believe me?) Have I ever lied to you?

RUBEN: No.

CARMELA: Ruben, when are we leaving? I can't stand living with your mother anymore. She hates me. She calls me a puta (whore). Tell her to stop calling me that or I'll leave.

RUBEN: I won't tell her... She doesn't mean it.

CARMELA: I'm pregnant. Do you want your bastard child to be raised by a puta?

RUBEN: Don't talk that way.

(BEAT)

CARMELA: What if I went to talk to her and begged her to give you the divorce? I'll tell her I'm pregnant and she might understand.

RUBEN: She won't do it. She wants to see me in hell and then maybe she'll give me a divorce.

CARMELA breaks down crying. He tries to hold her but she pushes him away.

CARMELA: You said we would go to el norte! You said we wouldn't hear all the things that people would say about me.

RUBEN: Just ignore them.

CARMELA: No. Ruben, make me a decent woman. Marry me!

RUBEN: You know I can't do that now!

CARMELA: Then I'm leaving you.

RUBEN: Are you crazy?!

CARMELA: I was when I decided to leave with you.

CARMELA takes off her apron and throws it on the floor. She walks out.

Lights fade out.

End of Scene 4.

SCENE 5

(MEXICO: 35 YEARS AGO)

Lights fade in. It is night and CARMELA'S MOTHER, an older stocky woman, is on her rocking chair knitting. CARMELA, at 20, watches her from a distance. She whispers to the moon.

CARMELA

Mamacita, he regresado,

como he llorado,

al saber que tu sufres.

Tengo una tristesa profunda,

una canción moribunda,

de un amor que no fue.

(Oh, mother, I have returned,

how I have cried,

to know how you have suffered.

I have a deep sadness,

a melancholic song,

about a love that can not be.)

CARMELA gets the courage to walk up to her mother.

CARMELA (CONT'D): Mamá, ya regresé. I came back.

CARMELA'S MOTHER: Me regresaste panzona. You're pregnant.

CARMELA: Who told you?

CARMELA'S MOTHER: I know... The curandera (a psychic) told me. She told me he's married and my daughter will have bastard children for ten years. I wanted to pay her to do a cure or a prayer to save you. But I want you to suffer. Your daughter will do the same to you... All your sisters married in the church. They were virgins. They waited.

CARMELA: I'm 20 now. Papá never let me talk to any boys because I was his youngest daughter. But he forgot I grew up and I turned into an old maid. Ruben was the only man who wanted me.

CARMELA'S MOTHER: No. You deserved better than just a handsome man. No te diste tu valor. (You did not value yourself.)

CARMELA: Sí. You always said I was the lazy one, que no valia nada. (that I was not worth anything) That no man would ever marry me because I didn't make good tortillas or cleaned properly, or dressed nice. Not like my sisters.

CARMELA'S MOTHER: No me heches la culpa. Don't blame me for your sins.

CARMELA: No. I made a mistake.

CARMELA'S FATHER, an older man with a cane, enters. He can barely see in the night.

CARMELA'S FATHER: Who are you talking to?

CARMELA: Tu hija, Papá. Your daughter.

CARMELA'S FATHER: Yo solo tengo dos hijas. (I only have two daughters.)

Maria, come into the house now. There are ghosts in the yard.

CARMELA'S father goes inside the house.

CARMELA'S MOTHER: Until you come back properly married, you're dead to us.

CARMELA'S mother goes inside the house too. CARMELA is left outside with her shawl and her few belongings. She uses the shawl to wipe her tears.

Lights fade out.

End of Scene 5.

SCENE 6

(BOYLE HEIGHTS, PRESENT)

Lights fade In. Spotlight on DALIA in the center of the yard.

DALIA: I'm an "old maid." I came back home as an old maid. Broken and broke, with nothing to say, and no where to go. If there was a balcony to scream from I would climb it and shout "Oh, woe is me, come rescue me." And I guess I have to wait until my brown or white, or whatever color prince I haven't tried yet, comes... Yeah, right...

DALIA stares at the vines leading up to the roof. She goes to the vines and climbs up to the roof.

DALIA (CONT'D): Oh, woe is me. All I do is write bad poetry.

Lights fade out.

End of Scene 6.

SCENE 7

(LOS ANGELES, 15 YEARS EARLIER)

Lights fade in on the Rosales' house and front yard. JAIME, at 26, appears at the front gate. He is very careful not to make any noise. ROSANA, at 19, sneaks out of her house through the front door. She is carrying a small suitcase with her few belongings.

ROSANA: Jaime, ¿eres tu? (is that you?)

JAIME: Sí, are you ready?

ROSANA: Jaime, I'm scared...

JAIME: Come with me.

He reaches for her lips with his hand. He caresses her chin.

ROSANA: My parents will never talk to me again. My brothers and sisters will think I'm a slut. Everyone in this barrio will talk about me.

JAIME: We'll go far.

ROSANA: Far? Far enough to escape the gossip? Far enough that my parents will forgive me someday?

JAIME: We'll go to the suburbs.

ROSANA: The suburbs?... Wherever, as long as it's not Boyle Heights... You promise?

JAIME: Sí, I give you my word. We'll live in the suburbs if you come with me.

ROSANA considers her options. She looks at her house and looks at her few belongings.

ROSANA: I'm going to miss my parents. Mi Amá (my mother) prayed so much that I'd get married in white in a Catholic church full of people and all her family. Why don't we wait?

JAIME: Because it won't help to wait. I'm a Jehova's Witness

ROSANA: Then maybe we shouldn't be together.

JAIME: But I love you!

ROSANA: Yo también te amo. (I love you too.)

He grabs her hand and pulls her toward him. He kisses her melting her resistance.

JAIME: Let's go.

ROSANA looks at her house painfully.

ROSANA: Adiós Mamá. Adiós Papá.

ROSANA extends her hand to JAIME. He leads her away.

Lights fade out.

End of Scene 7.

SCENE 8

(LOS ANGELES: 15 YEARS EARLIER)

Lights fade in. ROSANA, at 19, is outside in the front yard wearing an apron. She is cleaning the china plates. ROSANA looks out as if searching, impatiently waiting for JAIME. She wipes the China and starts crying. Her tears land on the China plates. JAIME, at 26, enters and sees her crying.

JAIME: ¿Porqué lloras? Why do you cry?

ROSANA is startled. She stands up and drops some plates. They crack. She quickly gets on her knees and picks up the pieces as if playing with a jigsaw puzzle.

ROSANA: Ayyy, no! Your mother is going to kill me. This is her favorite china... She already thinks I'm good for nothing.

ROSANA has to pick up every single piece of porcelain.

JAIME: Just leave it. I'll get a broom later and sweep them off.

ROSANA: No. If she sees them she'll make me pay for them...

JAIME: You're lying. Mi Amá (my mother) wouldn't do that.

ROSANA: ¿Porqué no me crees? Have I ever lied to you?

JAIME: No.

ROSANA: Jaime, when are we moving out to the suburbs? I can't stand living with your mother anymore. She hates me. When you are gone on your business trips for days she calls me a puta (whore). Tell her to stop calling me that or I'll leave.

JAIME *(menacingly)*: You won't leave me.

JAIME grabs her arm tightly.

ROSANA: Please don't hurt me... I'm pregnant.

JAIME releases her arm and lovingly embraces her.

ROSANA (CONT'D): I just found out today.

JAIME: I love you.

ROSANA *(hesitantly)*: I love you too.

JAIME touches her abdomen.

ROSANA (CONT'D): What if you became a Catholic? What if you just

went through the ceremony pretending you're Catholic?

JAIME: You know I can't do that.

ROSANA breaks down crying. He tries to hold her but she pushes him away.

ROSANA: You said we would go live in the suburbs! You said we wouldn't hear all the things that people would say about me. We live so close; I know how my parents are suffering. I hear what they say about me!

JAIME: Just ignore them.

ROSANA: No. Jaime, make me a decent woman. Marry me in a Catholic church!

JAIME: You know I can't do that!

ROSANA: Then I'm leaving you.

JAIME: Are you crazy?!

ROSANA takes off her apron and throws it on the floor. She walks out.

Lights fade out.

End of Scene 8.

SCENE 9

(LOS ANGELES: 15 YEARS EARLIER)

Lights fade in. It is night and CARMELA, at 40 is on the porch in her rocking chair knitting. ROSANA, at 20, watches her from a distance carrying her small suitcase. She whispers to the moon.

ROSANA:

Oh, mother, I have returned,

how I have cried,

to know how you have suffered.

I have a deep sadness,

a melancholic song,

about a love that can not be.

ROSANA gets the courage to walk up to her mother.

ROSANA: Amá, ya regresé. I came back.

CARMELA: Me regresaste panzona. You're pregnant.

ROSANA: Who told you?

CARMELA: I went to a curandera (a psychic) and she told me... She also tells me he beats you and I wanted to pay her to do a cure or a prayer to save you. But I want you to suffer. I know what I did and you will know what you did when you have a daughter, también. (too)

ROSANA: I'm 20 now. Papá never let me talk to any boys because I was his oldest daughter and he didn't want me to do what you did. But I loved Jaime. He was the only man who wanted me bad enough to deal with my father's old fashion ways and beliefs.

CARMELA: No. You deserved better than a "Pocho" (American born Latino) who couldn't respect us. You left because you thought he was going to give you a better life. You betrayed us... Pero no te diste tu valor. (You did not value yourself.)

ROSANA: Sí. I made a mistake.

CARMELA: Now go back to him. Raise your daughter not to do what you did. Go be with the man you left. You are not welcome here.

ROSANA: I can't go back!

CARMELA: Yes, you can. I did.

CARMELA goes inside the house and shuts the door. ROSANA is left outside with her suitcase. She wipes her tears and leaves through the gate once more.

Lights fade out.

End of Scene 9.

SCENE 10

(BOYLE HEIGHTS: PRESENT)

Lights fade in. DALIA is on the roof. No one is outside; all is quiet. In the background we hear "firecrackers" just barely. CARMELA comes out of the house and sits on the steps, crying. DALIA stands above her, watching her for a few seconds.

DALIA: What's wrong?

163

CARMELA is startled. She stands up scared.

CARMELA: What are you doing up there?

DALIA: Just thinking. Why are you crying?

CARMELA doesn't answer her. DALIA climbs down.

CARMELA: I liked Craig. I really thought it was going to work out between you and him. I thought he would be the one to marry you.

DALIA: Me too. Things were going really well. I did everything I could, but...

CARMELA: Why don't you go back to him?

DALIA: I can't.

CARMELA: Why do you always make it difficult for men to love you?

DALIA: I don't. I just won't take any crap from men.

CARMELA: You shouldn't have lived with him. The way all your cousins gossiped about you for doing that. Ay, why don't you try to make it work with him? Why don't you go back with him?

PAUSE.

DALIA: He hit me.

CARMELA: What did you do?

DALIA: What did I do? Nothing. I just told him the truth about his so-called friend and he punched me.

CARMELA starts crying.

CARMELA: I can't go back to Mexico knowing that you are alone. I worry about you. I worry you'll get AIDS and die. I worry you'll never marry and end up all alone like my aunt who ended up dressing saints, or dressing drunks like my mother.

DALIA and CARMELA embrace each other and cry together.

DALIA: I'm not going to end up dressing saints or drunks. I might be alone, but I still have places to see, and things I've got to do.

CARMELA: What are you looking for?

PAUSE.

DALIA looks for an answer...

DALIA: I don't know.

Lights fade out.

End of Scene 10.

SCENE 11

Lights fade in on the Rosales' house. DALIA is on the roof writing poetry from her notebook.

DALIA:

Dear God,

Diosito por favor,

mándame un hombre con un corazón

calientito.

Send me a man,

who is not afraid or threatened by my

sexuality and who doesn't want to tame

down my originality.

Send me a strong man with a gentle smile,

who doesn't scream,

who is not scared of my power,

who doesn't force me to climb ivory

towers to get to his heart,

and occasionally brings me flowers...

That's all I ask.

Is that too much?

Well, for once in my life I can say I

deserve it.

So send me a man who deserves me!

And if you can't, then send me an angel.

Their neighbor, CHAVA, 26, is by the right side fence. He has been watching her and listening to her.

CHAVA: Hey, tonta (dummy), what are you doing up there? You can fall and kill yourself.

DALIA: That's exactly what I don't want God. I'll try again.

DALIA prays again.

DALIA (CONT'D): Dear God, Diosito por favor...

CHAVA: Hey, you're the weird sister in the family, aren't you?

DALIA: Who told you that?

CHAVA: The whole neighborhood knows. So why did your ex-boyfriend dump you?

DALIA: He didn't dump me!

CHAVA: That's not what I heard.

DALIA: You're so nosey... So what did you hear about me?

CHAVA: That you're on boyfriend number 23 and you live with guys, and you can't keep a job.

DALIA: That's not true! It's number 20 and I've only lived with one guy and I don't like regular jobs like you people.

CHAVA: Like "us people." Excuse me.

DALIA: You're excused. Now can I get some privacy?

CHAVA: Then go inside your house

DALIA: Are you kidding? Privacy? That doesn't exist in Mexican households. That's why I'm on top of the roof talking to the moon. No one in my family can keep secrets, so I just talk to the moon and people think I'm weird.

CHAVA: Yeah, you are weird, but hey you're cool. I just thought I'd say "hi" 'cause I wasn't sure if you were planning to jump because if you were I was gonna tell you, you would survive it and you would only get a broken leg and a real bad headache. I tried it once when I was a kid 'cause I thought I could fly and I was in a cast for three months.

DALIA: You thought you could fly?

CHAVA: Yeah. I use to draw myself flying when I was a kid. I would put on a beach blanket on my back like a cape and jump off of the stairs. But stupid me, I always wanted to go higher and higher…

DALIA: Me too, I use to be a super-hero. But I wouldn't rescue anybody. I'd just stay on the roof and look at people like little ants.

CHAVA: Anyway, I should let you go back to your talks with the moon. Sorry for interrupting.

DALIA: No, problem… What's your name?

DALIA climbs down from the roof with the help of the vines.

CHAVA: Salvador Ramirez. But they call me Chava.

DALIA: My name is…

CHAVA: I know what your name is.

DALIA: What do you do?

CHAVA: I make deliveries… But I kinda paint. I paint murals.

DALIA: You do? That's pretty cool!

CHAVA: Yup.

DALIA: Did you go to school to study that?

CHAVA: Well, I studied painting at Otis, but they didn't have a class for the mural work that I do.

DALIA: Wow, can I see some of your work?

CHAVA: Yeah, just go check out the freeway on Cummings Street.

DALIA: Oh, you're the one who did that! So you make deliveries and spray paint freeways on the side?

CHAVA: Right.

DALIA: Wow, you know it's so rare to meet an artist, especially one who has gone to school. I went to UCLA. I'm a writer and a poet, but I haven't found a job I can do right now. Maybe they're hiring where you work.

CHAVA: Nah, you wouldn't want to do what I do. It's too dangerous.

DALIA: I'm a good driver.

CHAVA: It takes more than that to do what I do.

DALIA: Oh, well. Maybe some time we can have some coffee.

CHAVA: Coffee! I'm not a gringo. Coffee? What about tacos? I'll do tacos with you.

DALIA: Okay.

CHAVA: Does this mean you like me?

DALIA: No! It's just nice to meet someone from this neighborhood who actually graduated from high school and is an artist. I just like having somebody who can understand where I'm coming from.

CHAVA: Well, I think you're cute.

DALIA: Yeah, okay.

DALIA walks away blushing.

CHAVA: But don't let it go to your head okay, Cutey?

Lights fade out.

End of Scene 11.

SCENE 12

Lights fade in on the Rosales' house. It is day and RUBEN is gardening. He speaks to his roses. DALIA is on the porch writing. She observes her father.

RUBEN: Aver mis chulitas, (Now my little darlings) get ready for your daily shower. Don't worry, I'll be gentle. (*He hoses them gently.*) Mira que bonitas se ven. (Look how pretty you look.) Now you're all clean. Mmmm, and your fragrance.

DALIA (reading):

Roses are red,

get off my bed.

Then get out.

All right, you can stay.

Make love to me as though

I were a rose.

Porque es tu calor mi amor

that makes me unfold before you.

Porque es tu calor mi amor

that makes all my fragrances

run free.

No need to force it, just let

it be.

RUBEN: What did you say? Yes, mi vieja (my old woman) can be a real mule. What does she think she's going to do without me? ¿Qué, qué? (What, what?) Nombre, (No way) she would never leave me... For another man? No!! (*He cuts off the head of the outspoken rose.*) I want you all to know that another stupid remark like that will cost you your head... Okay, pues (then). That's better... And where's Ernie? I don't think he's my son. He's so lazy. A good kid, but lazy. Bueno, (Well) I guess God is punishing me for my sins... How do I know? I have three daughters.

DALIA: I heard that!

RUBEN (*whispering*): Three nosey daughters... So where is your brother?

DALIA: I think he's on the phone talking to his girlfriend.

RUBEN: He can barely wipe his butt and he has a girlfriend? Go inside and tell him to come out here and do the grass right now.

DALIA goes inside the house. She comes back quickly. A few seconds later ERNIE drags himself outside. He is wearing baggy pants and a loose shirt.

RUBEN (CONT'D): Lift up those pants! Tuck in that shirt. Why do you dress like that? You look like a cholo. (gangster). One of these days someone's gonna shoot at you thinking you're in a gang.

ERNIE tucks in his shirt and lifts up his pants.

DALIA: Ernie, I think my father is trying to tell you he loves you.

RUBEN shoots DALIA a look. She smiles at him. He gets embarrassed.

RUBEN (*whispers to ERNIE*): She's such a metiche (nosey).

ERNIE: Yeah.

They tap fists in brotherly agreement. RUBEN is hipper than he lets on. ERNIE gets the lawn mower and cuts the grass. They get busy taking the job seriously.

DALIA observes her father.

DALIA (*reading*):

There is no one who can

take the place of my father.

Who can not tell me

he loves me, but instead

fixes everything for me.

If I weren't scared of

you I would hug you,

save you from your solitude,

save you from tradition,

save you from your loneliness.

If I weren't scared I would

tell you I love you,

instead of just writing

everything about you.

A STREET VENDOR selling paletas (popsicles) passes by sounding his bells.

STREET VENDOR/"PALETERO": ¡Paletas! ¡Paletas!

ERNIE and RUBEN are sweating. They stop when they hear the bells.

RUBEN: Aver, let's see how those paletas taste.

The STREET VENDOR stops and opens his cart.

STREET VENDOR/PALETERO: ¿Qué sabor? (What flavor?)

ERNIE: I want tamarindo.

RUBEN: Give me a watermelon and a tamarindo.

DALIA coughs.

RUBEN (CONT'D): Do you want one?

DALIA: Mango.

RUBEN: And a mango paleta.

The STREET VENDOR hands them the paletas and RUBEN pays him. RUBEN and ERNIE go rest with DALIA on the porch. They suck their paletas passionately. Their eyes follow a car in front of them. They whisper to one another.

DALIA: Why does the police always come by and stop right in front of our house?

RUBEN: ¿Quién sabe? (Who knows?)

ERNIE: Maybe our neighbors are in a gang.

RUBEN: Yeah, they dress like you.

ERNIE: It's just a fashion statement, Papá.

RUBEN: No seas tonto, m'ijo. (Don't be dumb, my son.) Don't dress like those pendejos (idiots).

DALIA: What happened to our Japanese neighbors on both sides?

ERNIE: The little Japanese viejita (little old lady) on the right broke her hip coming down the stairs. So her family took her to live with them. And the other little Japanese viejita on the left died.

DALIA: She died?!

ERNIE: She was 96.

DALIA: Man, I remember when we were the first Mexican family to move into this block. Everybody was Japanese-American. This used to be little Tokyo.

ERNIE: No way! Little Tokyo!

DALIA: And before that, this neighborhood used to be Jewish and Italian. That's why there are Jewish temples around here.

ERNIE: What's a temple?

DALIA: It's like a church, but for Jews.

RUBEN: How do you know this?

DALIA: I took a class at UCLA about this neighborhood.

RUBEN: ¿Pa qué? (For what?) You studied this neighborhood pero (but) that hasn't helped you get a job.

DALIA: No, Apá, I'm a well-educated bum. I'm a bohemian.

RUBEN: ¿Bo - qué? (Bo-what?)

ERNIE: Look, they're leaving.

DALIA: I remember when there were no fences on any of the houses. Except our house, it was already here.

ERNIE: Yeah, when the Gonzalezes moved in they copied us and added a fence.

RUBEN: They even hired a gardener to compete with my roses. But those smelly gardenias look like wrinkled chicharrones. I just hope the new owners of this house keep up the garden like I do.

DALIA: Apá, you're not really going to sell this house and retire in Mexico.

RUBEN: I'm counting the days.

ERNIE: Nah, Apá, you'll probably go to Mexico and live a couple of months and you'll want to come right back.

RUBEN: I'm tired of this country. Too many taxes and you gotta have insurance for everything.

DALIA: Ernie, what are you going to do when our parents leave? What am I going to do?

ERNIE: Leech off another boyfriend.

DALIA: Shut up! You'll probably end up knocking up your girlfriend and marrying her like every other guy in this neighborhood.

RUBEN: Hey, don't talk that way to your brother.

DALIA: Well look at the way he talks to me.

RUBEN: Si te cabe el zapato, póntelo. (If the shoe fits, wear it.) Ernie's 18, so my legal responsibility for all my children is over.

ERNIE: Oh, well, Dalia. Two more months of free rent and that's it for us.

DALIA: Hey, isn't that Rosana's car?

RUBEN: What's your sister doing here?

ERNIE: I thought she was scared to come to this neighborhood.

DALIA: I think she is going to invite us to paint her white picket fence.

ERNIE: Nah, I already painted it last month. She probably wants Apá and me to help her remodel her kitchen. You know how cheap Jaime can be.

ROSANA enters through the gate.

ROSANA: Buenos dias. (Good afternoon.)

RUBEN: Buenos dias. What a surprise.

ROSANA: I was in the neighborhood buying pan dulce. (Sweet bread.)

RUBEN: Vamos, (Come on) Ernie, we have weeds strangling my roses.

ERNIE and RUBEN finish their paletas and get back to work. ROSANA approaches DALIA.

DALIA: Hey!

ROSANA: What are you doing?

DALIA: Writing bad poetry.

ROSANA: Good, I'm not interrupting... Hey, ah... You want to go to Paris with me?

DALIA: I don't have a job.

ROSANA: You speak French, don't you?

DALIA: No, I speak Italian, but I can speak a little French.

ROSANA: Jaime said he would let me go to Paris and he'll pay for your plane ticket if you come with me.

DALIA: Really?!!

ROSANA: He doesn't want me to go by myself, but he doesn't want to go.

DALIA: Oh my god, of course I'll go!

DALIA (CONT'D): But I still don't have any money...

ROSANA: I'll lend you some money.

DALIA: Magnifique! Merci beaucoup! Vive la France!... Ah, shit, we're going to Paris!

Lights fade out.

End of Scene 12.

SCENE 13

Lights fade in on the Rosales' house. It is night and DALIA is on the roof writing. JUAN and MARGIE are tip toeing from the back. JUAN and MARGIE are about to sneak out the front gate when DALIA catches them.

DALIA: You know, my father has a key to the back door that leads to the alley. When he sleeps at 9:37 p.m. you should sneak into his room and there's a hardware store still open on Mott St. Make a copy, that way the whole neighborhood won't know each time you have sex at the Carol Motel.

JUAN: What are you doing up there?

DALIA: You ever hear of Neighborhood Watch?... Nah, I'm paying tribute to Coatlicue, the goddess of the moon.

MARGIE: Leave her alone, she's just weird.

JUAN: I don't like doing this. Now, everybody knows.

MARGIE: No they don't.

DALIA: Margie, I found out from our neighbor what you do. And he found out from the neighbor at the corner. She's my mother's friend. It's only a matter of another conversation before she finds out and forces you to marry him because she'll want the neighbors to stop talking.

MARGIE: I can't believe how nosey people are!

JUAN: Why don't they keep their mouths shut... Margie, I hate sneaking around. Why don't you let me talk to your father? If they're leaving to Mexico, then you're not going to be a family anymore, so he'll be happy you and I will start one.

MARGIE: Because you don't have a good job. My father's not going to like that. I make more money than you, he's going to look at it like I'm supporting you and laugh at your face. He did that to Jaime when he came to ask for Rosana.

JUAN: But that was 15 years ago. Your father has changed.

DALIA: I'm afraid machos (men) don't evolve.

MARGIE: Stay out of this.

DALIA: Then go inside the house if you don't want the whole neighborhood to butt in... Look, (*pointing*) there's Doña Nacha, she's on her porch staring at you pretending to be reading.

They all look at her.

MARGIE: Her husband used to beat her. She kicked him out, and now she's got a boring life...

JUAN: Look, if everyone already knows we do it at the Carol Motel then let's go talk there.

MARGIE: All right.

They exit through the gate waiving goodbye at all the nosey neighbors. DALIA continues writing. CHAVA sneaks up behind her and tickles her. DALIA screams.

DALIA: ¡Cabrón! (Pig!) You could have killed me!

CHAVA: Don't you remember I used to do that to you?

DALIA: What? When did you used to do that to me?

CHAVA: In third grade. You used to have a mean ol' crush on me.

DALIA: Yuck! No, I didn't.

CHAVA: I gave you your first kiss.

DALIA: Liar! You're making it all up.

CHAVA kisses her passionately. DALIA is moonstruck. She can't believe what just happened.

CHAVA: Now don't go writing about that... You know, you're like your mother except you write about it.

DALIA: What do you mean?

CHAVA: Your mother tells wonderful stories, chisme, (gossip) at the beauty salon when she gets her hair dyed and cut. You probably tell good stories and poetry too. But you write about it. You write about everything.

We suddenly hear a car screeching and a spray of bullets.

DALIA: Who's popping fire crackers this late at night?

CHAVA: Are you joking? Those were bullets.

DALIA: But the police station is three blocks away. If they were bullets the police would have been here by now.

CHAVA: Is that what they taught you at that white arts college? How could you be so naive? Open your eyes and ears, esa. Those were gun shots. This neighborhood isn't the way it used to be when you were growing up here.

DALIA: How do you know so much about me?

CHAVA: We grew up together. I used to have a crush on you for the longest time.

DALIA: Used to?

They kiss again.

DALIA (CONT'D): Did everybody see that?

CHAVA: Yup... Hey, I just came to tell you I'm going to miss you. Have a great time in Paris... Just don't take your notebook. Just be present to what you see.

DALIA: All right.

DALIA looks away for a few seconds. CHAVA disappears.

DALIA (CONT'D): Chava? Chava? How did you know I needed to be kissed?

Lights fade out.

End of Scene 13.

SCENE 14

Lights fade in on the Rosales' house. It is day. The Rosales' house is brewing with activity. JAIME and ROSANA are talking on the porch.

JAIME: Now don't take any free drinks from any man at a bar you don't know. They may slip a drug in your drink and take advantage of you. Let your sister try it first...

ROSANA: What?

JAIME: Just kidding.

DALIA, CARMELA and RUBEN come out of the house.

CARMELA: Bring me back a real nice perfume or a real handsome Frenchman.

RUBEN: What did you say?!

CARMELA: Okay, okay, just bring me the perfume. Eventually all men wrinkle and get cranky. Your Papa used to be real handsome too, and look what he's turned into.

RUBEN tries to ignore the comment, but starts straightening out his clothes and fixes his hair.

MARGIE: What are Ernie and his girlfriend talking about?

JUAN: Yeah, they look like they're arguing.

DALIA and ROSANA are comparing notes, and then slowly everyone turns to look at ERNIE arguing with his girlfriend. ERNIE finally comes to the gate. Everyone wants to know what's going on.

ERNIE: What's everybody looking at?

DALIA: What happened?

ERNIE: Aren't you going to miss your plane?

CARMELA: Why is your girlfriend crying?

RUBEN: Hijo, ¿qué pasa? (Son, what happened?) What's wrong?

ERNIE: I just found out she's pregnant.

DALIA: We are going to miss the plane if we stay for this.

ROSANA: Yes, we better go, Jaime.

JAIME: But this is going to get good.

ROSANA: It's none of our business.

JAIME: We're all family.

Ernie spills the beans that he got his girlfriend pregnant.

Photo by Hector Rodríguez

ROSANA: Goodbye!

ROSANA drags JAIME to the gate. DALIA drags the many suitcases.

JAIME: Make him marry her Don Ruben!

Lights fade out.

END OF ACT ONE

BOYLE HEIGHTS

ACT TWO

SCENE 1

Lights fade in on a hotel room with a bed. As DALIA and ROSANA enter the bedroom we hear "La Vie En Rose," by Edith Piaf. They are both drunk and throw themselves on the bed.

DALIA: How many did you have?

ROSANA: I lost count after the fifth glass.

DALIA: You're crazy, woman. You're crazier than me!

ROSANA: Free at last! Free at last! No kids, no husband!

ROSANA gets on top of the bed and starts taking off her clothes. She is laughing so hard she starts crying.

ROSANA (CONT'D): We're in the city of love, but I've never been in love.

DALIA: Sure, you have. Jaime and you love each other.

ROSANA: I know he loves me, but I don't... I don't want to go back home.

DALIA: You're just drunk.

ROSANA: Tell me what it's like to be in love. I wanted to be a slut like you.

DALIA: Hey, hey. I prefer you call me sexually liberated, okay.

ROSANA: I always wanted to know how it feels to be kissed by someone you...

DALIA: Love? It feels great. I don't have much to show for my life, but I have really loved and been loved. I know what chispas, sparks feel like. I have had a very romantic life.

ROSANA: I want romance. I want to know what being madly in love feels like.

DALIA: It's so wonderful. I surrender completely and magic happens. I don't think of the consequences. I live in the moment and then it's gone.

ROSANA: You surrender? But what about when they leave you?

DALIA: It hurts like hell. But you can't truly love unless you completely surrender.

ROSANA: No, I can't do that. I see you constantly giving yourself completely to these boyfriends of yours and then they leave you and you're left like a sad puppy.

DALIA: Hey, just because you're drunk doesn't mean you can talk shit about my life. I'm proud of my life.

ROSANA: Why? What have you done that you are so proud of?

DALIA: I got an education.

ROSANA: Big deal! You don't have a house or a car or anything. You don't even have a job.

DALIA: You're right. I don't have a job like you, I have a career. I love what I do. I love my life. I have loved and been loved by many men. I have traveled all over and seen a lot of the world. What have you done with your life? You got married. Big deal. Any idiot can get married; work like a mule, buy material things and have a life already lived.

ROSANA: Yeah, I got married. Rosana got married and had children. That's my story.

ROSANA starts crying. There is an uncomfortable silence between them.

DALIA: Where do you want to go tomorrow? What do you want to see?

ROSANA remains silent.

DALIA (CONT'D): Who is your favorite author?

ROSANA: Why are you asking? You just want to show off how educated you are?

DALIA: What?

ROSANA: In all of our conversations since we got here all you do is talk about yourself to anyone who asks. You're constantly trying to prove how educated and smart you are.

DALIA: No. I'm just asking because there are so many cafés where famous authors used to hang out and drink coffee. I wanted to know who your favorite author is so that maybe we can go to a café where he or she went.

ROSANA: Who cares? That's so dumb.

DALIA: Okay, where do you want to go?

ROSANA: To the Coco Channel Couture house.

DALIA: For what?

ROSANA: To see the window displays.

DALIA: Why?

ROSANA: To take pictures in front of it and show all my co-workers. The designer I assist used to work in Paris.

DALIA: All right... Let's go, but can we go to the Picasso museum after?

ROSANA: But he's dead and his paintings are ugly.

DALIA: You know, I'm so glad I came with you to Paris because I used to think you were ignorant, now I know you are!

ROSANA: So you think I'm stupid. Well I guess I was stupid enough to bring you.

DALIA: I didn't say you were stupid. I said you were ignorant. There's a difference between stupid and ignorant.

ROSANA: Shut up!

DALIA: You shut up!

ROSANA: You know what. (*She reaches into her purse. She pulls out some money and throws it at DALIA.*) Here! Bon chance! (Good luck!) You're on your own.

DALIA: Hey, I studied French in college; I speak enough French to get by. I guess you'll have to smile and flirt and use your pretty looks to get a guy to rescue you like Jaime did.

ROSANA wants to respond, but can't fight back.

Lights fade out.

End of Scene 2.

SCENE 3

Lights fade in on DALIA who is roaming the streets of Paris. She stops by a bridge where many Parisians and tourists play music and listen to music. DALIA sits on the ground "Indian" style and writes poetry.

DALIA: I guess this dream came true... I'm running out of money. I'm a starving writer in Paris. It doesn't get more real than that.... "Paris from a bridge."

Sun rays shine,

someone sips wine.

St. Germaine dances,

a tourist prances.

Coins drop,

I want to hop.

My sister roams free.

Dixie music colors our ears,

this feeling won't leave me

for years.

Birds chirp,

I blow bubbles.

I'm a writer,

I starve.

Hemingway, Porter, Fitzgerald,

Stein,

they drank coffee, I'll drink

sunshine

Lights fade out.

End of Scene 3.

SCENE 4

Lights fade in on ROSANA getting off the "Metro" at Champs Elysse. She looks at her map and is very confused. A very handsome FRENCHMAN comes up to her.

FRENCHMAN: Vous êtes perdu? Are you lost?

ROSANA: Yes.

FRENCHMAN: Are you an American?

ROSANA: Yes. I mean no. I'm Mexican-American.

FRENCHMAN: That's better. Can I help you find your way?

ROSANA : I'm looking for the Coco Chanel Couture house.

FRENCHMAN: I know where it is. I'll take you.

He sticks out his hand like a "gentleman"

Lights fade out.

End of Scene 4.

SCENE 5

Lights fade in on DALIA getting out of the "Metro" at Bastille Circle. There is a lot of commotion going on. We hear loud music. A lot of "busy bees" circle around DALIA, who walks with heavy feet. She finds a nice bench in the midst of the storm. She takes out her notebook and writes.

DALIA:

A song of protest to a carnival *(BEAT)*

The police hurry off.

I stop.

The world spins,

a little Haitian boy sits next to me.

Bastille doesn't stand still.

I came here when there was light,

the music brought on the night.

The clouds rise like blue ink

dropping in water.

I hope it doesn't rain.

The golden angel at the very top

tip toes with a torch as the moon

lights the kiss of two lesbians now

sitting next to me.

There is poetry everywhere,

Francs nowhere.

But Bastille doesn't stand still.

If I sit still a man might ask...

FRENCHMAN #2

"Are you waiting for someone?"

DALIA (writing)

I'll simply say, (to the man) my sister is late.

DALIA gets up and walks away from him.

Lights fade out.

End of Scene 5.

SCENE 6

Lights fade in on ROSANA in the arms of the handsome FRENCHMAN in a cafe at Bastille Circle. They are drinking wine and the Eiffel tower is in the background. The moon is out and it's definitely a Kodak moment.

FRENCHMAN: You are so beautiful. I didn't know Mexican girls could be so beautiful.

ROSANA: Merci. (*She giggles, quite tipsy.*)

FRENCHMAN: Rosana, why don't we go back to my apartment?

ROSANA: Your apartment?

He kisses her neck. He knows where to touch her and what to say. ROSANA loves it. She doesn't recall wishing on a star, but her dream came true. It doesn't get any more romantic than this.

FRENCHMAN: Your husband must be very lucky.

ROSANA: He's a good man.

FRENCHMAN: Do you love him?

ROSANA: Do I love him? No... I've never have.

(BEAT)

FRENCHMAN: I want to make love to you.

ROSANA: You do?... I want to make love to you too.

FRENCHMAN: Then let's go.

ROSANA: I can't... I ah... I'm supposed to wait for my sister here. But she's late.

FRENCHMAN (*more aroused*): You have a sister? Well, I'll wait with you.

ROSANA (*lying*): Ah, she's a lesbian... She'll tell on my husband if she sees me with another man.

Just then DALIA (by incredible coincidence) happens to be walking by. DALIA and ROSANA are surprised and relieved to see each other.

ROSANA: There she is. That's my sister.

FRENCHMAN: Enchanté. Nice to meet you, you are pretty like your sister.

DALIA: Bonjour.

ROSANA: It was great talking to you. Goodbye.

They swiftly lose the FRENCHMAN.

FRENCHMAN: Au-revoir Mexicaines! (Goodbye Mexicans!)

DALIA and ROSANA sneak into a cafe. They sit at a table and are quickly

given menus. They remain sitting for some time before ROSANA finally speaks.

ROSANA: How was the Picasso Museum?

DALIA: Pretty fantastic. How was Coco Chanel?

ROSANA: It was... It was just nice to look at... Why do you dress the way you do?

DALIA: Do you want to start up with me again?

ROSANA: Why don't you care what people think about you?

DALIA: Because people are going to think whatever they want to think about me.

ROSANA: You don't dress with nice clothes or have fancy quality things.

DALIA: Everything tears; all things come to an end. No matter what I dress in it's still Dalia.

ROSANA: It has always been my dream to come to Paris to shop. I always wanted to have nice things. I always wanted people to respect me. When I was a little girl in Mexico, we used to be so poor; my mother would buy the fabric left over from potato sacks and make me dresses out of it. I was so embarrassed. I felt like I was nothing. I learned how to sew so I would never have to dress like that. I learned how to look pretty and flirt and smile and say all the nice things to boys so I would never have to dress like that...

DALIA: Is that why you became an assistant fashion designer?

ROSANA: Yes, and that's also why I married Jaime. My parents didn't want to talk to me after I married Jaime. Then when they saw the house we bought in the suburbs and all the nice cars and things we have they forgave me... I've been walking around the streets of Paris wondering what people think of me. But nobody knows me, nobody cares. I've lived my life always being observed by our macho father, and then by my husband who always has an opinion about things and me. Today there was no one watching me. I didn't know what to do, who I should please. It felt so nice to not care what people think of me.

DALIA: Now you know.

ROSANA: Yes. And now I can't go back...to the way things were... I'm getting a divorce.

DALIA: Are you sure about that?

ROSANA: I've been thinking about it for fourteen years.

They are both silent.

DALIA: You know what, I've been thinking about coming to Paris for almost fourteen years too. But you know what, after spending all these days here, I miss home. I actually miss Boyle Heights. Paris is so wonderful, but I'm ready to go back.

ROSANA: Me too.

Lights fade out.

End of Scene 6.

SCENE 7

Lights fade in on the Rosales' house. DALIA is on top of the roof. JAIME is at the bottom screaming at her.

JAIME: What did you tell her? If we get a divorce it's your fault!

DALIA: If she divorces you, it's your fault!

JAIME: Come down so I can talk to you. You want the whole neighborhood to hear?

DALIA: You're getting a divorce, Ernie knocked up his girlfriend, look we're officially Mexican trash now. We fit right in.

The neighbors throw tennis balls at her. She artfully dodges them.

JAIME: Come down. I just want to talk to you... Look, I'll pay you some money if you come down.

DALIA: I'm not for sale.

JAIME: I'll publish your poetry.

DALIA: What did you say?

JAIME: I was looking through your poetry book the other day and it's not bad.

DALIA: Why were you looking at my book?

JAIME: I want to know what you told her. It had to be you telling her some of your feminist bullshit to get her to do this. She would never have done this. We're about to buy a bigger house and I let her go to Paris and she's got no reason to be upset with me.

DALIA: Jaime, I'm not coming down no matter what you do or how much you offer to pay me.

CHAVA comes out of his house and is by the gate.

CHAVA: Come on Dalia, come down "Miss Holier Than Thou". Come down and smell las rosas.

DALIA: Hey, Chava! Where are you going?

CHAVA: I'm going to make this city pretty, by painting my graffiti.

DALIA: Can I come?

DALIA climbs down from the roof and runs to the gate as fast as she can. Jaime follows her.

CHAVA: This isn't some field trip; this is dangerous.

DALIA: I have my tennis shoes on in case the cops come. I'll run as fast as I can.

CHAVA: Are you sure you want to do this?

DALIA: It's either go with you or listen to my brother-in-law complain.

CHAVA: All right, but you have to be quiet when I'm working.

DALIA: Yeah, sure.

Lights fade out.

End of Scene 7.

SCENE 8

Lights fade in on CHAVA and DALIA by a freeway wall. CHAVA is tagging away as DALIA sits by observing him. He has already done a lot of work on something that is somewhat pretty but not decipherable.

DALIA: So, why do you do this?

CHAVA: It's the art of the people; it's about taking pride in your community.

DALIA: Yeah, but what I don't get is, if you're taking pride in your community, how come you're doing it on public property?

CHAVA: Because we're reclaiming it for ourselves—we're saying, "This community belongs to us."

DALIA: But it does belong to us.

CHAVA: No, it doesn't. We just live here until our lives get better and we move to Montebello or some other stupid suburb with the uppity Mexicans.

DALIA: Don't you plan to leave Boyle Heights?

CHAVA: No. The only way I'm leaving is in a casket.

DALIA: That's so dramatic. Straight out of a telenovela. (soap opera)

CHAVA: I don't watch that shit.

DALIA: Me neither.

CHAVA: Hey, you were supposed to be quiet and let me get my work done.

DALIA: I still don't get why you have to paint on public property and not on a canvas or paper.

CHAVA: Because that way everybody in this neighborhood can see it. It belongs to everybody. How many people get to read your poetry?

DALIA: My poetry? Me.

CHAVA: So what good is it if you write it just for yourself? What good is it, if you left Boyle Heights and got your education, but you keep it all to yourself?

DALIA: My poetry is not very good.

CHAVA: It's not a matter of whether it be—

Suddenly a shower of bullets is heard. CHAVA falls over. He was shot. DALIA is absolutely stunned.

Lights fade out.

End of Scene 8.

SCENE 9

Lights fade in on the Rosales' house. It is night and DALIA is still on top of the roof. CARMELA comes out.

CARMELA: Dalia, come down. It's too cold for you to stay up there.

DALIA doesn't respond. She's in shock.

CARMELA (CONT'D): What are the neighbors going to think? That you finally lost it? M'ija, ya bajate. (Come down now.)

CARMELA gets a blanket with her as she climbs up to the roof.

CARMELA (CONT'D): Now the neighbors know that we're definitely crazy.

CARMELA gets on the roof and covers DALIA with a blanket.

DALIA: Gracias.

CARMELA: Your Papá says you're from his side because he had a crazy aunt and you act just like her. But I think you're more like me than him... M'ija, did you love that guy?

DALIA: Please don't ask me that.

CARMELA: Well you fall in love so easily. I don't know what your heart is made of, but you keep getting it broken. Yo que tu, I would stop loving men. No valen la pena. (They aren't worth it.)

RUBEN walks outside unaware of CARMELA and DALIA on the roof. He overhears the conversation.

DALIA: Is that what you did?

CARMELA: No, I was a pendeja (idiot), I fell madly in love with a handsome man and it's been hell ever since.

DALIA: Is it really that bad?

CARMELA: No, the fighting actually makes this life livable... Have you seen the moon? Que bonita se ve. (How pretty she looks.) Her smile reminds me of the Mona Lisa. Look at her; she's smiling at us... Did you see the Mona Lisa?

DALIA: Yeah, she looked better in my mind.

CARMELA: That moon reminds me of the moon we saw in Venice. Remember when we went? N'ombre when I was in the rancho I used to dream about going to Venice. And then you took me. That's when you had money from winning that poetry contest and that grant. It was the most romantic night of my life. We were on that river by that big bridge--

DALIA: --The Grand Canal.

CARMELA: Sí, ese. And in the background they were playing and singing "Cielito Lindo."

DALIA: That was so beautiful... Amá, did you see?

CARMELA: I saw everything. I always thought those plants were for limpias not for smoking.

DALIA: I can't believe Chava used to sell it. I can't believe what has happened to our block. It was never like this before. Maybe we ought to move?

CARMELA: Pos your Papá is leaving and he's set on selling the house. So you're going to have to.

DALIA: Are you going with him?

CARMELA: I don't want to go back to our pueblo.

DALIA: ¿Porqué no? What would you do without my father?

CARMELA: I don't want to go because I'm worried about your sister and about you.

DALIA: Rosana is finally thinking for herself, she's thinking straight and she's got a good job. And for me...

CARMELA: Es que tu estás muy loca. You're so crazy. I guess it's my fault for letting you be who you wanted to be.

DALIA: Mamá, thank you for letting me be. I love my life. It may not make sense, but it's exactly what I designed it to be. When it's no longer working for me, well then I'll change.

CARMELA: It's just that by now you should be married to a good husband who will take care of you. I don't like it that you're always struggling and suffering. It's very hard to see one's children suffer.

DALIA: Yeah, I suffer, but it's 'cause I love drama, I love being dramatic. I get a kick out of it. It makes my world go 'round. Some people like gossip. I like drama…and I have to be true to myself, even if it doesn't make sense to anybody else... So don't worry about me. If things really get that bad I'll get a normal job as a secretary or a teacher or anything. I have an education.

CARMELA: Tu y tu education. (You and your education.) Bueno (fine), then I'll leave without looking back.

DALIA: Sí, Mamá. (Yes, mother.) Go back to Mexico and enjoy the rest of your life. Be with your mother before she dies.

DALIA cries. CARMELA puts her arm around her.

CARMELA: Yeah, I have to talk to my mother and forgive her. I don't want to see her, but she's leaving quickly too... When she wouldn't take me back after I eloped with your father. I hated her. But I hated her more when I returned from el norte having bought this house and bringing her back money and beautiful things. I came back a respectable worthy daughter and I bought her love back... I even bought the rancor of Ruben's first wife with money. She signed the papers because she needed to buy Ruben's daughter clothes for school. So, I don't want to go back. I've seen enough, I've heard enough of chisme and insults. If you think the gossip is bad on this block, a

pueblo where not everyone has T.V. is worse.

DALIA and CARMELA embrace. CARMELA leaves DALIA to her thoughts. CARMELA climbs down. On her way down RUBEN gives her a hand and CARMELA lands in his arms.

CARMELA: The last balcony I climbed down, it was to flee with you and I've regretted it ever since.

RUBEN: Has life with me been that bad, mujer?

CARMELA: Worse.

They sit on the porch together. Upstairs, DALIA writes in her notebook.

DALIA:

They sat together on the porch,

a Rockwell for the barrio.

When they rocked in their chairs

no one would ever know all the witchcraft,

curses and prayers she did to keep him.

No one would ever know all the betrayal,

all the abuse and pain he inflicted.

They just smiled,

as father and mother,

nodding peacefully, thinking...

CARMELA/RUBEN: At least we have each other.

(BEAT)

RUBEN: So what did you decide?

CARMELA: What do you think?

RUBEN: Pos I don't know; that's why I'm asking.

CARMELA: Do you deserve me?

RUBEN: Ay, that again? Mujer (woman), stop it with that; tell me yes or no, but don't do this!

CARMELA: Do what?

RUBEN: Make me admit I need you!

CARMELA: Well do you?

RUBEN: Well what do you think?

CARMELA: I don't know; that's why I'm asking. You act like you don't need anybody all the time, like you're such a man that you don't need anyone and I…I'm not like that. I need to hear it.

(BEAT)

RUBEN: Well I need you. Why do think I make you believe I don't need you; so you'll never leave me… Don't leave me… Ya, I said it… Please don't make me repeat it.

(BEAT)

CARMELA: I'm going back with you.

RUBEN: Yo sabia. I knew it.

CARMELA: But it's not because I love you. It's because you kept your promise. When you were in Los Angeles you could have stayed and never returned for me and your children like a lot of no good husbands did and left their women to fight for themselves in Mexico. And not just hunger but the dirty chisme (gossip) of the pueblo (people) when they were abandoned. Pero tu no. (But not you.) You're not so loving, you're not so handsome anymore, and you're getting shorter, pero (but) you came back. So, it's only fair that I keep my word and go back to Mexico with you.

RUBEN reaches for her chin like he did the night they eloped. He is about to kiss her when CARMELA stops him.

CARMELA: No, don't do it here. The neighbors are going to see.

RUBEN: Pos que vean. Let everybody see and know I love my wife.

They kiss. On the roof DALIA is composing more poetry.

DALIA:

I have named you my Prince.

There are more taller than you, more taller.

There are more courageous than you, more

courageous.

There are more loving than you, more

loving.

But you are my Prince.

When you walk down the streets no one

recognizes you,

no one sees your golden sword,

no one sees your white horse,

that on which you ride on,

the one only I can see.

*And when you look at me,

*all the rivers of my body flow,

*you shake the bells in heaven,

*and a hymn fills the world.

*Only you and I.

*Only you and I, amor mio,

*love of mine,

*can hear it.

(* This is an homage to Pablo Neruda's poem *La Reina*... The sentences with an * come from that poem.)

RUBEN grabs her by the hand and they go inside the house.

DALIA laughs and then suddenly a bright white light appears before her.

DALIA (CONT'D): Who's that?

CHAVA appears as an angel.

CHAVA: Put your pen down I'm not going to hurt you. Get off the roof, Dalia and start your life. Poetry is being...being alive.

DALIA: Why are you here?

CHAVA: I came to say adiós. Goodbye Boyle Heights. Adios Mamá y Papá and all your sacrifices. Goodbye to my marijuana plants and my homeboys who looked to me for help. Goodbye to the oldies and all the things I never knew I loved. Goodbye to all that I loved. Goodbye Dalia. May you realize how wonderful this world is like all the great poets who did. Goodbye Mariposa street. Adíos mundo. (Goodbye world.)

CHAVA disappears. DALIA searches for him. He is gone. She gets down from the roof by climbing the vines. The vine tears and she falls to the ground. She picks up the vine and sees it's got potential. She goes to the spot where CHAVA was shot. She digs the dirt and plants the vine. She kneels in front of it and begins to pray.

DALIA: Dear God, Diosito porfavor, send me a tree...

Lights fade out.

End of Scene 10.

SCENE 11

Lights fade in on the Rosales' house. It is day. JUAN and MARGIE enter together through the front gate. JUAN knocks on the door and RUBEN comes out.

RUBEN: Yes.

JUAN: Señor Ruben, I have come to ask for your daughter's hand in marriage...

RUBEN : Son, what took you so long? Here in the U.S. men are not as aggressive. I practically stole my wife.

JUAN: I thought about it, but your daughter kept telling me you might kill me.

MARGIE playfully punches him.

RUBEN: That's before. Now that we're leaving, it's up to my children to decide what they want to do with their lives. You don't happen to have a brother who might want to take Dalia?

DALIA comes outside with the portable telephone.

DALIA: I heard that, Apá.

RUBEN: Let's go inside and tell mi vieja (my wife).

DALIA: Craig, I guess I'm just shocked to hear from you. It's been three months... You want me back?... Yeah, I love you too, but I gotta tell you... I've been doing a lot of thinking and a lot of writing and I wrote you a poem. You want to hear it? Okay. Let me read it to you. This is dedicated to you. (*She clears her throat.*) It's called "My Low Self-Esteem Days."

Si te quise fue porque I had low self-esteem.

If I swore I'd always be by your side,

was because I had nothing better to do.

Si te dije you were a great lover,

was because I had nothing to compare it to.

If I said you and me were meant to be,

was because I thought I couldn't find any better.

Si te dije que te amaba con toda mi alma,

was because I hadn't found myself.

If you think that now that time has passed,

and my low self-esteem days are gone,

that I'm a bitch, a whore, a liar.

Well then go ahead!

Cause you ain't my master, my father,

my hero, my lover...

Shit! I ain't even gonna bother...

To address your remarks.

Time has proved me stronger,

I don't need your approval any longer.

So today, I ain't even gonna bother...

To let you know how good it's been...

Without you.

Goodbye, Craig.

DALIA hangs up the phone. ROSANA appears at the gate.

DALIA (CONT'D): What are you doing here?

ROSANA: Looking at houses.

DALIA: For you?

ROSANA: I'm ready to move out of the suburbs.

DALIA: You want to live in this neighborhood?

ROSANA: Is Papá home?

DALIA: He's inside talking to Juan. Margie and Juan are getting married.

ROSANA: She's too young... Oh, well, like grandma used to say que cada quien haga con su culo un papalote. (May each person turn their asshole into a kite.)

DALIA: I think she was going senile when she said that.

ROSANA: But sometimes it makes sense... I'm going to buy this house.

DALIA: Now that doesn't make sense.

ROSANA: I want my kids to grow up in a Latino neighborhood. My daughter wants a cappuccino machine for her 12th birthday. I'll get her a churro maker instead.

DALIA: So could I live with you if you bought the house?

ROSANA: Yeah, but you would have to baby sit and you can't bring all your boyfriends over.

DALIA: I'll just bring one.

ROSANA: Maybe.

DALIA: So Jaime is really going to give you the divorce.

ROSANA: No, but it's nothing a good curandera (a psychic) who performs white magic can't take care of.

197

DALIA: I see...

Lights fade out.

End of Scene 12.

SCENE 13

Lights fade in on the Rosales house. It is spring and all the roses are blooming. There are many boxes and suitcases on the porch. ERNIE and RUBEN and JUAN are busy carrying them into RUBEN'S truck off stage. When they finish carrying the last items they stop to wipe off their sweat.

RUBEN: I guess we're ready to go.

JUAN: That's a really nice truck suegro (father-in-law).

RUBEN: And it's all paid for. Now in case your mother-in-law wants to leave me at least I have my truck.

DALIA, CARMELA, ROSANA, and MARGIE come out of the house.

CARMELA: I guess this is it. I hope you come and visit us and please bring my grandchildren to visit us so they know where they came from.

MARGIE: Of course, mamacita.

MARGIE and ROSANA hug CARMELA. JUAN and ERNIE hug RUBEN. It's a tearful goodbye. DALIA hugs her father.

RUBEN: Remember, you're old enough to know what you're doing.

DALIA: I love you too Papá.

RUBEN finally breaks a tear. DALIA embraces her mother.

DALIA (CONT'D): Adiós Mamá.

CARMELA: No. No digas adiós. Don't say goodbye. Just say hasta luego. Until we see each other again.

DALIA: Sí. Sí. Hasta luego, Mamá. Until we see each other again.

CARMELA and RUBEN exit through the gate. ERNIE, ROSANA, MARGIE, JUAN, and DALIA wave goodbye. They slowly stop waving and go inside the house. DALIA continues waving. She finally stops and sits down on the stairs. She remains on the stairs until she can't see her parents anymore. She stares at her poetry book. DALIA reaches for it. She picks up her pen and is about to write. She stops.

DALIA (CONT'D): Poetry is being... Being here... Being home... Boyle Heights.

My beautiful little barrio.

Since I can remember I swore I'd leave you like all the rest,

But when I'm in Paris, Rome, or New York I just want to come back.

Everyone thinks you're East L.A.

But I know who you really are.

I know what they say on the five o'clock news isn't true.

I know you are a beautiful place where families like me loved and lived.

I know you are located near the L.A. River, somewhere close to my heart.

DALIA puts the pen down and closes her book. She gets up and goes into the house.

Lights fade out.

The End

Lola Goes to Roma

a new play by Josefina López

LOLA GOES TO ROMA

PLAYWRIGHT'S NOTES

I took my mother to Italy and we both kept travel journals. We would sit down and write about our amazing trip that started in Rome and ended in Venice. One of the most romantic nights of my life happened on the Grand Canal on a gondola with my mother and a singer singing "Cielito Lindo". I remember how close I felt to my mother and how much I loved her and was so happy that I had just made one of her dreams come true. I wrote Lola Goes to Roma as a screenplay first and then adapted it as a play. This is my most cinematic play, although some of my critics will argue that this is not "theater." I like calling it "Cineatro" – it's cinema and teatro – Cineatro! I have written many screenplays and I have spent the last 20 years trying to get films made; so unless I have a couple of million dollars to make these movies, I can forget about them getting made for now since they are all about Latina women who are not stereotypical – "Not commercial" as most typical Hollywood producers would say. I've decided to take some of my screenplays and turn them into plays and this is my first one... I like it that the scenes are short and it moves fast and that there are too many scenes. When I directed it on stage I had so much fun doing it, and when an audience saw it they were moved and touched. It's a different type of play, but it still makes you laugh and cry.

This play was inspired by the many bitter women I have met who never had the courage to leave loveless and passionless marriages. I have met too many women who had to grin and bear it so I wanted to write something to

remind me that regret kills the soul. It was also inspired by my love of Italy and I wanted a reason to remember Italia every time I read this play.

Josefina López

March 1, 2011

LOLA GOES TO ROMA

ACT ONE

The stage is completely white except for the outline of a giant postcard on the central wall where slides will be projected. The ceiling is painted with a light blue sky with white clouds.

PHOTO SLIDES: CEMETERY HEADSTONES

SCENE 1

ROMA RODRIGUEZ, a 26 year old overachiever Latina with a slightly visible moustache she's had no time to pluck, (ROMA looks like a young Frida Kahlo with black framed glasses with two braids up in a bun), stands in front of the PowerPoint presentation.

Spotlight on ROMA.

ROMA: ...and that's the end of my presentation on the European influence on cemetery headstones in colonial Mexico of the 1700s. Any questions?

PAUSE

DEAN STEWART (*V.O.*): ... Having successfully defended your dissertation, your committee hereby bestows upon you a Doctorate in Anthropology. Congratulations Dr. Roma Rodriguez.

Lights fade out.

SCENE 2

Lights fade in. ROMA does a mini victory dance thinking no one is around. ALEX MARTINEZ, 25, approaches her and startles her. She quickly puts her "Professor" hat back on and pretends it didn't happen.

ROMA: Alex, how are you?

ALEX: I just heard, so I wanted to be the first to congratulate you.

ROMA: Oh, it's not a big deal; I knew they would have to give it to me.

ALEX: Oh, yes it is a big deal. I know in my family it would be. Your family must be so proud.

ROMA: Oh, yeah. I'm the first to go to college and get my Ph.D.

ALEX: Maybe now that you're not as busy we can go get some coffee and discuss Mayan hieroglyphics or the latest Almodovar film. You want to go see a movie--?

ROMA: Actually, I'm going to be out of the country. I'm rewarding myself by going on a two month vacation to Europe.

ALEX: Well, what about when you get back?

ROMA: I'm going to be busy teaching four classes and trying to get published, because you know me, I'm going to get tenure.

PAUSE

ALEX: You ever think about that night?

ROMA: Alex, we said we would never talk about that…I had failed my first exam, I was desperate; I was drunk--

ALEX: But wasn't it good?

ROMA: I have to go.

ALEX hands her a present. She quickly tears it open.

ROMA: Oh, I already read this. This isn't the best translation of Pablo Neruda's poems, but thank you.

ALEX: Aren't you going to celebrate at all?

ROMA: Didn't you get the e-mail for my graduation party? I'll send you another one. I have to go.

Lights fade out.

SCENE 3

Lights fade in on the RODRIGUEZ FAMILY LIVING ROOM. A CORONER hands BELLA, 38, ROMA's older sister, beautiful and graceful, a clipboard and a pen.

CORONER: Just sign here so we can take the body.

BELLA signs and he takes the clipboard and pen and hands her a receipt. He exits. BELLA whimpers and blows her nose. Just then ROMA enters.

ROMA: Dad?

BELLA: It finally happened.

ROMA: I'd always thought he'd be around.

BELLA: Ten years was too long to suffer... Where were you? I've been leaving you messages all morning.

ROMA: I defended my dissertation today and I got my Ph.D.!

BELLA: Oh.

BELLA blows her nose again.

BELLA (CONT'D): Go say hi to Mamá, she doesn't want to talk to anyone. I'm going home to tell my husband. Keep Mamá company.

BELLA leaves. ROMA walks over to a door and knocks.

OLDER WOMAN'S VOICE: Vállanse a la chingada! (Go to hell!)

ROMA: Mom, it's me, Roma! Let me in.

ROMA stops knocking and DOLORES, 60, opens the door wearing dark sunglasses.

DOLORES: Pos que chingados quiere?!

ROMA: Nice to see you too.

DOLORES: Ah, I thought it was that man from the funeral home. I don't want to talk to him.

ROMA: How are you feeling?

DOLORES: How am I supposed to feel?

ROMA: You can feel like crap, you can feel relieved, you can feel however you want to feel. Every response is appropriate. You know death is seen differently in many cultures. You're lucky this isn't India in the 1800s and we

don't have to toss you with your dead husband to burn to death with him.

DOLORES: It was a rhetorical question.

ROMA: I thought maybe you were testing my expertise. You know today I got tested.

DOLORES: What do you mean?

ROMA: I defended my dissertation and I was awarded my doctorate.

DOLORES: Ah, que bueno. Maybe now you'll work on your "M-R-S" degree because my neighbor has been asking if you're a lesbian and just using the education excuse to get out of getting married.

ROMA: A lesbian? Just because I'm not like her "chola" daughters who spread their legs and breed with anything that has a social security number doesn't mean I'm a lesbian.

DOLORES: Don't get upset Dr. Rodriguez.

ROMA readjusts her glasses and controls herself.

ROMA: Fine. *(BEAT)* Don't worry about the wake. I was planning to have a graduation party here in three days for me so it will be Dad's wake instead.

Lights fade out.

SCENE 4

Lights fade in on LIVING ROOM. ROMA carries a tray of appetizers. The house is full of relatives in black eating ROMA's food. The doorbell rings and no one answers.

ROMA: Hold on!

She answers the door and ALEX is outside holding a bouquet of flowers.

ROMA (CONT'D): Alex, I didn't expect you.

ALEX: I thought you were having a graduation party.

ROMA: Oh, didn't you get my e-mail? It's my father's wake instead.

ALEX hides the flowers.

ALEX: What? How? Ah -- I should go; this is a family gathering...

ROMA: Come in. Maybe you can give them to my mother instead.

ROMA drags him in.

DOLORES is seated with her COMADRES. DOLORES is dressed in black with a shawl over her head. ROMA drags ALEX to meet her mother. She makes ALEX give DOLORES the bouquet of flowers.

ALEX: I'm very sorry Mrs. Rodriguez.

DOLORES takes the flowers and cries uncontrollably. All the COMADRES try to cheer her up. She gets up and screams up to God.

DOLORES: Why didn't you take me instead?

DOLORES exits with her entourage of MOURNERS.

ALEX: Okay, I think I'm going to go now.

ROMA: I'm sorry about the mix-up.

ALEX hands ROMA another copy of Pablo Neruda's poetry book.

ALEX: This is the best translation available according to the head of the literature department. (*ASIDE*) Have a nice life.

ROMA takes it and before she has a chance to say "thank you" ALEX has already left. BELLA walks over to ROMA.

BELLA: Roma, we have to do something about Mamá. Help me gather all our brothers and sisters. We need to talk.

Light changes.

BELLA, ROMA and their three siblings, ARMANDO, 33, JULIA, 29, PEDRO, 27, are in the midst of a serious conversation.

BELLA: If we don't do something, Mamá is going to die in two years just like every spouse does who has been married over 40 years.

ROMA: But that's just the husbands. Women survive longer because they have better support systems and coping skills for grief.

BELLA: Could you stop being "Dr. Rodriguez" for a minute and be my sister? What if she does die?

ARMANDO: Yes, she's a mess; we have to do something.

JULIA: I don't think it's up to us to decide if we should sell the house. It's her house. Why didn't we talk about this when Dad was alive?

PEDRO: But Mamá should not live alone.

ARMANDO: Why don't we put her in a home for old people?

BELLA: We are Latinos; we don't do that to our family.

ALL Oh, no, no, of course.

ARMANDO, JULIA, and PEDRO give a dejected look and mutter aside, "Oh, man!"

BELLA: So who is going to take her?

They all look at each other.

JULIA: I love Mamá, but she can be...a bitch-- I'm sorry I said that, but--

PEDRO: --I could have been married by now if it wasn't for Mamá telling my fiancée about how bad her teeth were.

JULIA: Her teeth were bad.

PEDRO: Yeah, but I loved her and I have dental insurance.

BELLA: Armando, what about you?

ARMANDO: No way! I'm a bachelor. My mother would kill my action. Women are going to think I'm a dork if I live with my mother.

PEDRO: What about you Bella?

BELLA: I can't convince my husband. He's afraid she'll be a bad influence on the kids.

JULIA: But you would get free baby-sitting.

BELLA: Mamá refuses to baby sit, so I don't know about that.

They silently ponder their options. All the siblings turn to ROMA.

ROMA: Don't even think about it. I worked so hard for my Ph.D. I'm going to Europe on vacation.

BELLA: Take her with you!

ROMA: You take her. Take her to Disneyland or wherever, but I'm not ruining my vacation.

JULIA: Come on, she would love that. I remember when we were kids she mentioned how much she loved Italy and wanted to go back someday.

ROMA: Are you crazy, I'd kill her or she'd kill me in a week.

BELLA: Come on, take her with you. Give us two months to figure out what to do with her, maybe by then we will have an extra bedroom built in my house so she can come live with my husband and me...for a while.

JULIA: When Dad was sick you were never here helping out. You were always studying.

PEDRO: It's your turn to do something for the family.

ROMA: No.

(BEAT)

BELLA: All right, we'll disown you. We'll stop talking to you. From this day forward you are not our sister.

They proceed to have a conversation without her and ROMA tries to talk to them but they ignore her until she agrees to take her mother with her.

ROMA: All right, all right!!! But if I kill her I'm burying the body over there!

Lights fade out.

SCENE 5

Lights fade in on DOLORES' ROOM. ROMA is about to knock on her mother's door when it opens slightly.

DOLORES (O.S.) (*Sotto*): Oh, God, take me, take me!

ROMA walks in and searches for her mother. A YOUNG MAN, 30s, handsome, kisses her mother's neck. ROMA does a double take, then, sees him massaging her neck. DOLORES sees ROMA and turns to the YOUNG MAN.

DOLORES: You can go now. That neck massage really helped.

The young man exits in a hurry. ROMA is about to comment, but she shakes her head and moves on.

ROMA: I'm glad you're feeling better... I don't know how to say this... I got a big grant and I am planning to go to Europe for two months... Would you like to come to Europe with me?

DOLORES looks from underneath her sunglasses.

DOLORES: Who put you up to this?

ROMA: Nobody. I want to do this because I think it would be a good idea to get your mind off of death.

DOLORES: Is that why you're going?

ROMA: It's my reward. I start teaching in the fall and I need a break because after that it's ten years before I get tenure.

DOLORES: Ten years? That's how long your father was sick.

DOLORES puts her sunglasses back on and sobs. She sits on her bed and caresses the bed.

ROMA: Mom, it would mean a lot to me if you joined me.

DOLORES: No, no. I can't go... What would people say? My husband dies and I take off with my youngest daughter to go "live it up" in Europe? No, it's just not done. Eso no se hace... (It's just not done.) I have to stay here and suffer.

ROMA: Mom those are such antiquated beliefs! You've suffered enough. We're not going to go party it up in Europe; we would simply go there to get our minds cleared and ready to face new challenges.

DOLORES: But if we went to Paris we would most likely "go paint the town red" como dicen los gringos. (like the white people say)

ROMA: No, we wouldn't, I'll make sure of that.

DOLORES thinks about it and is about to say "yes", then:

DOLORES: No, I can't go. Luis is watching me from heaven and I don't think he would like that.

ROMA feigns sincerity and begs.

ROMA: Papá loved you so much he would want you to enjoy the rest of your life. You were always there for him.

DOLORES: I was; que no? (wasn't I?)

ROMA: You couldn't have done anything more for him.

DOLORES: I tried. My life was devoted to him.

ROMA: Now it's your turn to live your life.

DOLORES sobs again. Then a few seconds later:

DOLORES: All right. I'll go with you. But nine days from now. After nine days of praying for Luis it will be all right. I'll go, I'll feel guilty, but I'll go.

ROMA: How wonderful. I can't wait to tell the rest of the family.

DOLORES: So where are we going exactly?

ROMA: Well, I was thinking of starting in the west and heading south east, beginning with Lisboa, Portugal, and then Spain, France, England, maybe

Germany or the Netherlands, and then Italy, ending up and returning from Rome.

DOLORES: Rome? I don't know if we should go to Rome.

ROMA: I thought you might want to see the Pope in the Vatican.

DOLORES: Oh, yes, my comadres would love for me to get them rosaries blessed by the Pope.

Lights fade in.

SLIDE: MAP OF EUROPE

SLIDE: PORTUGAL

SLIDES: TOURIST SIGHTS OF PORTUGAL

SLIDES: TOURIST SIGHTS OF BARCELONA

SLIDE: SAGRADA FAMILIA

SCENE 6

Lights fade out on ROMA and DOLORES in front of Sagrada Familia. They sit at a bench. ROMA hands DOLORES a travel journal and takes out another one for herself.

ROMA: Here.

DOLORES: What is this?

ROMA: I got you a travel journal. So you and I can keep track of our travels. Isn't that great?

DOLORES: O, sí... Thank you.

ROMA: So here, write something.

ROMA hands DOLORES a pen. ROMA writes in her travel journal with so much joy. DOLORES writes in hers too.

ROMA (V.O.): I am now in Barcelona in front of the Sagrada Familia...

DOLORES (V.O.): Roma bought me this travel journal...so I'm pretending to write in it or she'll never let me hear the end of it... Blah, blah, blah, blah, blah, blah, blah...

In the distance we hear someone shouting "Lola! Lola!" A YOUNG MAN/ SERGIO runs to DOLORES and hugs her tightly.

YOUNG MAN/SERGIO: Lola, what are you doing here?

DOLORES: Sergio, what are you doing here?

ROMA approaches them.

DOLORES (CONT'D): Sergio, this is my daughter Roma.

SERGIO: Lola, you have such a beautiful daughter.

SERGIO shakes her hand. ROMA is taken by his charm and good looks.

ROMA: You look familiar... How do you two know each other?

SERGIO: I met Lola in church.

DOLORES: His mother is my comadre. We run the bingo games.

ROMA: Why do you call her "Lola"?

SERGIO: "Lola" is the nickname for Dolores.

ROMA (*playing it off*): Oh, that's right, I knew that.

SERGIO: So where are you two staying?

ROMA: At the Christopher Columbus Hotel close to Las Ramblas.

SERGIO: Me too!

DOLORES/LOLA: No!

SERGIO: Sí!

ROMA: No!

SERGIO: Yes!

ROMA: Are you here by yourself?

SERGIO: Yes! I would have brought my mother but she doesn't like to travel. What are you doing for dinner? Do you mind if I join you?

ROMA looks to DOLORES, they both nod their heads.

Lights fade out.

SCENE 7

Lights fade in on CHRISTOPHER COLUMBUS HOTEL ROOM. ROMA is on her cell phone. LOLA is in the shower.

ROMA: Mamá's been having a great time. I'm sorry Bella, you were right... Yeah, tomorrow we take off to France. I'll call you next week, bye.

LOLA comes out of the bathroom with a towel around her head.

ROMA (CONT'D): That Sergio really knows how to dance.

LOLA: He certainly does.

ROMA: I thought only gay men could dance like that.

LOLA: He's certainly not gay.

ROMA: These three days hanging out with him have been very exciting.

LOLA: Yes, I would say so.

They both sigh.

ROMA: You know, Mamá, I was thinking... Do you think Sergio would like to join us in France?

LOLA: Hmmm... It would be safer to have a man with us on our trip.

ROMA: Should we ask him?

LOLA: ¿Pues por qué no? (Well why not.)

(BEAT)

ROMA: Mom, can I confide in you?

LOLA: Of course, m'ija soy tu Mamá. (darling, I'm your mother.)

ROMA: Do you think Sergio is an honest guy?

LOLA hesitates to answer.

LOLA: Yes, I think so.

ROMA: Mom, I think he likes me.

ROMA giggles like a teenager. LOLA looks at her and nods.

LOLA: Yes, I think he does.

ROMA falls back on the bed like a hopeless romantic.

ROMA: Wow, you think so too?

LOLA: I see the way he looks at you when you're not looking.

Lights fade out.

SCENE 8

LIGHTS FADE IN ON THE SAME HOTEL ROOM. Several hours later,
ROMA and LOLA now wear pajamas and get into bed.

ROMA: I'm so happy Sergio is joining us on this trip! What a great guy.

LOLA: It's going to be fun with him around. Buenas noches. (Good night.)

ROMA: Good night, Mom.

Lights fade a little.

Loud snores fill the darkness. ROMA uncovers herself wearing a nice dress. She
tip-toes out of the room.

LIGHTS CHANGE - HOTEL HALLWAY.

ROMA makes her way down the hallway to another hotel room. She primps
herself and is about to knock on the door when it opens slightly by itself.
ROMA walks in tip-toeing.

LIGHTS CHANGE - SERGIO'S HOTEL ROOM.

LOUD MOANS become more audible as ROMA walks through the tiny
hallway. ROMA walks in and catches sight of LOLA on top of SERGIO in the
heat of passionate, dirty, love making.

ROMA: Mom?!! Yuuuuck!!!

ROMA runs to the bathroom and vomits. She quickly cleans herself and rushes
back in. By now LOLA and SERGIO have covered themselves with their own
bed sheet.

LOLA: I can explain--!

ROMA: This is disgusting! How could you, Mom! You knew I liked him!

SERGIO: Let me explain--

ROMA: What the fuck is wrong with you Sergio? She could be your mother!
You mother fucker!

SERGIO: This isn't what you think. I care for your mother!

ROMA: Oh, God, you have an Oedipus complex. My mother is 60, you're
like my age!

LOLA: Calm down, Roma.

(BEAT)

ROMA: Wait a minute! You're the "masseure"! I can't believe what a pendeja I've been. You two knew each other in L.A. and you've been fucking him even before Papá died. You're a puta!! (whore)

LOLA gasps.

SERGIO: Have some respect for your mother!

ROMA: I'm going to go tell the whole family right now!

ROMA runs out of SERGIO's room.

Lights fade.

LIGHTS CHANGE - ROMA'S HOTEL ROOM AGAIN.

ROMA runs in and dials on her cell phone. LOLA takes the phone away and hangs it up. LOLA is wearing her clothes backwards.

LOLA: You don't understand. You have never been married. You don't know what it was like.

ROMA: You're supposed to be a suffering widow, not a...

ROMA can't hold back the tears. After a few seconds LOLA wipes ROMA's moustache. ROMA pushes her hands away.

LOLA: You had a little bit of vomit on your...

ROMA: You cheated on a dying man. My father loved you!

LOLA: Yes, he did...

ROMA: And why would Sergio choose you over me? What do you have that I don't have-- don't answer!

ROMA gets up and throws pillows everywhere. After she calms down, LOLA readjusts her clothes and proceeds to explain.

LOLA: You knew your father as your father, but I knew him as a man. After he got sick we had no sex life. Even when he could get it up, he didn't like sex and he was a lousy lover.

ROMA: Don't say that!!

LOLA: Well, it's true! You want to know the truth, pues here it is.

ROMA: Shouldn't you be mourning over him?

LOLA: I did. I mourned him long before he was dead. That man had already given up; he was just waiting for his body to catch up.

ROMA: I don't want to hear anymore! I'll never forgive you for this!

ROMA undresses and hides in her bed under the blankets. (BEAT) ROMA sticks her head out.

ROMA (CONT'D): Needless to say, Sergio is not coming with us. If I find out you're still seeing him on this trip, I swear I'll tell Bella! And she'll tell everyone and we will never forgive you! Good night!

Lights fade out.

The sound of train is heard.

SLIDE: FRENCH COUNTRYSIDE

SIDE SLIDE: MONET LIKE VISTAS

SCENE 9

Lights fade in on EURORAIL TRAIN. ROMA turns to LOLA and is about to say something, but then she closes her mouth and turns away. LOLA continues reading her romance novel. ROMA turns to LOLA and is about to say something, but then she closes her mouth and turns away again. LOLA closes her novel and gets up.

LOLA: While you figure out what you want to say, I'm going to go pee.

LOLA proceeds forward on the train. LOLA struggles to keep her balance. She's tossed towards the bathroom and a HANDSOME FRENCH MAN, early 30's, catches her a la romance novel. They both laugh and exchange looks.

FRENCH MAN: C'est la vie. (That's life.)

LOLA: Thank you so much, you saved my life.

FRENCH MAN: My pleasure.

LOLA: No, it was my pleasure.

He laughs again. Their laughter dies down. Clearly there is chemistry. He pulls out his pack of cigarettes and offers her one. LOLA takes one lovingly. She knows how to work the cigarette. She licks the cigarette butt and sticks it in her mouth. He lights her cigarette and then his. She grabs his hand and holds it close to make sure she gets a good whiff.

Meanwhile ROMA reads her "Encyclopedia of Cemeteries." She sniffs.

ROMA: Yuck, somebody is smoking! Those damn French --!

ROMA looks up and sees her mother smoking with the FRENCH MAN. Even from far away ROMA sees what's going on.

FRENCH MAN (*Re: bathroom*): What is taking so long?

LOLA: Maybe it's not just one person in there.

They look at each other with a devilish look. They laugh again. The bathroom door finally opens. A LITTLE OLD LADY with a poodle comes out.

FRENCH MAN (*Re: bathroom*): Please, go right ahead.

LOLA: No, gentlemen go first, you saved my life it's the least I can do.

FRENCH MAN: Then please let me be a true gentleman--

LOLA: No, I insist.

They both look around to see if anybody is watching so they can both go in together. ROMA gets up and goes to her mother and takes the cigarette out of her mouth. ROMA drags LOLA back to their seats.

ROMA: Do you know how embarrassing it looks to see a grown woman, make a fool of herself like that?

LOLA: What are you talking about?

ROMA: I can't believe the way you were throwing yourself at that poor man.

LOLA: Me? He started talking to me. We were just killing time.

Just then the FRENCHMAN walks by and hands LOLA his card.

FRENCHMAN: Call me when you get to Paris.

LOLA takes his card and winks.

ROMA: ¡Cochina! (Dirty girl!)

LOLA: You don't know how to have any fun. We're on vacation, like they say - chill out.

ROMA: Did you even love my father?

LOLA: No.

ROMA gasps.

LOLA (CONT'D): Look, I took care of him, I would make sure he would be happy, but no, my heart was not his.

ROMA: Don't say that!

LOLA: M'ija (my darling), I love you... I love all my children... I'm just happy I had good children in spite of my horrible marriage.

ROMA turns to the window and wipes off her tears.

LOLA (CONT'D): Why don't you look at me just as a woman on this trip and not as your mother?

ROMA gets up and walks off to the bathroom without saying a word.

Lights fade out.

SLIDES: TOURIST SIGHTS OF PARIS

SLIDE: THE EIFFEL TOWER

SCENE 10

Lights fade in on EIFFEL TOWER. TOURISTS swarm around. A MIME pantomimes for coins. ROMA walks quickly to get to the line for the EIFFEL TOWER. LOLA can't keep up with ROMA.

ROMA: Hurry up, Mamá!

ROMA stops to wait for LOLA. When ROMA turns back a few TOURISTS get in line ahead of her.

ROMA (CONT'D) (*mutters*): Fucking great! (*to her mother*) Look at the line to the Eiffel tower? Look what happened! Why do you have to drag your feet and take forever to get anywhere?

LOLA can hardly catch her breath much less respond.

ROMA (CONT'D): It's exhausting trying to get to places with you constantly taking your sweet time.

LOLA: I have arthritis. I'm walking as fast as I can.

ROMA: Oh, yeah, but it sure doesn't keep you from--

LOLA: What is the hurry? We're on vacation! No one is expecting us; we're not going to be late for anything.

ROMA: There is a lot to see and I want to see it all before we have to leave for England.

LOLA: We don't have to go to England if we don't want to.

ROMA: We have to. I've never been there and we are not going to miss it because you're too slow.

LOLA: Then maybe I can wait for you here and on your way to Italy we can meet again.

ROMA: No.

LOLA: Why not?

ROMA: Because I say so! That's why.

LOLA: Roma, I'm tired of you treating me like a child. Since Barcelona you have been cold, inconsiderate, and a real bitch.

ROMA: A bitch? Me, a bitch?

LOLA: Yes!

(BEAT)

ROMA: I didn't want to bring you in the first place, but Bella and the rest of my brothers and sisters forced me to do it.

LOLA: You're lying.

ROMA: No, I'm not.

LOLA: Then you lied when I asked you who put you up to this.

ROMA: Nobody wanted you so they made me baby-sit you while they figure out what to do with you.

(BEAT)

LOLA: At least you brought me so your trip wouldn't be an entire disaster. You don't know how to have fun, you're just like your father; you're so boring! You're only 26, but you act like you were 56.

ROMA: I do know how to have fun. Ask-- Yeah, I always--, of course, that's so--

LOLA: When was the last time you made love?

ROMA looks around. People in line listen to their conversation closely.

ROMA gets in LOLA's face about to say something, but then she can't respond.

LOLA (CONT'D): All right, when's the last time you had sex or at least a one-night stand?

All of a sudden people in line behind them and in front of them get closer. Everyone wants to know.

ROMA: That's none of your business!

LOLA: Well, then why is it your business that I have fun, my kind of fun?

ROMA: Because you're my mother!

LOLA: Well then, from this moment on, I'm not your mother. I'm your friend.

GERMAN WOMAN IN LINE: The line is moving.

The line keeps moving. They get closer to the point of no return. ROMA and LOLA hold up the line with their heated conversation.

ENGLISH MAN IN LINE: Ladies, please move ahead or move out.

ROMA: I wouldn't have a friend like you. And since you are not my mother I don't have to continue on this trip with you.

ROMA walks out of the line and walks away.

LOLA: Where are you going? Come on, you were the one who wanted to come here.

The MIME gets in ROMA's way and won't let her pass by until she punches him in the face. The MIME gets in LOLA's face and she knees him.

Lights fade out.

END OF ACT ONE

LOLA GOES TO ROMA

ACT TWO

SLIDES: EIFFEL TOWER FROM ABOVE

SCENE 1. Lights fade in on TOP OF EIFFEL TOWER. LOLA looks down. A YOUNG ITALIAN MAN, 23, taps her on the shoulder. He is holding a disposable camera and signals for her to take a picture of him.

LOLA: Ah, sí, sí. (yes, yes.)

He poses for his picture.

LOLA (CONT'D): Uno, due, tre! (One, two, three.)

LOLA takes his picture.

LOLA (CONT'D): Let me take another one.

He poses for the picture.

LOLA (CONT'D): But this time, do this.

LOLA gives him a suggestion for another pose, a sexier pose. He does it.

LOLA (CONT'D): One, two, three!

LOLA takes another picture. LOLA keeps taking pictures of him.

LOLA (CONT'D) : You are a handsome man, I can't stop taking pictures.

He smiles and plays along, it's obvious she's flirting with him and he loves the attention.

Lights fade out.

SLIDE: *CAFE IN MONTMARTRE*

SCENE 2

Lights fade in on an OUTDOOR CAFE IN MONTMARTRE. LOLA and the YOUNG ITALIAN MAN drink two blended margaritas.

YOUNG ITALIAN MAN: So, how long has it been since you were in Italy?

LOLA: A long time ago... How long will you be in Paris?

YOUNG ITALIAN MAN: I have to leave tomorrow to begin summer school.

LOLA: That doesn't give us much time.

They toast.

LOLA (CONT'D): To youth!

YOUNG ITALIAN MAN: A la giovanessa. (*To youth!*)

LOLA (ASIDE): To a young ass.

They both drink. LOLA stirs her Margarita with her straw. She fills her straw with Margarita juice and points it at him. He stops to look at her and smiles. LOLA blows on the straw and spits out Margarita juice all over his face. He is startled, shocked, turned on. He doesn't know whether to be offended or what.

(BEAT)

LOLA smiles at him, he smiles back. He wipes the juice off his face. He sticks his straw in the Margarita and spits the Margarita juice at LOLA's face. She is taken aback. She didn't expect it. She wipes her face and smiles back at him. They look around to make sure no one is watching them.

LOLA spits Margarita juice at his face and he practically melts. This is the coolest form of foreplay. Now it's his turn. He spits the Margarita juice into her cleavage. LOLA's mouth opens wide with ecstasy. After she recovers from the ice passing through her breast she raises her hand.

LOLA: Check please!

Lights fade out.

SLIDE: *PERE LE CHAISE CEMETERY*

SCENE 3

Lights fade in on PERE LACHAISE CEMETERY in PARIS. ROMA pulls out her Encyclopedia of Cemeteries and wanders the cemetery.

SLIDE: "JIM" IN GRAFFITI ON A CONCRETE WALL

TWO WEIRDOS dressed in black clothes come out of an aisle of tombs. ROMA walks the other way. The "Weirdos" enthusiastically talk about Jim's tomb. ROMA sits on a tomb and unpacks her journal and jots down a few thoughts in her journal.

ROMA (*V.O.*): I am in Pere Lachaise cemetery in Paris surrounded by the most exquisite tombstones. I am sitting on Voltaire's tomb, just touching it has made this dark night more...

SLIDE: A FULL MOON

ROMA looks up and sees the moon.

ROMA (*to herself*): What time is it?

ROMA looks around. There is no one in sight. ROMA packs her things and gets up. She looks around for an exit.

ROMA (CONT'D): It has to be that way.

Photo by Leslie Holtzman

Lola and the Italian student.

223

Footsteps are heard.

ROMA walks faster. She bumps into a TALL MAN who looks like a vampire. ROMA screams and pulls out her keys ready to attack.

JIM: Stop! I'm not going to hurt you.

ROMA freezes and notices his face. He's not a creature, but a man with black eyeliner. He looks like Jim Morrison.

ROMA: Who are you?

JIM: I'm Jim. I'm an American... I'm lost too.

ROMA relaxes the hand with the keys.

ROMA: I thought you were...

JIM: Jim Morrison?

ROMA: No... How do we get out of here?

JIM: I think it's that way.

ROMA looks in the direction he's pointing and then looks at the opposite direction. She considers both options.

Lights fade for a transition.

Lights fade in.

ROMA and JIM arrive at the main gate. It is closed.

ROMA: It's closed! No, fuckin' way!

JIM: Oh, well.

JIM gets comfortable and sits by a corner.

ROMA: What are you doing?

JIM: They'll open it in the morning.

ROMA: I'm not sleeping here!

JIM: It won't be the first cemetery I've slept in.

ROMA: But we're all alone and it's cold.

JIM: Yeah, but we're all alone, and if we see something, cool. Maybe Jim Morisson walks around at three in the morning.

(BEAT)

ROMA: Wow, you're right.

ROMA and JIM sit on a tomb next to each other. He puts his arm around her to keep her warm.

ROMA: So where are you from?

JIM: L.A.

ROMA: Me too!

JIM: So how long have you had this love for cemeteries?

ROMA: You know, I don't know... Maybe after I found out my father had cancer that I figured might as well make the best of it. So I started doing research about which cemetery would be best and what kind of tombstone and it became like a hobby... It's sick, huh?

JIM: No. My dad owned a funeral home and I always wondered why a body when it was alive weighed 3 ounces more than when it was dead... Does our soul only weigh 3 ounces?

ROMA: Wow...that is so deep... You know, now that I'm getting a closer look at you, you really do look like Jim Morrison.

JIM: Thanks.

Roma at Pere Lachaise with a Jim Morrison wannabe.

Photo by Leslie Holtzman

(BEAT)

JIM attempts to suck ROMA's blood from her neck. ROMA grabs her heavy bag with her Encyclopedia and pushes him away. She gets the hell out of there.

Lights fade out.

SLIDE: PLAZA WITH A FOUNTAIN

SCENE 4

Lights fade in on a PLAZA WITH A FOUNTAIN. LOLA sits on a park bench near the fountain and writes in her journal.

LOLA (*V.O.*): Pinche Roma, where are you? It's been three days and I haven't seen or heard from you.

On another park bench opposite the fountain, ROMA writes in her journal.

ROMA (*V.O.*): As annoying as it was to be with my over-sexed mother, I miss her.

She closes her journal. ROMA walks around the fountain.

LOLA writes in her journal.

LOLA (*V.O.*): As controlling and boring as my daughter is, I miss her.

LOLA walks around the fountain. Suddenly LOLA and ROMA stand in front of one another, speechless. They don't know where to begin. They sit down by the fountain. They turn to look at one another and notice each other's hickies, they say nothing about them.

ROMA: How long are you staying in Paris?

LOLA: I don't know.

ROMA: Are you leaving soon?

LOLA: I don't know.

ROMA: Are you going north or south?

LOLA thinks about it.

LOLA: Maybe north. I hear Amsterdam is fun.

ROMA: Fun? I think I can do fun.

Lights fade out.

We hear a train passing.

SLIDES: ENDLESS FIELDS OF TULIPS

SLIDES: POSTCARD PERFECT VISTAS

SLIDES: A WINDMILL

SLIDE: MUSEUM OF SEX IN AMSTERDAM

SCENE 5

Lights fade in on LOLA and ROMA at a BULLDOG CAFE. They walk in, in mid-conversation.

ROMA: I can't believe you tricked me into going to the sex museum instead of the Anne Frank Museum!

LOLA: It was educational.

ROMA: Hmmm, you're right; I didn't know women could ejaculate.

LOLA: Like fountains.

ROMA: Okay, I am not against porn or for that matter legalized prostitution, but how come most of the women on display are women of color?

LOLA: Quien sabe. (Who knows.)

ROMA: I know. It's women from third world countries who come here for the sex trade. How can prostitution be a choice when the economics of a country force women to go into this in the first place? How can that be free will?

LOLA: Can't you wait until the fall when your classes get started to start lecturing?

ROMA: Are you saying I'm lecturing you?

LOLA: No, but I think the whole point of going on vacation is to forget about things and just relax.

ROMA pauses to consider.

ROMA: Okay, you're right. I'll try to "chill out". So why are we here?

LOLA: Sit here. I'll order.

ROMA sits and waits. She sniffs and sniffs and can't quite make out the smell.

LOLA returns with little dessert cakes. ROMA is about to get one when LOLA pulls them away.

LOLA (CONT'D): These are for later.

ROMA: What did you order us to drink?

A RASTA WAITER walks up to their table with a tray with a big joint and accessories for a more enjoyable time.

ROMA (CONT'D): What's this?

LOLA doesn't answer and puts the joint in her mouth.

ROMA (CONT'D): What are you doing?

LOLA smokes the joint like a true "pot head" with impeccable technique. LOLA takes a good hit and presents it to ROMA.

LOLA: Here, your turn.

ROMA: No!

LOLA (*imitating ROMA*): Fun? I can do fun.

ROMA: Just because I don't smoke pot doesn't mean I'm not fun.

LOLA: All those years in college and a joint never made its way to you?

ROMA: I was busy studying.

LOLA: ¿Y para qué? (For what?)

ROMA: For my Ph.D.! I'm one of a few Latinas in this field with a Ph.D.

LOLA: Y so what? You're going to die without having learned a thing about life.

ROMA: And you know everything about life?

LOLA: No. But one thing I know is that you'll regret the things you don't do more than the things you do.

ROMA: Okay, maybe I lecture all the time, but right now you're starting to sound like a fortune cookie.

LOLA: Look, don't pay attention to me, fine. Just smoke the joint because we're wasting expensive grass.

ROMA: No! (*BEAT*) And how do you know how to do this?

LOLA takes another hit.

LOLA: Your dad smoked it for medicinal purposes.

ROMA: He what?!

LOLA: He smoked it to relieve some of the pain from his cancer. So I smoked it with him just to make sure he didn't fall asleep smoking and burn the house down.

ROMA shakes her head.

ROMA: Next thing you're going to tell me is that you and Papá were swingers.

LOLA: No, I tried to get him to do it, but after he couldn't get it up anymore he didn't feel like a man... I know you don't want to hear this, but he never said it in words, he just made sure I knew that it was okay for me to find "happiness" someplace else.

ROMA fights tears.

ROMA: So how do you do it?

LOLA hands it to her. ROMA puts it in her mouth. LOLA lights it.

LOLA Takes a puff, inhale, start by inhaling a little bit, then try to hold it in for ten to twenty seconds and slowly exhale.

ROMA tries it but ends up coughing up too much smoke.

LOLA (CONT'D): You inhaled too much, try it again, this time, take a smaller hit. You'll get used to it.

ROMA tries it again and doesn't cough. ROMA and LOLA finish the last dessert cakes.

ROMA: This tastes sooo damn good. It's better than sex!

ROMA cries.

ROMA (CONT'D): The last time I got laid I had a B.A. It was with a guy named Alex. I had failed a test, and he was trying to comfort me, we got drunk and...it was good...

ROMA laughs uncontrollably, then instantly turns serious. She has whipped cream on the sides of her mouth.

ROMA (CONT'D): I really need to get laid... I'm going to turn into an old maid. (chuckles) That rhymes! Wow, I'm a poet... (*cries*) I will have no time for men as soon as I start teaching, I know it... I'll never get a man and I'll die all by myself and my 50 something cats will eat me.

ROMA lowers her head on the table and sobs uncontrollably. LOLA puts her hand on her head and caresses ROMA's hair.

LOLA: If you let me pluck your moustache and eyebrows I will teach you the secrets of seduction that were passed on to me by my grandmother. Let's go back to the hotel.

Lights fade out.

SCENE 6

LIGHTS FADE IN on a BATHROOM IN A HOTEL ROOM in AMSTERDAM. LOLA and ROMA stand in front of a mirror. They are still high and out of their minds. LOLA, tweezers in hand, plucks ROMA's "Frida Kahlo" eyebrows.

LOLA: And now; your moustache.

ROMA: I don't have a moustache.

LOLA: Yeah, and Jennifer Lopez doesn't have a butt.

LOLA proceeds to pluck.

ROMA: Ouchh!!!

ROMA pushes LOLA's hands away.

LOLA: Are you going to let me do my job or do you want to be eaten by cats?

ROMA: Okay, okay, home girl, yeah, what up. (*chuckles*) I sound like a "chola"! (*laughs*) Hey, why don't you give me "chola" eyebrows?

LOLA: Hey, don't move, I almost got your nose hair instead of your moustache.

ROMA (*sad*): I didn't know my moustache was that bad.

LOLA (*teasing*): No, it's not; it just looked like Emiliano Zapata's moustache.

ROMA: No!

LOLA (*teasing*): No, it looks like Cantinflas' moustache.

ROMA: No!

They both laugh.

LOLA: It looks like...

ROMA: Like whose?

LOLA doesn't respond; her mind is someplace else.

ROMA (CONT'D): Like whose?

LOLA (*whispers*): Like Lorenzo.

LOLA sits on the toilet shaking her head. ROMA sits next to her.

ROMA: Who's Lorenzo?

LOLA: I can't tell you.

ROMA: I told you I hadn't had sex. Now you tell me who he is! Come on!

LOLA: You really want to know who Lorenzo is?

ROMA: Yeah. Tell me.

LOLA: When I was 18 years old I was awarded a scholarship to study art in Rome. One day the most beautiful man I had ever seen in all my life walked in. He was the figure model. He would get naked everyday for us and I would do everything I could not to look him in the eyes. Then one day I did. We locked eyes for a few seconds and I felt like his spirit went right though me. I looked away, but after that we couldn't stop looking at each other. Then a few days later after class I was walking by the Spanish Steps and he drove up to me on his Vespa and asked me to show him my drawings. I didn't think they were very good, but he liked them. He told me he wanted me to come to his apartment to teach me how to really draw. I quickly told him, "Look, I'm not your typical American girl, I'm Mexican... American and my parents didn't raise me that way and—", then I kissed him. So I went to his apartment and there among his many canvases was a portrait he had drawn of me. Through his eyes I was so beautiful. He sat me down on his artist bench and put a pencil in my hand. He told me, "Lola, your drawings are beautiful, but the figures are missing a soul. I can tell you have decent technique, but il cuore non ce, the heart is not there. Where is it?" I told him I didn't know. He said, "I'll help you find it." He took my hand softly and said, "Don't push - pull. See the beautiful Virgin? See the Crying Mother? See the Wise Woman? Pull them out of the paper. Give them life... Your hand must be limp. Surrender and let the spirit take over. That's how you'll find your soul...for your drawings." We fell in love and a week before I was to return to Los Angeles we went to Fontana Trevi. We threw coins in the fountain and we made wishes. He wished I could stay. I told him I couldn't, but he practically proposed so I would stay. My heart was telling me to stay, but my mind was thinking, "This is just a 'summer love'... It's just lust"...I knew my mother and father would never let me, they sacrificed so much to give me a good life and I couldn't do that to them. But somehow

I got the courage to ask my mother if I could stay because I was truly in love. She told me I was an idiot for believing Lorenzo and she threatened to disown me and never speak to me again if I didn't come back. I was their only daughter how could I betray them? I couldn't get myself to tell Lorenzo that I had to go back. So I pretended like I was staying. The night before I was supposed to go back to the U.S. I told him I wanted to make love to him. He was so happy because I had told him from the beginning that I was going to stay a virgin until my wedding night. He was so happy he told me, "Questa notte e per noi. This night is ours." I made love to him as if it were the last time I would ever make love to anyone. I caressed his face until it was etched in my memory forever. I kissed all of his beautiful body, the body I had studied for one whole summer…I left my heart in his hand. The next morning when I woke up I heard birds chirping. It was such a beautiful morning. It was too beautiful a morning for me to have walked out of Lorenzo's bed forever without even saying goodbye. When I got back to Los Angeles I cried for nine days until my eyes hurt like they had been cut by razors and there were no tears left. And just when I thought things couldn't get worse I found out I was pregnant with Lorenzo's baby. I tried to keep it a secret from my parents but my mother quickly found out. So my parents forced me to marry Luis, the only man who was interested in me. Poor Luis, he really loved me... I had the baby eight months later and I called her Bella.

LOLA cries. ROMA puts her arm around her and LOLA cries her heart out. LOLA continues crying her heart out. LOLA finishes crying and lifts her head up.

LOLA (CONT'D): I wanted to call her Roma, but I thought your dad might get suspicious.

LOLA and ROMA chuckle.

ROMA: So Bella is my half sister? (*then:*) I always knew you liked her better.

LOLA: Yes, I did. Face it; she's the pretty one.

ROMA cries.

LOLA (CONT'D): But you're the intelligent one!

LOLA hugs ROMA. ROMA finally cuts loose and let's herself cry too.

Lights fade out.

Lights fade in. ROMA lifts her head up, wipes her face, but quickly puts her head back on LOLA's shoulder and continues crying.

Lights fade out.

Lights fade in. ROMA stops crying and regains her composure.

ROMA: So all those years you had to pretend...

LOLA: Yes, I had to bury my love for Lorenzo so I wouldn't go insane. I had thought about divorcing your father when my father died, but then I found out Luis was sick. So I couldn't leave him. He waited for me for so many years so that I would change and eventually love him, but when he realized that I couldn't love him back he got cancer.

ROMA: It wasn't your fault.

LOLA: Yes, it was! I killed his spirit. He was just waiting for his body to catch up. It seemed the more I rejected him the more he loved me until he couldn't go on.

ROMA: I wish you could have told me this growing up. I would have understood.

LOLA: I didn't want to ruin your childhood entirely.

ROMA: No, I would have understood. I would have wanted both of you to be happy.

LOLA: You say that now, but when you have children you'll understand.

ROMA: Children? I have to have sex first in order to have children. I don't think that's ever going to happen.

LOLA: Yes, it will. And someday you'll even fall in love.

ROMA: No, no - forget it. As soon as I open my mouth and men find out how intelligent I am they run the other way. Let's face it men get intimidated by a woman like me.

LOLA: No, they feel useless around you. If men don't feel needed they won't stay. Now, your father, he was different, but that's another story.

(BEAT)

ROMA: Mom... I'm ugly. You said so yourself. Maybe if I were pretty enough for you I wouldn't have spent all these freaking years trying to make you proud of me at least.

ROMA sobs.

Lights fade in and lights fade out a few seconds later.

LOLA puts her arm around ROMA.

LOLA: M'ijita, it's not about the way you look. Looks are such a small part

of it. It's about the way you make a man feel like a man around you... I bet you with a little bit of make-up and a change in attitude you will find a man who will treat you like a queen... Or at least! make you cum like a fountain.

ROMA blushes, then playfully slaps LOLA on the arm, then:

ROMA (*sincerely*): Mom, help me.

LOLA: I'll help you. But you have to do everything I say no questions asked.

ROMA: All right. I'll do it.

Lights fade out.

A train is heard passing.

SLIDE: (READS IN ITALIAN:) BIENVENUTO A ROMA (WELCOME TO ROME)

SLIDE: SHOPPING DISTRICT.

SCENE 7

Lights fade in on SHOPPING DISTRICT STREET. LOLA and ROMA stroll; window-shopping.

LOLA: Roma, you need to get a hair cut.

ROMA: No... I'd rather not.

LOLA: You said you would do it, no questions asked.

ROMA: Okay, well, I didn't mean--

LOLA pushes ROMA forward towards the hair salon, but ROMA pushes back and creates a scene. People walk around them as best they can.

ROMA (CONT'D): No, I won't do it!

LOLA: You said you wanted my help.

ROMA: No! Why do I have to do such drastic things? Why can't a man just love me or lust after me the way I look? Why do I have to succumb to the pressures of society's standards of beauty--! What's wrong with having a vagina and an opinion? I refuse to be a sex object!

An ITALIAN STALLION walks by and they both stop arguing and watch him strut by. They return to their argument without missing a beat.

ROMA (CONT'D): You know what I mean!

LOLA: You need a haircut. You need a new hairstyle.

ROMA: No! I won't do it.

ROMA walks away and bumps into an ART STUDENT and spills her art supplies. She mutters obscenities even though LOLA and ROMA help her pick up her art supplies.

ROMA (CONT'D): Sorry... There's an art school? Where do you go to art school? La scuola- dove? (Where is the school?)

The ART STUDENT points to a direction, grabs her supplies, and whisks off.

ROMA (CONT'D): Where is the art school that you went to Mom?

LOLA: I don't remember.

ROMA: Haven't you ever wondered what happened to that man you fell in love with?

LOLA: Wondered? That's all I thought about for years.

ROMA: Why don't you try to find him? Maybe the art school still has records. Let's go check.

LOLA (*angry*): No. That's so silly. I don't want to go digging up the past.

ROMA: Oh, but I'm so good at it. I spent eight years doing it; I bet I can find him for you.

LOLA: No. I don't want to know anything more about him. Let's go.

ROMA: All right. I'll let you give me a whole make-over if we go to the art school after...

LOLA: Let's give you a make-over and afterwards we'll see.

Lights fade out.

SCENE 8

Lights fade in on "GILDA" NIGHT CLUB. ROMA and LOLA walk into the club. LOLA and ROMA have sexy outfits on and look amazingly vibrant. ROMA attempts to walk on high heels, but she can't quite do it.

LOLA: Walk like this...

LOLA demonstrates, ROMA imitates.

LOLA (CONT'D): A little more grace. Like this.

LOLA walks with grace and sexual appeal. They walk to the bar and sit down. There is hardly anyone there.

ROMA: Why are we here?

LOLA: Because this is where the men are.

ROMA: There's nobody here.

LOLA: The party doesn't get started until at least eleven p.m. This gives us enough time to practice.

LOLA and ROMA walk around the nightclub eyeing the men. They walk up to the bar counter.

LOLA: Two dirty Martinis.

The bartender serves them the Martinis. LOLA and ROMA lift their cocktail drinks. ROMA takes a sip and spits it out.

LOLA (CONT'D): It's all in the eyes. Look at a man from across the room and stare a little longer than you should and then turn away like you don't care. Watch me.

LOLA walks around the nightclub with her cocktail in hand. She makes her round shooting looks at men. LOLA returns to the bar counter.

LOLA (CONT'D): Your turn.

ROMA takes a large swig of her cocktail. She takes a deep breath. ROMA takes her first steps, but then turns around.

ROMA: No, I can't do this. I feel naked. I feel like a piece of meat on heels with a bunch of lions ready to eat me.

LOLA: Yes, but you can choose which one.

ROMA: It doesn't make me feel any better. I think this is wrong to reinforce these gender stereotypes. I hate playing this game-- The man is the hunter and I'm the pray and I do this and he reacts this way and--

LOLA: Save the lecture! Fine, don't do it. I give up. I can see you have no talent for this. Let's go back to the hotel.

LOLA stands up, pays the bill, and heads for the door. ROMA follows after her. IN SLOW MOTION: TWO STYLISH ITALIAN MEN walk past them. One catches ROMA's attention and she stares at him longer than she should. He notices her and looks back at her.

ROMA: Wait! Let's stay. I'll try.

Photo by Leslie Holtzman

Lola and Roma are ready for a night out in Rome.

LOLA: Men like it when you smile and they especially love it when you laugh at their jokes; no matter how stupid they are. Just imitate me.

LOLA smiles and laughs at an imaginary man's joke. ROMA imitates. LOLA plays with her hair. ROMA imitates. LOLA touches her chest with her fingertips. ROMA imitates. A catchy dance beat plays and EVERYONE heads to the dance floor. LOLA dances, ROMA just shakes with no rhythm.

LOLA: How did you get no rhythm? You're a Latina for God's sake!

ROMA: I just never had time to dance.

LOLA takes ROMA's hand.

LOLA: Just follow me, chickadee.

LOLA grabs her hips and moves them the right way. ROMA let's go and finally it comes together. She gets her wings. "VOLARE" plays on the dance floor. Everyone sings and dances to the beat. LOLA and ROMA go sit down to catch their breath.

ROMA: I have to go to the bathroom.

ROMA takes her purse and walks to the ladies room. On her way there the STYLISH ITALIAN MAN turns to look at her. ROMA exits the ladies room and the STYLISH ITALIAN MAN stops her.

FABRIZIO: Balliamo? (Want to dance?)

ROMA nods. He takes her hand and they dance. From a distance LOLA gives ROMA a thumbs up. ROMA turns away embarrassed. FABRIZIO takes her by the hand to a quiet corner.

FABRIZIO (CONT'D): Come ti chiami? (What's your name?)

ROMA: No parlo Italiano. Solo Inglese o Spagnol. (I don't speak Italian. I only speak English or Spanish.)

FABRIZIO: Pecato! (Darn!) Io sono Fabrizio. (My name is Fabrizio.)

ROMA: Roma.

FABRIZIO: Roma? Ti chiami Roma, ma tu non parli Italiano? Pecato! (Your name is Roma but you don't speak Italian? Darn!)

ROMA just smiles and giggles. It works! FABRIZIO calls a CLUB WAITER over and orders wine. From a distance, LOLA watches her ROMA with pride and does hand gestures to remind her of what techniques to use. ROMA flirts with FABRIZIO. She plays with her hair; she caresses her chest with her fingertips. ROMA grabs his hand. FABRIZIO turns to her. ROMA gets very close to him as though she is about to kiss him, but pulls away leaving him wanting more. FABRIZIO stands up and extends his hand to her.

FABRIZIO (CONT'D) (*seductively*): Andiamo? (Shall we go?)

ROMA turns to LOLA. LOLA motions with her hand for her to go. ROMA turns to FABRIZIO and back to her mother. LOLA waves with her hands telling her to go. ROMA takes his hand and they leave together.

Lights fade out.

SLIDE: A FULL MOON SLIDE: THE COLISEUM

SCENE 9

Lights fade in on a HOTEL ROOM IN ROME. ROMA enters with her head still in the clouds. ROMA throws herself on the bed.

ROMA: Mom, oh, mom! It was the most romantic-- I had my very first--!

ROMA (CONT'D): Mom, where are you? (then:) Where are her bags?!

Lights fade out.

Lights fade in. ROMA lies on the bed. The phone rings. ROMA quickly picks up.

ROMA: Mom? Oh... Yes, tomorrow I'll need a shuttle to the airport... How many passengers? Two. I mean one... Can I call you back and let you know if it's one or two? Grazie. (Thank you.)

ROMA hangs up. She lies back in bed. Then ROMA sits up and picks up the phone and dials.

ROMA: Bella? I have bad news. Mom is missing... I don't -- Oh, wait. I'll call you back later!

ROMA grabs her purse and runs out.

Lights fade out.

SLIDE: TREVI FOUNTAIN

SCENE 10

Lights fade in on TREVI FOUNTAIN. ROMA walks around the fountain. COUPLES kiss; TOURISTS make wishes and toss coins into the fountain. LOLA sits on a bench by herself.

ROMA (*to herself*): There she is!

ROMA walks over to LOLA. She negotiates the crowd and sees an older gentleman with a moustache approaching LOLA. This is LORENZO, 30 years later, still a handsome man with gentle eyes. ROMA stops in her tracks and sits. She watches them from afar. LOLA and LORENZO talk and laugh.

LOLA hands him a picture of BELLA and he breaks down crying. LOLA puts her arm around him and can only shake her head in apology. LOLA and LORENZO are the last two people at the fountain. They say nothing. They walk to the fountain. LORENZO hands her a small rolled up painting. LOLA takes it and they walk their separate ways.

ROMA approaches LOLA who is wiping her tears.

ROMA (CONT'D): Are you ready to go home?

LOLA shakes her head and goes to a bench to sit down. She cries another round of tears. ROMA pats her on the back. LOLA can't talk. ROMA sits next to her and patiently waits for her mother to come back to the present. ROMA takes the rolled up painting and opens it up. It is a portrait of LOLA at 18.

ROMA studies it.

ROMA (CONT'D): Who is this?

LOLA: That was me.

LOLA cries some more.

ROMA: It almost looks like me.

LOLA: That's what I looked like in love.

ROMA: Are you ready to go back?

LOLA sits up; there are no more tears left.

LOLA: I don't want to go on pretending I'm a suffering widow. I can't do it anymore.

ROMA: I won't let you. Everyone should know how wonderful and passionate you are.

LOLA: No, it's convenient that I play the role of grandmother. No one wants to know who I really am. Look how you reacted, look at the way you used to see me.

ROMA: Yes, I was selfish. I didn't know... What I do know is that you are not a coward.

LOLA: Yes, I am. I'm a coward and I got the life I never wanted.

ROMA: Mom, please don't say that.

LOLA: I was a terrible mother and a bitter wife. I have nothing but regret.

ROMA: No, you have five children who love you.

LOLA: Love me? You guys don't know how to get rid of me. You were the unlucky one.

ROMA: No, I was the lucky one. I got to see who you were before you became my mother. We do love you; we just never learned how to express our love.

LOLA: I neglected you. I was never there for you emotionally. I never gave of myself more than I had to.

ROMA: You weren't a bad mother because you couldn't have raised a daughter like me. I'm not that bad.

LOLA: You're actually too good.

ROMA: Are you going to run away from your life?

LOLA shakes her head.

ROMA (CONT'D): But if you really want to stay, I'll tell them whatever you want me to... I promise not to...

(BEAT)

LOLA: No, my life is with all of you. I have to go back.

They embrace and then walk away

ROMA: Wait.

ROMA stops and hands LOLA a coin. They walk back up to the fountain, turn around, and make a wish with their backs to the fountain and toss in their coins.

Lights fade out.

SCENE 11

Lights fade in on the RODRIGUEZ FAMILY LIVING ROOM. ROMA's siblings wait around nervously. JULIA peeks through the curtains.

JULIA: The taxi is here...and they're together!

JULIA sticks out her hand to ARMANDO and he hands her a $20 bill.

ROMA and LOLA, looking like they just stepped out of Vogue, make their grand entrance. After the hugs and kisses they both sit on the couch. EVERYONE surrounds them with nervous energy.

BELLA: So what did you do in Europe?

ROMA: We smoked pot and got laid.

EVERYONE LAUGHS. LOLA and ROMA look at one another. ROMA winks at LOLA.

SILENCE

BELLA: Well, ah, I have some bad news. You see, Mama, Roma, ah... I tried getting a building permit to add the extra room, but when I tried to get it, it turns out I didn't have the right kind of insurance coverage and then we had to fill out some papers, but we needed a--

ROMA: Mom, would you like to be my roommate?

Everyone stares at ROMA, after a few seconds

They turn to LOLA.

LOLA: That's so sweet, Roma. I'd love to...but I'd rather live alone...in my house.

BELLA: Are you sure?

LOLA: I don't blame any of you for not wanting me around. I know none of you want to get stuck with me. I know I wasn't a loving mother. I was a terrible, cold-hearted bitch.

JULIA: Mama, you weren't that bad--

PEDRO: Yes, she was.

LOLA: Yes, I was. I don't deserve you. You are all good children, and I never let you know that I loved you. You see, when I was 18 years old--

ROMA: Mom, you don't have to tell them.

LOLA: Yes, I want them to know. I want them to understand. When I was 18 years old I fell madly in love with a man in Italy and my parents didn't let me stay with him. So I made passionate love to him--

PEDRO/ARMANDO/JULIA (*uncomfortable*): Mamá!

LOLA: I know it makes you uncomfortable to think of me as a human being, but you'll get over it. (*then*) So I returned to Los Angeles pregnant and my parents forced me to marry your father.

PEDRO, ARMANDO, and JULIA GASP.

BELLA: You mean Dad is not my father!

BELLA sits down.

BELLA (CONT'D): Who is he? What's his--

ROMA: Bella, let her finish. You have the rest of you life to figure it out.

LOLA: So in time I learned, or at least I tried, to love your father, but I hated myself for being a coward and I took it out on you. I'm sorry I never told you I love you. I'm sorry I never kissed you and hugged you and made you feel special. Pedro, I'm sorry for interfering with you and your fiancee. So what if she had terrible teeth. Julia, I'm sorry I never told you you were pretty. Armando, I'm sorry I never told you I was proud of you. Bella, I'm sorry I never told you about your father. And Roma, I'm sorry I always made you feel like you weren't good enough.

By now there isn't a dry eye. LOLA walks up to the children and hugs them one by one

LOLA (CONT'D): Luis was a good father and a good husband. I didn't deserve him, but we were all very lucky to have him be a part of our lives.

EVERYONE nods in agreement.

LOLA (CONT'D): And I want to be a part of your lives from now on. If you'll allow me.

EVERYONE nods in agreement.

PEDRO: We've always wanted that, Mamá.

EVERYONE nods.

LOLA: But you see now I'm ready to be your mother... And the first thing I want to do as your mother is to propose a toast.

JULIA: A toast?

BELLA: I need a drink.

BELLA runs to the kitchen.

ARMANDO: Mamá, I didn't know you drank.

LOLA: There are a lot of things you don't know about me.

ROMA (*ASIDE*): Hey, what happened in Europe stays in Europe.

LOLA (*ASIDE*): Don't worry; your secrets are safe with me.

BELLA returns with a tray full of tequila shots for everyone. They all grab a shot glass.

LOLA (CONT'D): I want to toast to Roma for being one of the youngest and the first member of our family to get a Ph.D.

They all raise their drinks to her. ROMA turns away embarrassed.

ROMA: No, no. Please don't embarrass me like this.

LOLA: Roma, I am so proud of you and we love you. To Professor Rodriguez!

EVERYONE: To Professor Rodriguez.

They all drink to ROMA.

Lights fade out.

SCENE 12

Lights fade in on ROMA who stands in front of a door on which a name plate reads: PROFESSOR ROMA RODRIGUEZ. ALEX passes by nonchalantly.

ALEX: Hello, Dr. Rodriguez.

ALEX continues walking. ROMA turns around.

ROMA: Alex, wait.

He turns around.

ALEX: Yes, Dr. Rodriguez.

ROMA: You can still call me Roma.

ALEX: Certainly.

ALEX continues walking.

ROMA: I read the book you gave me. I loved all the poems. I actually read the first translation you gave me and I was wrong. It's actually pretty good. A little raw and awkward here and there, but over all there was a lot of heart.

Alex finally has a chance with Roma.

ALEX: I thought so too... So, how was your vacation? You probably can't talk right now; you're probably very busy; I should go.

ROMA: No, I would love to tell you about my vacation.

ROMA plays with her hair.

ALEX: Would you like to have coffee some time?

ROMA: Yeah, I would love to have coffee. (*giggles*) Call me and let's have coffee. (*giggles*)

ALEX: All right. I'll call you.

ALEX walks away with a glimmer of hope in his eye. ROMA walks into her new office.

Lights fade out.

The End

CASA 0101

PRESENT ACTIVITIES

Every year, CASA 0101 produces live stage productions, and two 10-week sessions of classes in acting, screenwriting and playwriting. These classes are free to youth and teens ages 7 to 18, $10 for adults, and $5 for adult residents of the 90023, 90033, and 90063 zip codes. However, no one is turned away for lack of money. These courses all culminate in a performance or presentation that is open to the general public.

CASA 0101 has been honored to produce world premieres of works by our emerging Latino writers such as *Hoop Girls* by Gabriela López, *You Don't Know Me* by Patricia Zamora and *Little Red* by Anthony Aguilar and Oscar Basulto. CASA 0101 will continue to provide affordable and accessible programs in theater, film music, art and culture to teens and adults. In addition, CASA 0101 will further expand collaboration with community-based organizations to take CASA's programming to senior centers, high schools, and local health organizations throughout Boyle Heights. These programs will culminate in public performances.

THE ORIGINS OF CASA 0101

CASA 0101 was founded in 2000 by Josefina López who grew up in Boyle Heights to fulfill her vision of an artistic renaissance in East Los Angeles. From its modest beginnings CASA 0101 has grown into a respected theater with a team of dedicated artists that provides regular programming, including full length theater productions, an annual film festival and classes in acting, writing, production and performance/play development.

On September 9, 2011, the new CASA 0101 Theater opened at 2012 E. First, Los Angeles, CA 90033. Please support it with your donations and efforts.

Thank you, Josefina López

THEATER
FILM   MUSIC
ART
CULTURE
PASSION

STAFF:
JOSEFINA LÓPEZ

EMMANUEL DELEAGE
Director of Development

MARK KRAUS
Administrator

OUR MISSION
CASA 0101 is dedicated to providing vital arts, cultural, and educational programs—in theater, digital film-making, art and dance—to Boyle Heights, thereby nurturing the future storytellers of Los Angeles who will someday transform the world.

For more information go to www.CASA0101.org

CASA 0101 BOARD OF DIRECTORS:
JOSEFINA LÓPEZ
Artistic Director

GERARDO ALVAREZ
Treasurer

EMMANUEL DELEAGE

GINA LINN ESPINOZA

ALLEN GOLDEN

GIOVANII JORQUERA

GABRIELA LÓPEZ DE DENNIS
Secretary

MIGUEL MOUCHESS

EMMA NAVA

EDWARD PADILLA
President

MARIO PADILLA

LUZ VAZQUEZ-RAMOS
Vice-President

WHY THE NAME "CASA 0101"?
CASA means house and/or home in Spanish. 0101 is the original language of computers. It can also mean nothing and everything, yin and yang, male and female, life and death, individual and group, the self and the creator-self. It is a commitment to exploring the world and oneself, the good and the bad, the light and the darkness of our soul and our world to the point where there are no borders and "0" and "1" are one.

247

SUPPORT CASA 0101

CASA 0101 RELIES ON THE GENEROSITY OF DONORS LIKE YOU TO KEEP ITS DOORS OPEN. YOUR DONATION WILL HELP CASA 0101 CONTINUE TO BE A HOME FOR THE FUTURE STORYTELLERS WHO WILL SOMEDAY TRANSFORM THE WORLD.

YOU CAN DONATE VIA PAYPAL AT CASA0101.ORG,

OR YOU CAN ALSO MAKE A DONATION BY MAIL TO:

CASA 0101

2102 E. 1ST STREET

LOS ANGELES, CA 90033

CASA 0101 IS A 501(C)(3) NON-PROFIT ORGANIZATION

JOSEFINA LÓPEZ

Josefina López is best known for authoring the play and co-authoring the film *Real Women Have Curves,* a coming-of-age story about Ana, a first-generation Chicana torn between pursuing her college ambitions, a personal goal, and securing employment which is a family expectation. Along the way, Ana confronts a host of cultural assumptions about beauty, marriage and a woman's role in society. Although *Real Women Have Curves* is López' most recognized work, it is only one of many literary and artistic works she has created since her artistic career began at 17. Born in San Luis Potosí, Mexico in 1969, Josefina López was five years old when she and her family immigrated to the United States and settled in the East Los Angeles neighborhood of Boyle Heights. Josefina was undocumented for thirteen years before she received Amnesty in 1987 and eventually became a U.S. Citizen in 1995.

Josefina has been an activist and has been doing public speaking for over 20 years and has lectured on various topics including Chicano Theater, Women's History Issues, Minority representation in Cinema at over 200 universities such as Yale, Darmouth, and USC. She also has a magazine column called "Ask A Wise Latina". She has been the subject of countless TV and Radio interviews in which she has passionately discussed immigration issues and other controversial subjects concerning women and minorities.

Josefina is the recipient of a number of other awards and accolades, including a formal recognition from U.S. Senator Barbara Boxer's 7th Annual "Women Making History" banquet in 1998; and a screenwriting fellowship from the California Arts Council in 2001. She and *Real Women Have Curves* co-author George LaVoo won the Humanitas Prize for Screenwriting in 2002, The Gabriel Garcia Marquez Award from L.A. Mayor in 2003, and the Artist-in-Residency grant from the NEA/TCG for 2007.

Even though she is best known for the success of *Real Women Have Curves,* Josefina has had more than 80 productions of her plays throughout the United States. In addition, Josefina also paints, writes poetry, performs, designs, lectures on writing, Women's Studies, and Chicano theater. She currently resides in Silver Lake, and is the founder of Casa 0101 Theater Art in Boyle Heights, where she teaches screenwriting and playwriting and

nurtures a new generation of Latino artists. Josefina is actively working to create an Artist District in Boyle Heights where theater, arts, music can flourish and create opportunities for the many talented artists who reside in Boyle Heights or grew up in Boyle Heights and want to return to contribute.

Josefina is presently developing the musical version of *Real Women Have Curves.* Her first novel titled *Hungry Woman in Paris* came out in 2009. She wrote a play to protest SB1070 titled *Detained in the Desert,* which she is currently making into a film. She is working on her next novel *The Ave María Bed & Breakfast* and a cultural center in Boyle Heights that opened on September 9, 2011, where she continues to celebrate women and Latinos! For more information please go to www.josefinalopez.com, www.hungrywomaninparis.com and www.casa0101.org.

TIFFANY ANA LÓPEZ, PH.D.

Tiffany Ana López, Ph.D., is Associate Professor in the Department of Theatre at the University of California, Riverside. She is editor of the anthology *Growing Up Chicana/o* (William Morrow & Co., 1993) and coeditor of *Chicana/ Latina Studies: The Journal of Mujeres Activas en Letras y Cambio Social.* Her work has been published widely in numerous anthologies and journals, including: *Art Journal, Theatre Journal, Frontiers,* and *Paso de Gato Revista Mexicana de Teatro.* She is a dramaturge and community outreach scholar and is presently completing a book, *The Alchemy of Blood: Violence, Trauma, and Critical Witnessing in U.S. Latina/o Drama and Expressive Culture* (Duke University Press).

JORGE A. HUERTA, PH.D.

Prof. Huerta is a Chancellor's Associates Professor of Theatre Emeritus at the University of California, San Diego, where he began teaching in the department of Theatre and Dance in 1975. He has directed in regional theatres throughout the United States, including New York City's Puerto Rican Traveling Theatre, Gala Hispanic Theatre in Washington, DC, Seattle's Group Theatre and the San Diego Repertory Theatre. Huerta is also a leading authority on contemporary Chicana/o and U.S. Latina/o theatre who has lectured throughout the United States, Latin America and Western Europe. He has published many articles and reviews in journals and anthologies and has edited three collections of plays.

Prof. Huerta published the first book about Chicano theatre, *Chicano Theatre: Themes and Forms* in 1982; his last book, *Chicano Drama: Performance, Society and Myth,* was published by Cambridge University Press in 2000. Dr. Huerta was inducted into the College of Fellows of the American Theatre in 1994 and elected National Association of Chicana and Chicano Studies, (NACCS) Scholar, in 1997. In 2007 Huerta was awarded the Association for Theatre in Higher Education (ATHE) "Lifetime Achievement in Educational Theatre Award." In 2008 he was recognized as the "Distinguished Scholar" by the American Society for Theatre Research (ASTR), the Society's highest annual honor.

Enjoy more of Josefina's work in **REAL WOMEN HAVE CURVES & OTHER PLAYS BY JOSEFINA LÓPEZ***, a WPR Books: Latino Insights publication*

www.WPRbooks.com

Printed in the USA
CPSIA information can be obtained
at www.ICGtesting.com
LVHW010251040823
754218LV00001B/102